CUSTOM AND INNOVATION

JOHN MILLER + PARTNERS

black dog
publishing

london uk

CONTENTS

CUSTOM AND INNOVATION
John Miller

Much has happened since the publication of Colquhoun + Miller's first book in 1988. Alan Colquhoun left the practice in 1989 to continue his teaching appointment as Professor of Architecture at Princeton University. In 1990 the practice's name was changed to John Miller + Partners with Richard Brearley and Su Rogers, who had previously joined as partners in 1975 and 1986 respectively.

The title of the book *Custom and Innovation* refers to preoccupations that have persisted since 1961, when Alan Colquhoun and I decided to work together on our first commission, Forest Gate High School. It has been suggested that Tradition and Innovation might have been a better alternative title. But Custom implies meeting a client's expectations and requirements as well as the assimilation and re-interpretation of historical precedent. Innovation challenges precedent and the tension between the two, and their resolution has been a characteristic of our work ever since.

From the beginning we were predisposed towards classical organisation, that could be reduced to a typology of available forms and that could provide a counteraction to, the then, conventional dispersed plan. This approach required the classification of functions to create formal hierarchies and principal and local symmetries, which were then to be developed in the plan.

In our Forest Gate High School, the social space is contained by secondary or normative spaces. One is 'described' by the presence of the other. A similar hierarchic preoccupation is to be found in the laboratory building for Royal Holloway College and later and perhaps less overtly in John Miller + Partners' university work for the Universities of Warwick and East Anglia.

Following the introduction of Parker Morris Standards, which became mandatory in 1972 and the Local Authority housing programme, which blossomed in the decade that followed, Colquhoun + Miller received a number of commissions in London and Milton Keynes. There had been a shift in local government thinking, away from the utilitarianism of the high-rise era of the 1960s towards low-rise houses with gardens. This, it was argued, would meet public aspirations.

Alan and I found the challenge engaged our typological interests afresh, both in a re-evaluation of the villa type in the context of the London street and in a re-evaluation of the vernacular in Milton Keynes.

Where, initially, the typological approach centred principally on the plan, we now drew on historical context and extended it, three-dimensionally, to include facade elements, projecting bays, arcaded attic storeys, jettied windows and so on. The list had no limit. These typological forms were to be abstracted and put to appropriate use. This possibility of a multiplicity of forms ran counter to the convention of choice being reduced to a functional minimum.

A concern for architectural context developed at about the time Colquhoun + Miller became involved with housing design and with observations on the urban realm generally. We concluded that the way a project responded to its context, whether historic or cultural, depended on the degree of heterogeneity to be found or its opposite, contextual unity. In a heterogeneous context there seemed to be a greater freedom to develop experimentally, whereas contextual unity was thought to be fragile and easily damaged by the introduction of an aggressively novel element.

Latterly, much of John Miller + Partners' university work has been in the company of buildings that are within the broad compass of modernism and consequently the context inclines towards the cultural and less to historical precedent. However the typological approach developed earlier is still present.

Both the Queen's Building and the Elizabeth Fry Building share facade elements similar to those found in the Whitechapel Art Gallery or in our Milton Keynes housing. The Elizabeth Fry Building has benefited from a highly successful and innovative system for energy conservation, achieved without the fetishistic display of service paraphernalia as a means of expression.

The monotony of its conventional corridor plan is relieved by the displacement of the two stacked common rooms and the exhilarating space so formed connects the corridors above to the entrance hall below. The preoccupation with small innovatory shifts in plan or section, such as this, can be found in most of our projects and buildings.

Unlike more complex building types, such as university faculty buildings, art galleries have a greater freedom in the disposition of the plan, as functional connections are not as onerous.

Within the confines of an existing building, like Tate Britain, the presence of the existing footprint provides a framework, which paradoxically both restricts and liberates design. The space available for new work on the lower floor and the existing large courtyard, the 'site', is limited by the spine of the Duveen axis and the regularity of the structural bays, determined by gallery size, above. The site restraints encouraged invention and the plan developed empirically. The spatial experience is inevitably episodic. All so different from the axial symmetry of the Serpentine Gallery where the experience of one space anticipates the presence of its neighbours.

The enjoyment of the plan as an abstraction, the anticipation of tactility in the section and the value of the typological method, with the avoidance of the banality of operational incident, were the principal factors in Alan's and my work from its inception in 1961 as they are now in Richard's, Su's and my more recent work.

The selected projects and buildings that follow have been grouped under three categories, "Education", "Housing", and "Designing for Art" with a separate chronology that lists all buildings and projects from 1961 to 2008. Each have been attributed to either Colquhoun + Miller or John Miller + Partners, as appropriate.

JOHN MILLER: BIOGRAPHICAL NOTES
Deyan Sudjic

John Miller is a very English architect, the product of a particular moment in the history of post-war British architecture. And yet his architectural sensibility is more European than narrowly Anglo Saxon. Born in 1930, his is the English generation that was the first to take Modernism for granted. Tradition had already been overturned by the time that they got to be students, even if most of the country had failed to notice. For them, iconoclasm took the form of exploring a more sophisticated approach to the nature of the Modern Movement and an understanding that Modernism itself had a history, rather than relying on shock tactics. They started to look beyond the obvious names for inspiration, and became enthusiastic about the kind of architects—from Giuseppe Terragni to Gerrit Rietvelt and Jan Duiker—that Nikolaus Pevsner either disapproved of outright or whose contribution he underplayed. They were determined to look beyond the parochial and the provincial, and strip away the sentimental English gloss on contemporary architecture that had descended on the country. They were fascinated by the transitional figures, by Otto Wagner, and Hendrik Berlage.

But at the same time, Miller has always practised architecture in what might be characterised as the traditional manner; avoiding forced novelty, working in offices that are intimate and collegial rather than corporate or messianic, two options that have become increasingly popular alternatives. Miller was swept along with the mood of the post-war generation of architects without having any back story. He was leapfrogging from the orthodox cultural sensibilities of his upbringing (in which contemporary design of any kind was conspicuously absent), into the architectural climate of that part of London that turned its nose up at what it considered to be the saccharine quality of the Festival of Britain, and was looking instead for an altogether tougher approach.

His generation is old enough to remember World War Two and, in Miller's case, the dislocation of a series of evacuations to escape the blitz. He remembers picking up shrapnel and dud incendiaries on Hampstead Heath, after a night bombing raid, to swap at school the following day.

His father, who owned a hotel in London, wanted him to join the family business when he had completed his education, a prospect that he viewed with reluctance. Miller had already started thinking about architecture as an escape route from a career in hotels without being entirely clear about what it would entail. The idea was first planted in his mind in a random childhood conversation with a friend of his parents and it continued to reverberate in his thinking through his adolescence. While he was still at school, he developed his interest in drawing thanks to a sympathetic art master. And when he was 16, he went to see Britain Can Make It, the famous exhibition staged by the Victoria and Albert Museum in 1946. Before the museum's collection came back from the various mine shafts and quarries to which it had been evacuated for safe keeping during the war, the V&A was filled with what was intended as a morale booster to show what the future might offer now that peace had finally come. Designed by James Gardener and Basil Spence, the exhibition was a look at contemporary design of all kinds from bulbous Jowett cars to Murphy television sets fitted out in polished hardwood cabinets. Given post-war austerity, rationing, and a desperate need for foreign currency, the show was inevitably dubbed "Britain Can't Have It". Much of what was on display had been designed with the export market exclusively in mind and so was not available for home consumption. In its sense of brave optimism, it was the forerunner of the Festival of Britain, staged five years later, in changed political circumstances when a Conservative government had been returned to power. The exhibition had a significant impact on Miller: it offered a glimpse of a world with tastes that were very different from those of the comfortable suburb in which he had grown up, and he realised that architecture would be the way into it.

Britain Can Make It, exhibition guide, 1946.

He was introduced to Frederick Gibberd, who suggested that he should study at the Architectural Association. Miller went to have a look while he was still at school. He found the atmosphere full of ex-service men intimidating, and was advised not to apply straight from school. He decided to do his national service as soon as he finished school and apply for the AA afterwards. Before he went into the army, in September 1948, he worked briefly for Yorke Rosenberg and Mardall. By his own account he was somewhat naïve about design and got into trouble for lettering a drawing in italics. "Not our style" he was told, though FRS Yorke was more encouraging.

Once in the army, and with basic training complete, he boarded a troop ship, *The Empress of Australia*, *en route* for Libya, at that time under British administration after the collapse of the Italian colonial regime during the war.

Miller enjoyed his military service, but did not pursue officer training as might have been expected. Instead he reached the rank of acting drill corporal and found himself in the Western Desert steering Daimler armoured cars over sand dunes, under the command of a lieutenant no older (and certainly no more competent) than himself and barking orders on the parade ground. In Benghazi's city centre he saw a distant echo of the architecture of Fascist Italy. He went swimming in the Mediterranean, under the walls of ruined Roman cities. He came to know a landscape overlaid with the traces of Mussolini's colonists, who were settled in a rationalist grid of white cube farmhouses, positioned at precise half kilometre intervals, each set in a rectilinear olive grove.

In the barrack blocks, perhaps not so different from the dormitories at boarding school, he found himself making friends with people from very different backgrounds. He successfully sat his entrance exam for the Architectural Association at a solitary desk in Benghazi, invigilated by the Education Officer, and shortly after was bound for London again.

For Miller, his time at the AA was a happy one. He had a series of sympathetic, energetic, and even inspirational teachers. The first year was run by Leonard Mannaseh, whom he remembers with affection. The third year was in the hands of members of the Architects Co-Partnership such as Kenneth Capon; and his last year was memorably taught by Peter Smithson.

In 1950, the Architectural Association was divided between those students who had come straight from school, and those who had recently returned from national service as Miller had done. There was also another kind of division, the one between the students and the members. The balance of power between the architect members, a self-styled learned society that saw itself as a kind of architectural version of the Royal Academy, and the school had not yet shifted decisively towards the educational faction. The membership was made up mainly of practising businessmen architects and it nominally controlled the organisation. They treated the place less as an academy and more as a slightly shabby gentleman's club. In those days the AA still owned a cricket ground.

The two sides, one in duffel coats, the other in city suits, coexisted uneasily. The membership still clung to the faded Georgian rooms of Bedford Square. And the students left them alone. "It rarely occurred to us to go into the members' room" recalls Miller. "For us the cafe space with its outdoor tables in Ching's Yard was the heart of the school; there was as much work done there as in the studio."

It wasn't only the members who behaved as if they were still at school, the students did too. Every Christmas term they staged a carnival—part art school dance, part cabaret, and

Top to bottom *Empress of Australia*, troop ship; Miller, National Service, Libya, 1949; Miller's Daimler armoured car in Libya, 1949–1951; Italian colonnade in Benghazi; Ching's Yard, Architectural Association, c. 1952.

part pantomime—that attracted students from all over London. In 1950, Miller remembers that the cabaret included a cameo appearance from one student performer got up in an Edwardian straw hat and blazer. His song began: "I am one of the new first year, insincere and awfully queer." Alongside this, there were the beards and sandals of bohemia.

There were some overseas students: from South Africa, Israel, Greece and America. But it was still an overwhelmingly British environment, a school where domestic students of limited means could get grants. In Miller's year at the Architectural Association, there were just three women, one of whom was Denise Scott Brown. There was a dining room that the students shared with the men in suits, where they were served by a fleet of doting waitresses. Gwen the telephonist guarded the front door. Outside, beyond Bedford Square, London was still scarred by bomb sites, and Nissen huts built to provide emergency accommodation.

When Miller arrived at the AA, ex-soldiers were still getting priority for admission. The school was lead by Robert Furneaux Jordan, a left-leaning architectural historian whose book on Victorian architecture was to be the first to popularise the subject. Much later he attracted the contempt of David Watkin and Cambridge's more conservative architectural scholars, for what they termed Furneaux Jordan's vulgar Marxism. In his spare time he wrote detective stories.

Two years after Miller arrived, Furneaux Jordan was succeeded by Michael Patrick, a practising architect who personally designed a new studio complex on Morwell Street for the school, and who had some difficulty in following the popular Furneaux Jordan. Both Patrick and Furneaux Jordan presided over an ethos that made the school sympathetic to the herbivorous welfare-state-supporting climate of the time, without being in any sense ideologically driven.

But, as is usually the case, it was his fellow students who really shaped the nature of Miller's education. The Architectural Association was the largest school of architecture in Britain, with a scale that inevitably turned the place into a kind of pressure cooker, where ideas could quickly germinate and spread as if by viral infection. It was large enough to develop a critical mass which gave students the scope to shape their own direction within it. Almost alone in the world, it was, and still is, an independent academic institution focused exclusively on architecture. The result was a climate of ideas that sustained successive generations of students throughout their careers as they have crossed and re-crossed each other's paths.

The AA was a place that challenged Miller's assumptions about the world. He arrived temperamentally Conservative despite his experiences in the army where he came into contact with Labour-supporting working class people from all over Britain. He left the school with a different perspective. The Architectural Association was his first encounter with a sustained level of intellectual debate. Initially he was intrigued but also transformed by the experience.

On arrival, Miller was issued with a set square, a slide rule, and a selection of primitive drawing instruments, all packed into a plywood box. There was a set of instructions, and a timetable. He was given a stool and a drawing board that came with a T-square with a clear Perspex blade. Students were allocated their places in the studios on an alphabetical basis. After a while they spontaneously reshuffled themselves.

In the early 1950s, the Architectural Association had yet to develop the unit system that was later to make its own distinctive contribution to architectural education. The

Top to bottom AA Carnival, Adrian Gale on the left; Performance of the Duchess of Malfi, a section AA production; Stage design for the Duchess of Malfi; Primitive Hut, first year, 1951.

model for the course was the usual structured programme of design assignments of increasing complexity with each succeeding year, beginning with an individual building, and moving toward the urban scale.

Miller's formal architectural education began with a couple of simple exercises in the fundamentals of drawing, among which other things, included the freehand delineation of lettering. They were required to measure and draw a bicycle as well as an adjustable spanner. Later on in his studies, Miller earned some cash doing a survey of an Arts and Crafts building on the river in order to produce a measured drawing of it.

In parallel came the first real project, which was to design and model a primitive hut. The point was to select a specific environment, to realise the hut with the materials and techniques available to that particular location and to use them to address its constraints and demands. One student chose Papua New Guinea, allowing him to use a light frame structure made from a selection of exotic timbers. Miller suggests that he made something of an error in choosing to site his hut in the bitter cold of the far north. He made the model using wooden dowel, set in red Plasticine. As he worked on the model, it became more and more naturalistic, until it acquired a dusting of snow. Conceptually, it was not a success. Leonard Manasseh pointed out that the hut lacked a fire place, but Miller could neither find anywhere to put one, nor get his timber joints to line up.

Later in the second term, under the direction of Olive Sullivan, first year students went on to do a series of projects exploring colour and form. They worked in watercolour or poster paint to paint intricate gradations of colour in neat little squares, first from black to white, then from red to blue, and yellow to red. This was followed by an exercise using coloured paint on varying sized cards made of two-inch modules to make spaces of different temperatures. Then the students were asked to think about form-making and producing abstract sculptures in plaster.

The programme for the first year included a design for a workshop. Manasseh asked the students to design a workshop in the garden of a house in Hampstead. Miller remembers that Patrick Hodgkinson did a very mature scheme. "Even to an untutored eye, you could see it was head and shoulders above the rest."

As a student in the summer of 1951, Miller worked on the Festival of Britain site as a tea boy, based close to a cafe designed by Leonard Manasseh. Miller remembers the Festival as a world of spindly chairs, designed by Ernest Race, and a colour palette of lemon yellow and terracotta, pale blue and black. While Conservatives were predictably sceptical about the whole idea of a festival initiated by the outgoing Atlee government, not all those who might have been expected to be its natural supporters were impressed. James Stirling, whom Miller got to know well when he was at the AA, famously described his response to the Festival's prevailing Scandinavian-inspired aesthetic as "disgust" at the missed opportunities that it represented. But at the AA many of Miller's teachers had worked on the Festival, and there was a wide sympathy for its picturesque ideals among the staff. Most of the students were impressed at first, it was only later that they started to look for more rigour.

The Architectural Association was where Miller first met Kenneth Frampton who, as a student, had yet to manifest his preoccupations with history and theory. Patrick Hodgkinson was in the same year and stood out as a star for the maturity of his work and his bravura draftsmanship. Neave Brown and Adrian Gale were also there. They

Top Drawing exercise, first year.
Middle Festival of Britain.
Bottom Kenneth Frampton, c. 1951.

became a close-knit group of friends. Gale, who had been an ensign in a Guards regiment, surprisingly adopted the role of a revolutionary figure, leading the usual kind of student insurrections. He commandeered the scaffolding tubes used to form trestles in Michael Patrick's newly built studio work stations, and recycled them as an absurdist Heath Robinson design in Ching's Yard.

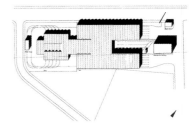

These were the friendships that were to shape Miller's career. His AA friends lived and worked in shared flats. In places such as Bayswater, Earls Court, and West Hampstead that were still in reach of student budgets. Miller initially lived at home with his parents in Hampstead, before moving out in his third year to share a flat (with an outside lavatory) in Devonshire Terrace near Paddington Station with the Israeli architect Ram Karmi, Ken Frampton, and David Jackson. The group moved together, from flat to flat, struggling to deal with landlords, their furniture and the challenging colour schemes that their rooms were painted.

And it was through the AA that Miller met Sam Stevens, a catalytic figure who kept an open house in Marylebone that encouraged conversation about architecture. James Stirling lived there for a while. Colin Rowe was also a visitor, as was Douglas Stephen. There were conversations that continued on Saturday mornings at the French pub in Soho, where Miller would meet Stirling and Douglas Stephen. At one end of the bar were the architects; at the other a group of London artists, with no contact between the two groups. Sam Stevens organised an exhibition at the AA of work by Liverpool University graduates, in which Stirling showed his thesis project. It was, Miller remembers, a jolt to the AA's preconceptions. Stirling and others produced drawings that were full of colour, and were prepared to attempt subjects far removed from the social responsibility that was taken for granted in Bedford Square. One Liverpool student had even designed a Turkish Bath.

An informal group drawn from this milieu went *en masse* one Saturday to see the newly completed Roehampton housing scheme, the London County Council's Architects' Department's translation of the parallel slab blocks of Le Corbusier's *Ville Radieuse* and *béton brut* to suburban municipal housing in South London. One of the other great talking points was the outcome of the Sheffield University competition, entered by many promising younger talents. Miller remembers it as the subject of an informal review, at which many of the participants got together to discuss their submissions, including Sandy Wilson, Bill Howell (who was later to establish Howell Killick Partridge and Amis), James Stirling and the Smithsons.

In their second year Miller and his cohort were set a project to plan the layout, and design of individual buildings for a satellite village in Kent. By this time the students were encouraged to work in groups. For this project, Patrick Hodgkinson and his team explored the picturesque, and did a contemporary version of a Cornish village, based on a sequence of winding lanes and roads. Miller, with Peter Forster, David Jackson and Grahame Herbert, worked on a radically different proposition that initially involved a mix of high-rise and low slab blocks. Encouraged by Colin Glennie, a fellow student who had been at Marlborough where the art master had introduced him to modernism of the Central European variety, they scrapped this version and suddenly took a plunge into radical instrumentalism. The group produced a plan that was surprisingly reminiscent of Hilbersheimer. It grouped the buildings so as to create a regular series of parallel blocks, spaced far enough apart and orientated to eliminate one block casting shadow on its neighbour, in a manner that Miller looks back on with dismay.

Top Bus station, roof plan, fourth year project, Neave Brown and John Miller, 1954–1955. **Bottom** Alton Estate, Roehampton.

Miller, who, prior to going to the AA, had read a book on perspective and, for the first time, had encountered a Le Corbusier axonometric drawn from beneath, initially struggled to understand the technique and then, when he started to master it, put it to work in his own projects. "I began to realise that there was more to it than just eye-level perspectives", he remembers.

In their approach to the second-year project, Miller's group took their idea of a rational machine age aesthetic approach to its logical conclusion, and elected to make their task as designers as rigorous as could be. They conceived of the village as a prefabricated construction, based on a modular system of factory-made components that would be assembled on the site. It was the conventional rhetoric of the period. Prefabrication would ensure high quality finishes by taking as much as possible of the construction process out of the endless unpredictability of the weather on a building site exposed to the elements. It would, in the long run, be cheaper, so it was claimed. In the set of drawings produced to underpin their design, every detail was related to an overall grid with a set of guiding dimensions in the manner of Le Corbusier.

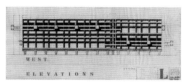

Miller's big awakening had come in the third year when he bought Le Corbusier's *Œuvre Complète* from a second-hand bookshop and, at the same time, began to discover the work of some of the less mainstream figures such as Pierre Chareau. He was fascinated by Le Corbusier's *Modulor* proportional system, and the Fibonacci series. He read about Neo-Plasticism and de Stijl, evidence of a willingness to explore beyond the conventional architectural wisdom by reading around the limits of the curriculum, in a way that was neither encouraged, nor discouraged, by the school, but eagerly pursued by his peers.

The group of students to whom Miller belonged was rediscovering the white and grey Modernism of the 1920s and early 1930s, cutting out all that had happened between 1938 and 1945. Some of the AA staff, as Miller remembers it, were puzzled by this kind of militant fundamentalism. "They thought things had moved on since then; they wanted to discourage this kind of abstraction. But we made buildings that were heavily influenced by Le Corbusier." As members of Miller's group left the AA and began, one after another, to build, you could begin to see the signs of a significant new body of work, representing a crystallisation of this mood. When Neave Brown worked for Lyons Ellis Israel, and Adrian Gale (who even worked briefly for Mies van der Rohe in Chicago) went to the office of Douglas Stephen, they started to build a series of militantly old-school modern projects. By and large it was a move based on an underlying conviction about the most appropriate architectural language open to them that was to stay with them throughout their careers, even if Miller himself, in the 1980s, was to come very close to the kind of spatial ambiguity in some of his projects that might be described as postmodernism. It's not a term that Miller is keen to accept, but he says that "sometimes you are faced with something so stylistically complete, that to insert a contrasting new fragment, would be to deface the context".

In their third year, Miller travelled to Rome with Neave Brown, Kit Evans, Adrian Gale, Janet Kaye, Rob Howard and Stuart Lewis to take part in an international congress of architecture students. They took a presentation of their recent work to put on show. The school had bought a very early model VW microbus, and they drove it to Italy with a box of drawings lashed to the roof rack. The twist was in their presentation style. They inserted their own work into images of historical buildings that they liked, such as Sir Christopher Wren's library in Cambridge. They mounted the highly professional looking drawings on grey card, and devised a scaffolding exhibition screen structure on which to show them. The whole thing created something of a stir at the congress and it seemed

Top Loughborough Road, model. **Middle** Loughborough Road, west elevation, 1954–1955, Forster Herbert Jackson Miller. **Bottom** AA exhibition in Rome, 1954, © Kit Evans.

to reflect a new direction in student work in Britain; one that followed at some remove the path being explored by Colin Rowe and James Stirling. It was a sign of a certain mood best expressed by Rowe's memorable title for his analysis of Stirling's design for Churchill College in Cambridge, which he called *The Blenheim of the Welfare State*.

Beyond the question of image, Miller was beginning to understand the need to learn the most vital of architectural lessons: to experience a building in three dimensions in his mind. "You began to visualise things in your head, and that was an amazing change. Until that happened, design was something distant on a drawing board; it existed on paper only and not in your imagination. It was not so easy to achieve that change."

In the AA's teaching priorities, an understanding of the nature of design and the design process came ahead of the practical skills needed to realise a building. "The Architectural Association's attitude tended to be that if you knew how to be a good designer, then all of the means of construction would follow", is how Miller puts it. As the course progressed, there was the beginning of a discussion of the nature of materials, a look at what needed to go into production information, and an appreciation of structural issues. By the time that they reached their third year, students were expected to be capable of producing elementary structural calculations to justify the plausibility of their designs. They needed to know how deep a beam had to be if it was to be able to carry a structural span. They needed to have a reasonable feel for how far apart the supporting columns would have to be. There was also a grounding in the basics of construction. But at the AA, the expectation was always that once they had shown that they were capable of a convincing level of design work and had graduated, students would be able to learn all the complex technical details of their profession when they were in practice. History was taught by Sir John Summerson, then embarking on his analysis of the making of Georgian London, and by Furneaux Jordan. Max Locke, deeply engaged with the practicalities, lectured in town planning. The brilliant engineer Felix Samuely did the same for structures. Among the other key figures in Bedford Square, was Peter Smithson, Miller's fifth-year master, who arrived at the AA just after completing the school in Hunstanton that brought him and his partner, Alison Smithson, mythical status. Miller, and a group of students from the AA, went to see Hunstanton School in the summer of 1953. Smithson, with his lugubrious style and portentous manner, became a towering figure at the AA and was to have a decisive influence on Miller's early career.

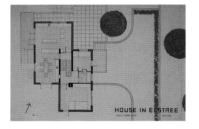

As a legacy of Britain's colonial tradition, the AA had established its own tropical school to specialise in architecture for non-European contexts. It was run by Maxwell Fry and Jane Drew who, at that time, were still working alongside Le Corbusier on completing the less memorable residential areas of Chandigarh and a variety of glum, naturally ventilated concrete structures from Nigeria to Jamaica. Miller, along with several others from his year, opted to join it, at least in part because it appeared to offer a possible introduction to an area that promised the chance of work. Miller designed a house as part of the tropical course. Looking back, Miller sees Fry and Drew primarily as practitioners, rather than inspiring teachers. "It was disappointing for us that they did not share our enthusiasms."

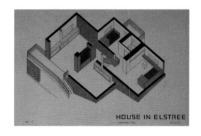

The group worked on the design of a series of projects set in the context of different climatic zones, from Accra to Chandigarh. The distinctive nature of the education offered at the AA, with the polite anarchy of its self-governing traditions, has survived to the present day; even as the kind of Englishness that shaped its origins and its ambiguous management structure has disappeared from the building.

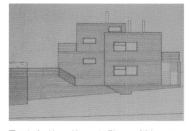

Top to bottom House in Elstree, fifth year project, 1955–1956, site plan, ground floor plan, axonometric and south elevation.

For the first three years that they were at the school, students were expected to work in the studios in Bedford Square. It was a way to develop a sense of cohesion and to encourage group working. Although it was discouraged, for most of the last two years many students disappeared to their own homes, for privacy and to work at another level of intensity. There was no 'year out' as part of the course in the 1950s. The only qualification was the diploma at the end of the fifth year, which brought with it exemption from the Part 2 exam of the RIBA. Although, as Miller remembers it, the school was pretty vague about how the ideas that it was teaching could be translated into the realities of finding work. "There was no system to help you find a job once you had left. It was only occasionally talked about at the AA."

Entry into the architectural profession was not handled with any more rigour by the Architects' Registration Council than the Architectural Association. "After graduation I got my professional practice certificate with an interview with Gontran Goulden following a rudimentary exam paper. It seemed perfunctory", Miller remembers, adding that Goulden seemed to take the fact that Miller had an AA diploma as sufficient evidence of his professional capabilities.

The constant conflict between succeeding generations of students and their examiners also continues. It is a predictable result of the way that assumptions and ideas confront each other, and which mark processes of succession. And the victories by the old over the young, not to say those of the young over the old, have a way of being no more than temporary in a pattern that keeps repeating itself. Just as Nigel Coates' students at the AA were failed *en masse* in the 1980s by James Stirling, who could not see the relevance of narrative architecture to the realities of building, so John Miller and a number of his year were failed in 1955 much to the consternation of the then chairman of the AA, by their external examiner, James Cubitt. Miller, Frampton, and several others were all failed on grounds that seem to have been somewhat subjective. Miller took it all philosophically enough, but Michael Patrick was disturbed at how this abrupt and violent move reflected on the school's reputation, as well as on the individual students who had spent five years getting to this difficult position but could not overturn the external examiner's decision. Those students who had been failed were set an extra project to design, and given the time to submit it in the autumn term. Miller duly did so, and got his diploma with honours.

He left the AA, with a certain sense of anticlimax, with no certainty of what to do next, and with no obvious route to build anything on his own account, or to find work in a stimulating office. Initially, he did not go far but took a job with a commercial firm of architects based in Bedford Square a few doors down from the AA, designing lacklustre supermarkets. It was a depressing interlude; one that he soon realised would serve no useful purpose for his career in architecture. He quit shortly afterward and, to fill up the time, he started going to the cinema day after day while he waited for something more promising and fulfiling to show up. The only break from this bleak routine was regularly meeting up with Ken Frampton. At one of these meetings, he and Frampton were walking aimlessly around Bedford Square. They encountered Peter Smithson coming in the opposite direction. It was 1956, and Frampton was waiting to go into the army. "What are you two doing now", the always taciturn Smithson asked them in his gruff way. Miller replied that he was out of a job, and was still trying to work out what to do next. "He pointed at me, and said, 'You, you should go and work for Lyons Israel Ellis.'" [Later to become Lyons Israel Ellis and Gray.] Smithson continued by offering to make Miller an introduction to the firm: "I'll talk to Tom Ellis, he is a friend of mine."

Top House in Accra, fifth year project, 1955–1956, southwest elevation. **Bottom** Clockwise, from top left: Lyons, Israel, Ellis and Gray, © David Gray.

Smithson did what he had promised, and the introduction was enough to get Miller started in what was, at the time, one of the more impressive architectural offices in London, although, over the years, one whose visibility has faded, despite the quality of such work as the Old Vic theatre workshop and the Titchfield Street building for Central London Polytechnic, now the University of Westminster.

The practice—finally dissolved in 1984—had first been set up by Edward Lyons and Lawrence Israel in 1932. Tom Ellis became the third partner more than a decade later, in 1947. It was an arrangement that had led to a certain confusion about the practice's identity. In the 1930s, Lyons and Israel built a town hall in the spirit of Swedish Classicism. After the war, before they were joined by Ellis, the work continued to have a faintly Scandinavian character. But with Ellis, who was keen to push the practice in new directions, its work began to move decisively toward what might be described as "Brutalism". There was an interest in the kind of Constructivist geometry and patent glazed aesthetic that set the mood, crystallised by Stirling and Gowan at Leicester; and it was reflected to some degree in the Royal Holloway College project that was Colquhoun + Miller's second design.

This was a development that was both fuelled by, and attractive to, a new generation of talented architects. Both James Stirling and James Gowan had worked briefly for the firm and it had begun to establish a reputation for rigorous and inventive work, almost exclusively for the public sector, with a string of social housing and schools projects. During the 1950s and 1960s, Lyons Israel Ellis was the office that attracted ambitious young graduates, drawn by its reputation for original thinking about design and the chance to build what the workload (fuelled by post-war reconstruction) offered. Neave Brown and David Gray, who eventually became a partner, joined the office in 1958.

This was the period in which Miller travelled to see the projects at first hand that he had devoured in the books he had started to buy. He had more than enough to think about in terms of architectural ambition. In 1957, Miller was in Paris, and went to see Pierre Chareau's *Maison de Verre*. He also travelled down to Marseille, to catch the boat to Israel, and found himself on the roof of the *Unité d'Habitation*, while Le Corbusier himself was conducting a site visit. Miller was also beginning to build up his library. From his collection of books and magazines he was able to explore the work of Mallet Stevens, and was fascinated by Adolf Loos' Chicago Tribune Tower. They appealed respectively to Miller's interest in a poetic understanding of modernity and intellectual rigour.

Working at Lyons Israel Ellis was also to have the important consequence of bringing Miller in contact with Alan Colquhoun, with whom he was eventually to set up his own architectural practice. Miller, in fact, was the first of a group of AA graduates that Lyons Israel Ellis had hired as an assistant. With the exception of Stirling, Gowan and Colquhoun, the other assistants in the drawing office had mostly come into architecture from training at night school, or had been part-time students.

When Miller arrived, the office was based in Portland Place in a domestically scaled Adam building almost directly across the street from the RIBA. The three partners sat in a row in one room. The rest of the practice was herded into the drawing studio. Colquhoun, nine years older than Miller, had become an associate some time earlier. Before that he had worked for Candilis and Woods, an impressive name to have on his *curriculum vitae*, given that Shadrach Woods had himself worked for Le Corbusier on the construction of the *Unité d'Habitation*. Woods had also been part of Team X, the

Top Le Corbusier on the roof of *Unité d'Habitation*, 1953, © Graham Herbert. **Middle** Jackson and Miller *en route* to Israel, 1953, © Graham Herbert. **Bottom** Miller seconded to Israeli Army to escort UN Officials in Negev, 1953, © Graham Herbert.

group attempting to breathe new life into the principles of CIAM, and had then gone on to build the Free University of Berlin's campus before his untimely early death.

Miller's desk was just inside the drafting room by the large mahogany door. Tom Ellis, the sharpest of the partners, became Miller's mentor; seeing him as one of his protegés, Ellis would take Miller, and Colquhoun, to the local Kardomah coffee house and talk about projects with them. He was looking for a critical debate about the schemes that he was working on. Ellis' approach to architectural design was triggered by thinking about the route and the architectural promenade as generating elements.

All three of the partners were impressively skilled draftsmen. Ellis had a particular flair for incisive perspectives and a detailed knowledge of the work of Le Corbusier. Lyons was an old-style watercolour perspectivist. Education was a mainstay of the practice. Local education authorities kept coming back, asking them to work on school projects. Miller's first job was to design and detail an external staircase for a school that Lyons was working on. Miller's staircase impressed Ellis enough to give his young assistant the chance of taking on more responsibility.

The practice was working on a scheme to remodel the Old Vic workshop. Ellis discussed the design at the conceptual stage with Colquhoun and Miller. Then, when the project went ahead, Israel (or Mr Israel as Miller called him, never Laurence) who had responsibility for building it, put Miller on the team. The Old Vic workshop was detached from but adjacent to the original Victorian building's scenery workshops, wardrobe stores and offices. Miller and Norman Pearl worked on Israel and Ellis' designs to produce the working drawings, while Christopher Dean designed the impressive concrete rear escape staircase. Miller helped to work out the shutter boarding finish for the concrete that has since been rendered over. He designed the north lights over the workshop, and worked on detailing the stairs and windows. He learned about using white sand in the mix for the concrete to make it lighter. He used Columbian Pine for doors, windows and cupboards. It was the Old Vic's combination of careful detail with a bold, overall conception that was behind the decision by the Department of Culture, Media and Sport to list the building in 2006. Miller did the site supervision with Israel, shuttling back and forth with him on the Underground from Oxford Circus to Waterloo.

When the project was finished, Miller was given a job of his own to take on, an extension to a school in Harrow Weald that he took from design to the beginning of the working drawings. It was a project based on Lyons Israel Ellis' previous approaches to similar briefs, which Miller was able to interpret in his own way. There was a central hall with a gallery running around it, with a number of classrooms opening off that in a semi-pinwheel arrangement, in a restrained palette of materials. The Lyons Israel Ellis office had provided an excellent grounding in the practical realities of building, and it had adopted, despite the ambition of the work that it produced a studiedly un-precious attitude to what might be called "the cultural aspects of architecture". As Miller remembers, "you worked intensively on the nitty-gritty of building during the day and then design was something that you did, or thought about, in the evenings or at the weekends".

His next job was in Cambridge with a practice that had a very different ethos from that of Lyons Israel Ellis. He was invited to join Sir Leslie Martin who combined practice with the headship of the school of architecture at the University. His office in which, two years earlier, Patrick Hodgkinson had been taken on to work on some housing in St Pancras and Harvey Court for Caius College in Cambridge, had already established a

Top Old Vic Theatre Annex, 1958, drawing by Tom Ellis, © David Gray. **Middle** Old Vic Theatre Annex, 1958, front elevation, © David Gray. **Bottom** Old Vic Theatre Annex, 1958, Miller on site visit, © Graham Herbert.

considerable reputation as an intellectual driving force for British architecture. When Miller joined, Hodgkinson was working on the design of the Oxford Law Library.

Martin, who had led the team designing the Festival Hall at the LCC, was an architect with a strong commitment to public service, as well as having a well-founded reputation for his generosity in pushing work in the direction of gifted young architects embarking in practice on their own account. Miller, who was by now married to his first wife Patricia, was ready to uproot his family and move to a house on the outskirts of Cambridge where his two daughters were born. It was a big step and one from which he had high expectations that were not entirely fulfiled.

Miller arrived in Cambridge, hoping to find an intellectual powerhouse in which he could thrive. Martin's was a relaxed office based in a converted watermill outside the city. Miller found himself being invited to feed the ducks on the mill pond on his first day. But after the pragmatism of Lyons Israel Ellis, Miller found it hard to settle and had trouble adjusting to the apparently idyllic rustic setting of the new office. For Miller, the intensity of the small community around the office, where work and life merged, was difficult to deal with. He had trouble finding enough to do in Cambridge. It was a sink or swim atmosphere with little managerial direction and, at times, even though nothing was said, Miller thought that he was sinking. He felt that he didn't fit in. It was only later, after he had left, that he began to appreciate the quality of the office. Martin's architectural workload at the time was mainly centred on universities and academic buildings. Miller was assigned a project to work on alongside Patrick Hodgkinson who, having worked for Alvar Aalto, was regarded as a star performer. Miller felt unable to make a mark on a project that Hodgkinson had already shaped.

Subsequently, he worked with Martin on developing a sketch scheme for restructuring the internal layout of the huge hulk of the French-Loire-Chateau-style Royal Holloway College at Egham, where the University of London had set up its first women's college in the prodigious Victorian mansion built by the nineteenth century patent medicine tycoon, Thomas Holloway, as well as on some more schematic proposals for building science laboratories and hostels in the grounds. In the end Martin passed on the project, but later, in a characteristically generous gesture, recommended to the University that Colquhoun + Miller be commissioned to design the laboratories under their own name.

Earlier, Thomas North, the East Ham Borough architect, had called up Lyons Israel Ellis to ask if the firm was interested in taking on another school for the Borough. He spoke to Israel who explained that, while Lyons Israel Ellis itself was too busy to consider it, he could recommend a well-qualified associate who had worked with the firm and was ready to go out on his own to do the work. He offered to pass on the job to Alan Colquhoun. Colquhoun and Miller had already discussed the idea of setting up in practice together at the right moment. "Alan called me in Cambridge, 'Shall I accept it?' he asked me, 'Definitely', I said."

And so Colquhoun + Miller was born. They set up their first office in Miller's house in Great Shelford on the outskirts of Cambridge. When he and Colquhoun felt confident to take the next step, they rented an office in London and Miller began to commute to Cambridge where his family still lived. Colquhoun + Miller were based in Alfred Place, just a few steps away from the Architectural Association. When they moved out, Cedric Price took over their old rooms. It was here that they invited Paul Yarker, who had worked alongside them at Lyons Israel Ellis, to join them.

Top Harvey Court, Gonville and Caius College Cambridge, Sir Leslie Martin.
Bottom Royal Holloway College, site plan, Sir Leslie Martin.

When completed, the Royal Holloway College laboratories, their second building, turned out as an impressive and sophisticated project, touched by the spirit of Italian rationalism. The laboratories were organised on a tartan grid, integrating services on the structural layout. They were arranged to step down a steep, sloping site. The concrete and patent glazing had a sharp astringency.

After Alfred Place, Colquhoun + Miller moved into the Sackville Street office, which they shared with Castle Park Dean Hook, friends from their days at Lyons Israel Ellis. They moved again to Neal Street in Covent Garden, and later to Camden.

John Miller's teaching career began in the 1960s, when he was invited to make the first of a series of visits to Cornell by Colin Rowe. After that he spent some years as a part timer at the Royal College of Art, where he was later to make his most substantial contribution to architectural education. When Miller first got there he was teaching on Hugh Casson's course, which had its roots in interior design more than architecture. "When Casson left, Lionel Esher (the Rector at the time) said to me 'Hugh is leaving, would you be a candidate?'." Miller set about becoming the head of what was then called the School of Environmental Design. He was interviewed by a panel that included the designer, Richard Guyatt, Iris Murdoch and Leslie Martin. Miller got the job, and spent ten years from 1975 to 1985 at the Royal College of Art running a department that he was to turn into a fully fledged school of architecture, while at the same time continuing to run his practice. "Lionel Esher said to me 'the college job is full time, four days a week, I expect you to keep up your practice so put in as much time as you need at the office.' It was a very clever strategy. You were not governed by bureaucratic demands, so you made yourself work doubly hard."

The Royal College of Art, one of the products of the Great Exhibition of 1851, was a very different proposition from the Architectural Association. It was and is Britain's only postgraduate college of art and design that has excelled by attracting an elite of gifted students across a wide range of disciplines, painting, sculpture, industrial and graphic design, automotive and fashion.

When Miller got there the College had a recently built new home, designed by a consortium of architects that included Jim Cadbury-Brown, Robert Gooden and Hugh Casson. It had skillfully managed to construct the trappings of an instant tradition for itself, complete with senior common room, college plate, medieval academic costume, and even a beedle.

What it did not yet have was a credible architecture school. There was an interior design programme, which gave graduates of art schools a further two or three years of study. But in the early 1970s, the majority of architectural degrees were five-year courses. The Royal College postgraduate degree did not fit comfortably with that pattern. For those students who planned to work as professional architects, the Royal College had the additional drawback of not meeting the demands of the Royal Institute of British Architects, needed to achieve exemption from their professional exams.

Miller's primary objective was to develop a programme for the College that would attract more mainstream architectural students by offering them a course that they could not find elsewhere, and a real school of architecture, with its courses gaining exemption from the Part 2 examination of the RIBA. At the same time it would provide interior design students an with understanding of the architectural context in which they would be operating.

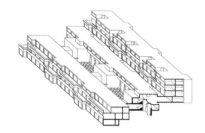

Royal Holloway College, Hostel block,
Sir Leslie Martin.

By this time, Miller's first marriage had ended. He was living with Su Rogers (with his two daughters and her three sons). They would later marry, and she would join Colquhoun + Miller as a partner. After teaching at the AA, Rogers moved to the Royal College where she worked in the College's Project Office, set up to take on live architectural schemes to provide students with practical experience.

The project office—which at one stage employed David Chipperfield—worked for George Howard at Castle Howard, on the interior of St John's Smith Square, on the gates at the V&A, forming a screen to its Exhibition Road entrance and on the Henry Moore Gallery, being an extension to the College's existing ground floor exhibition galleries.

For Miller, the Royal College of Art represented the possibility of building a unique architectural programme, aimed at postgraduates, and based within the context of an art school. He had an ambitious idea to create a school which looked beyond the parochial concerns of the British context, and which was ready to provide a viewpoint more definite than the well-meaning vagueness of most UK educational practice. It was, of course, a precise reflection of Miller's own architectural position and, translated into an educational programme, was to prove a highly influential one producing a course that was not available anywhere else.

With Ken Frampton recruited as a senior tutor, Miller began to map out a teaching programme that helped to establish the RCA as one of the most internationally influential centres for architectural education in Britain. It upset the heads of other architecture schools by attracting their brightest students to move after their Part 1 qualification and complete their educations with Royal College of Art diplomas. Even Alvin Boyarsky, by this time in command of the Architectural Association, was said to be looking at Kensington Gore with a little jealousy. Among the teaching staff, Edward Jones and James Gowan were consecutively senior tutors.

The course, as framed by Frampton and Miller, was prescriptive: it demanded that students knew history and were ready to venture beyond the familiar standbys. Miller says "we insisted that the students became involved with architecture in the context of the landscape. We worked on designing a curriculum, which did not depend only on purely functional issues. We did not simply want to hang architecture on a functional hook." A typical first project for new students would involve giving them the floor plan of a modern building, though not one so well known that they would be able to recognise it. Students were trusted to own up if they knew what their plans represented, and would be issued an alternative. Their task was to project the plans into three dimensions, to create a facade and a cross-section on the basis of the strictly limited information that they had to go on. It was a means of getting students to understand the spatial implications of the early Modern Movement, and at the subsequent "crit", students were asked to compare their work to the original in order to get them to think about historical precedent.

There was an impressive variety of visiting critics from every corner of architecture's ideological spectrum. They included Leo Krier, at that time still working for James Stirling and yet to ally himself with the Prince of Wales, Dimitri Porphyrious, Fernando Montez and Elia Zenghelis.

Students were expected to travel. Miller made the department budget stretch far enough to allow students to take regular study trips to Paris, Barcelona, Amsterdam, Rome and Vienna. On these excursions the students combined looking at key buildings, and

Top Su Rogers. **Middle** Henry Moore Gallery, Royal College of Art, © Peter Cook/View. **Bottom** Henry Moore Gallery, Royal College of Art, © Frank Thurston.

doing a project associated with the city. They got to meet locally based architects, such as Boris Podrecca in Vienna, and David Mackay in Barcelona. Podrecca, with his special expertise on the work of Jože Plečnik, was able to bring a new insight into an important historical figure still not well enough known in Britain at the time. And Mackay, as a member of MBM, gave advance warning of Barcelona's ground-breaking plans for large scale urban reconstruction after the end of the Franco dictatorship.

The students that the RCA architecture school, under Miller's leadership, attracted, included Russel Bevington, Tim Boyd, Norman Chang, Rachel Chidlow, Alex de Rijke, Mark Guard, Ben Kelly, Paul Keogh, Malcolm Last, Heidi Locher, Ken Mackay, David Nelson, Sheila O'Donnell, Eric Parry, Jose Santos, Ian Sharratt, and Patrick Theis.

It was during the teaching period that Miller began to work on the design of a series of exhibitions on art and architecture that both underscored and made use of the lessons of the European excursions that he was making with his students, and also began to lay the foundations for the work the firm was to do in the future, on the design of a series of art galleries.

Colquhoun + Miller was commissioned by Richard Francis, at that time at the Arts Council, to work on the design of travelling exhibitions. One looked at the work of Adolf Loos. Another was a show on the design of the modern house. At much the same time, Joanna Drew from the Hayward asked Colquhoun + Miller to design an exhibition on Dada and Surrealism, for Miller a richly rewarding project to work on. Through Francis, the firm was to meet Nicholas Serota who was shortly to move from the Oxford Museum of Modern Art to the Whitechapel. Serota was to be Colquhoun + Miller's client for the remodelling of the Whitechapel Gallery when he was the director, and again, when Serota had moved to the Tate, he found Colquhoun + Miller had already been commissioned by his predecessor, Alan Bowness to work on a masterplan for Tate Millbank. Serota wanted an architect sensitive both to art, and to historical context, and yet still firmly rooted in a contemporary architectural language to remodel the building.

Miller's practice has gone through a variety of incarnations. Richard Brearley became a partner in 1975 and Su Rogers in 1986. They continued to work with Alan Colquhoun until 1989 when he began to spend most of his time in America. The partnership was formally ended in 1990 and reformed as John Miller + Partners.

The Royal College itself went through something of a leadership change. Esher was succeeded by Lionel March, who soon resigned from the Rectorship declaring the College to be ungovernable. He was followed by Jocelyn Stevens, whose close connections with Margaret Thatcher and the Conservatives alienated some in the College, particularly when he started talking about making its courses more commercially relevant. He briefly suggested that architecture could usefully be transformed into a school of retail design. But Stevens' direct line to government helped to insulate the College from financial instability during a particularly bleak period. Indeed, Stevens managed to find the resources to fund an ambitious building programme, which turned into commissions for Colquhoun + Miller. The Jay Mews entrance to the college was remodelled and the Stevens Building, a complex mix of restoration and new building, was commissioned.

This was also the period of the redesign of the Whitechapel Gallery, and its extension. The commission to remodel the Whitechapel pushed Colquhoun + Miller's work in a new direction. It came at a time when Miller was growing disenchanted at the failure

Top 10 Twentieth Century Houses, catalogue cover, 1980. **Middle** Richard Brearley, 1977. **Bottom** Stevens Building and Jay Mews entrance, Royal College of Art, 1990, © Martin Charles.

of so many modern buildings to try to address the public role of architecture, or to work with historical, or the cultural, and geographic context. That is why the example set by Otto Wagner, Loos and others was so interesting for Miller. And it moved Miller to begin to explore the richer range of architectural flavours, which can be seen in the Stevens Building at the RCA, and also at the Whitechapel. It is a tendency that was most marked in Colquhoun + Miller's submission for the second stage of the National Gallery competition. For this highly charged site, overshadowed by the Prince of Wales' carbuncle speech, their design took the form of an Italianate palazzo, grafted onto the western end of Wilkins' original building.

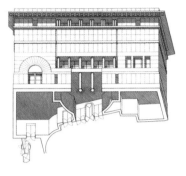

Given the multiple layers of the original Whitechapel building (an Arts and Crafts design with what might be understood to have an Art Nouveau rinse), it was perhaps inevitable that Miller's own work, always eclectic in its range of interests and influences, would be affected. What fascinates Miller is the idea of architectural innovation within the context of the customary and accepted methodology. Each of the practice's schemes is based on that play between custom and innovation; each of them has a twist of some kind. In Colquhoun + Miller's Oldbrook terraced housing project, for example, it is the plan. Colquhoun + Miller cranked the party wall to accommodate a staircase for each pair of terraced houses. It is an arrangement that allows for a corridor to drive through from front to back.

In their Hornsey Lane residential block, the brief was to provide accommodation for single people. The local authority client realised that paired bedsits would fit some needs for nurses hostels, and also for married couples. The ambition here was to achieve flexibility, within the context of a moderately high building, stretching the limits of reinforced brickwork. Few architects have been so urbane yet rigorous in their work as Miller, who has used his own designs as a kind of scholarly research into the essence of architecture. It has taken him from an interest in the French and Italian pre-war modernists, to turn-of-the-century Vienna. In Pillwood, the holiday house in Cornwall that he designed with Su Rogers, there is patent glazing and GRP high-tech. The gallery work is carefully respectful of the work of earlier architects, from Playfair in Edinburgh to Townsend at the Whitechapel, but also remarkably dexterous in making the most of complex plans and sections. In the University buildings at East Anglia, Miller has returned to the themes of the purist architecture of his own student days. The practice has built social housing in Milton Keynes, and in London, It has designed university buildings, and schools, a theatre and individual houses. In Alcoy, in Spain, there was a substantial urban expansion scheme, that remains unrealised.

As a body of work, it is impressive: an exemplary and highly accomplished model of what reflective architectural practice can be; and as a view of civilised architectural values, even more so.

EDUCATION

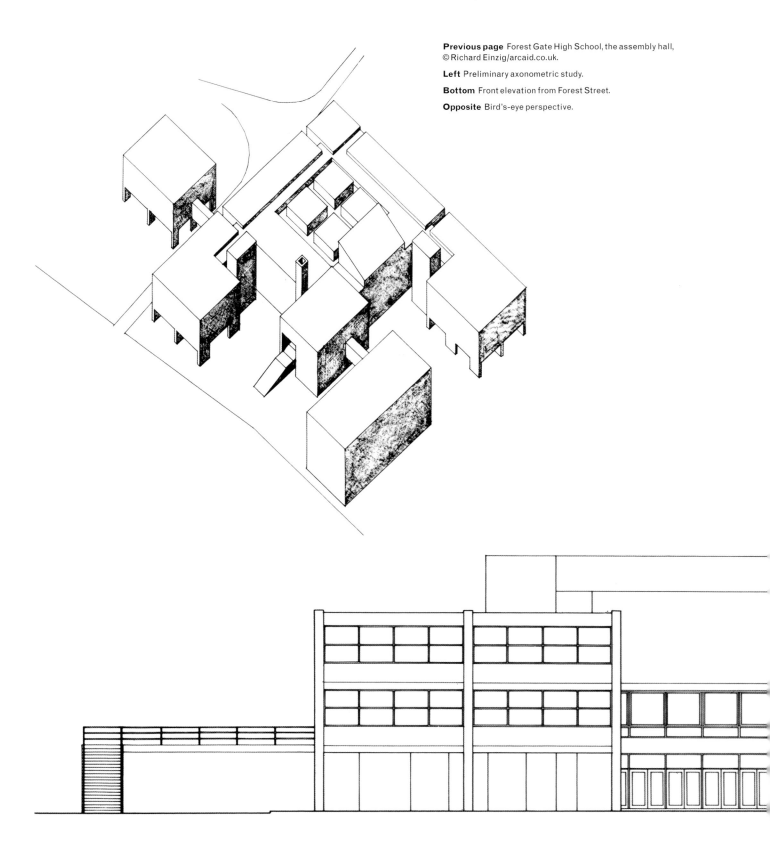

Previous page Forest Gate High School, the assembly hall,
© Richard Einzig/arcaid.co.uk.

Left Preliminary axonometric study.

Bottom Front elevation from Forest Street.

Opposite Bird's-eye perspective.

1965

FOREST GATE HIGH SCHOOL
London
Colquhoun + Miller

The school was Colquhoun + Miller's first building, commissioned by West Ham Borough Council to accommodate 780 mixed secondary school children.

The concept, with its square central assembly hall enclosed on two sides by classrooms set at right angles to one another, and with its remaining two sides fronting stage and small hall, shows the influence of Louis Kahn and of Frank Lloyd Wright's Unity Chapel with its four columns and associated access stairs. This compact arrangement is in part a critique of the dispersed school plan and in part a response to the severe restrictions of a small urban site. The arrangement of the enclosing classrooms and central hall produces a strong diagonal. A challenge requiring the need to frontalise the composition on Forest Street with the detached entry portico acting as the anchor.

Plain red brick is used throughout the exterior to be as near as possible to the original colour of clay. In retrospect, the expression of classroom cross-walls might have been omitted in favour of a simple overall surface, as is used in the gymnasium block, and as is suggested in the preliminary axonometric illustrated. This would provide greater homogeneity and remove the formal difficulties of the large end classrooms where the cross-walls are turned at right angles to the remainder.

A future extension for 120 school children was planned but not built. This was to be on the smaller piece of land approached by a bridge at first floor level.

The building has been much altered over 45 years and is now to be renovated.

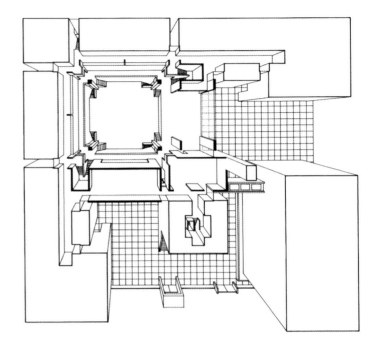

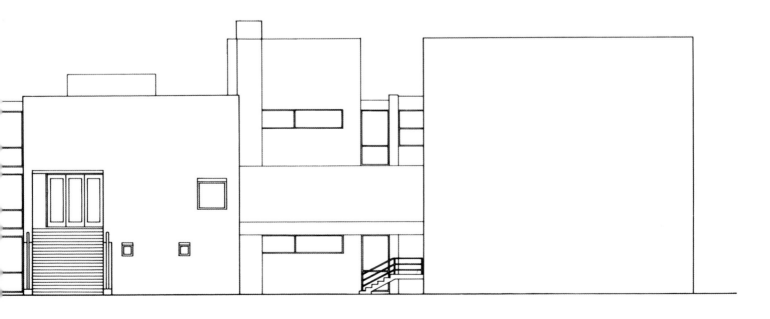

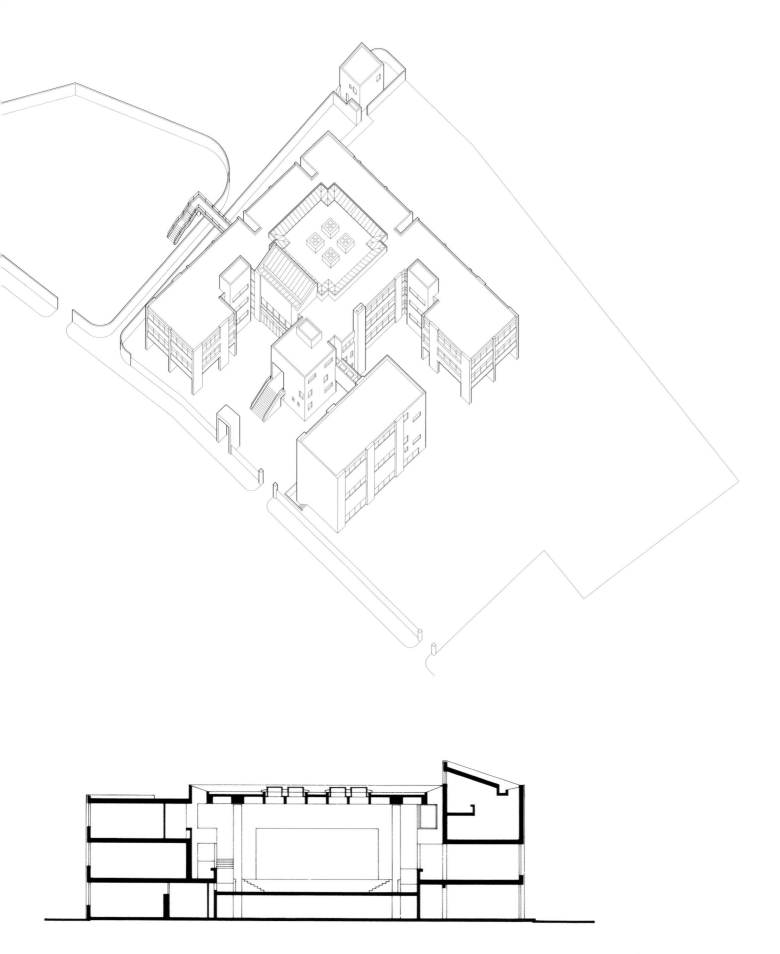

Opposite Lateral view across the forestage and part of the assembly hall, © Richard Einzig/arcaid.co.uk.

Below View of the stage and assembly hall, © Richard Einzig/arcaid.co.uk.

Overleaf Assembly hall, © Richard Einzig/arcaid.co.uk.

Top and bottom First floor; Ground floor.

Opposite top Library, © Richard Einzig/arcaid.co.uk.

Opposite bottom Second floor.

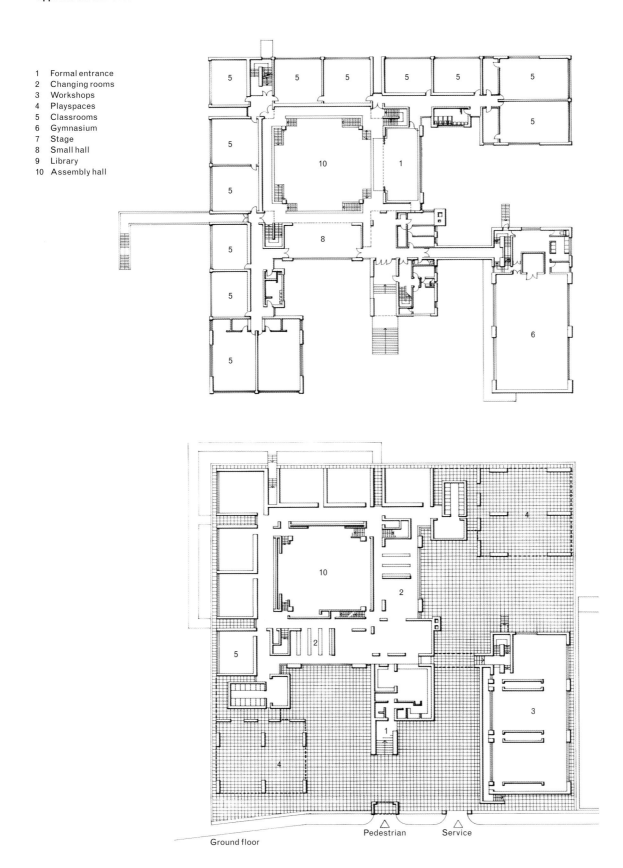

1 Formal entrance
2 Changing rooms
3 Workshops
4 Playspaces
5 Classrooms
6 Gymnasium
7 Stage
8 Small hall
9 Library
10 Assembly hall

Pedestrian   Service

Ground floor

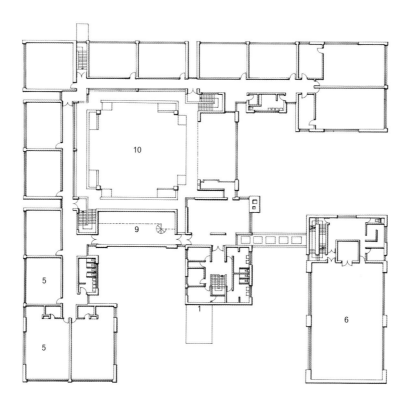

1971

CHEMISTRY BUILDING
Royal Holloway College
Colquhoun + Miller

Chemistry Building Royal Holloway College, site plan.

The Chemistry Building is the second of Colquhoun + Miller's built commissions.

Where Forest Gate is an exercise in compositional massing, the form of the Chemistry Building is determined by module, and the mechanics of service distribution set against the challenge of a sloping site.

The three foot four inch square module and its half module, anticipating the change to metrication, are used rigourously throughout. Thus, the fragment conditions the form of the whole. The structural bay relates to the space needed, for Lab bench, fume cupboard, fittings and personnel. This forms a planning sub-group offering a potential for future expansion whether lateral or longitudinal.

The need for future expansion and height control provides a spreading form in which daylight is provided by light wells. The accommodation divides into two types, linear and non-linear, corresponding closely to the two major components, research and teaching. The sloping site gives the opportunity of interconnection between them. The research sub-groups in the form of Ts are placed over the teaching laboratories below. Their ancillaries are located on the two long perimeters. The teaching sub-groups run laterally across the building at ground level and consist of a pair of two large laboratories with parallel ancillaries.

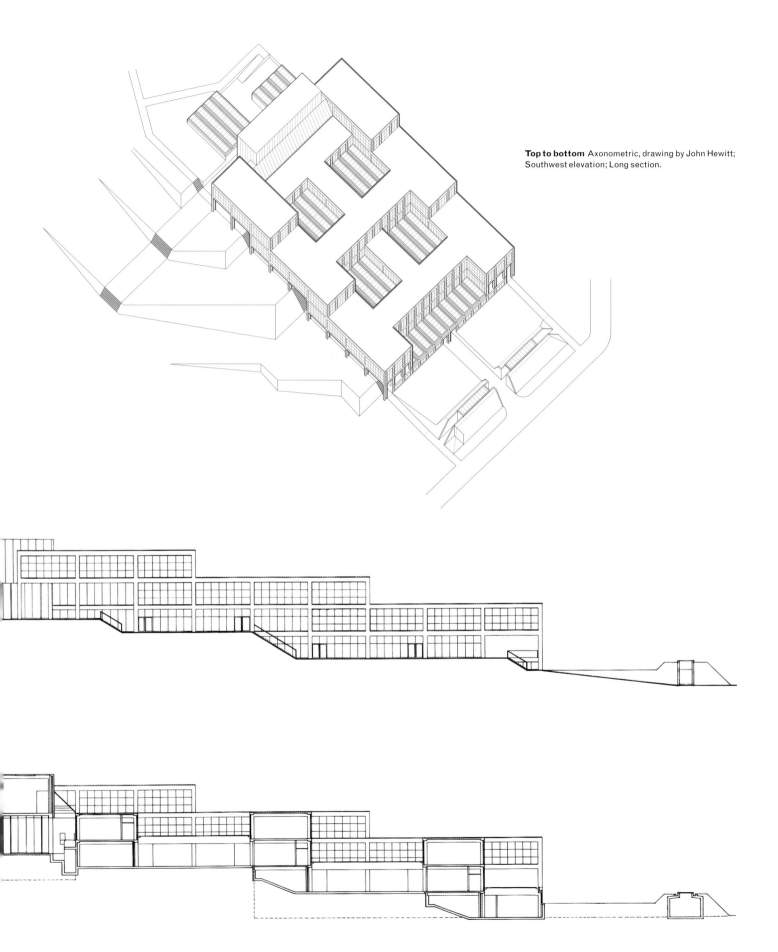

Top to bottom Axonometric, drawing by John Hewitt; Southwest elevation; Long section.

1 Stores
2 Workshops
3 Teaching laboratories
4 Research
5 Lecture theatre
6 Library
7 Administration
8 Entrance

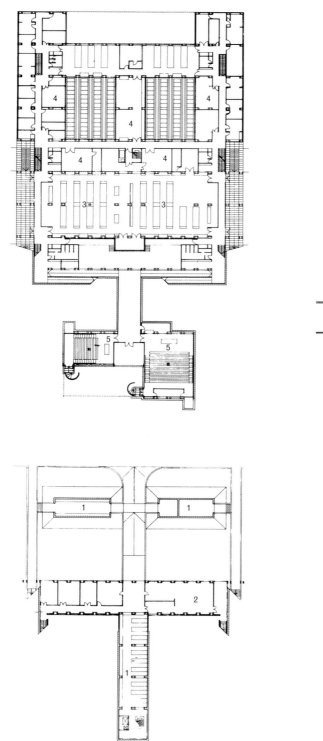

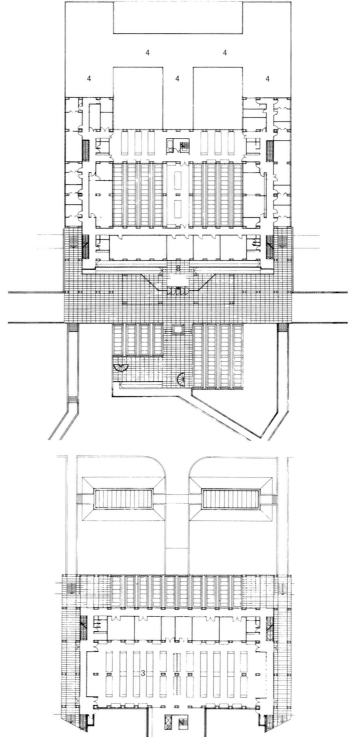

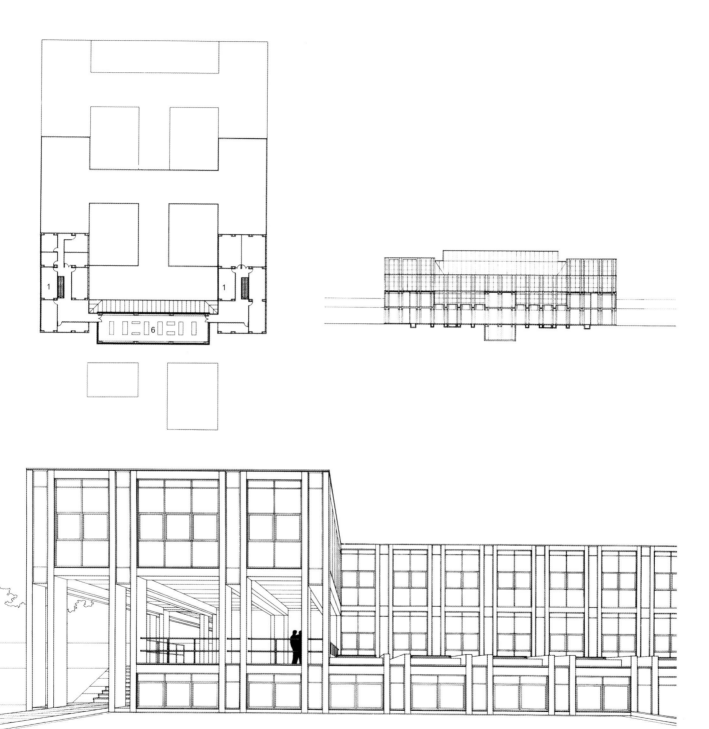

Opposite clockwise from top left Level 3; Level 4; Level 2; Level 1.

Clockwise from top left Level 5; Cross-section; Perspective from the access road.

Top and bottom Part view of the entrance hall; Entry to the library with views down to the entrance, © Richard Einzig/arcaid.co.uk.

Opposite Entrance hall, © Richard Einzig/arcaid.co.uk.

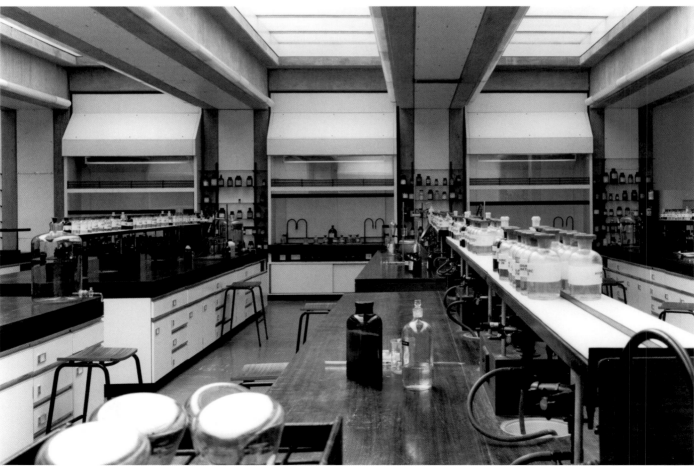

Opposite top and bottom Rooflight over the teaching laboratory; Teaching laboratories, © Richard Einzig/arcaid.co.uk.

Top and bottom Teaching laboratories and side collonade; Teaching laboratories, © Richard Einzig/arcaid.co.uk.

Top and bottom Service entrance; View from the Service Road, © Richard Einzig/arcaid.co.uk.

Opposite top and bottom Views of the rooflight to the workshops, © Richard Einzig/arcaid.co.uk.

Overleaf Perspective of the teaching laboratories with the research department over, drawing by Birkin Haward.

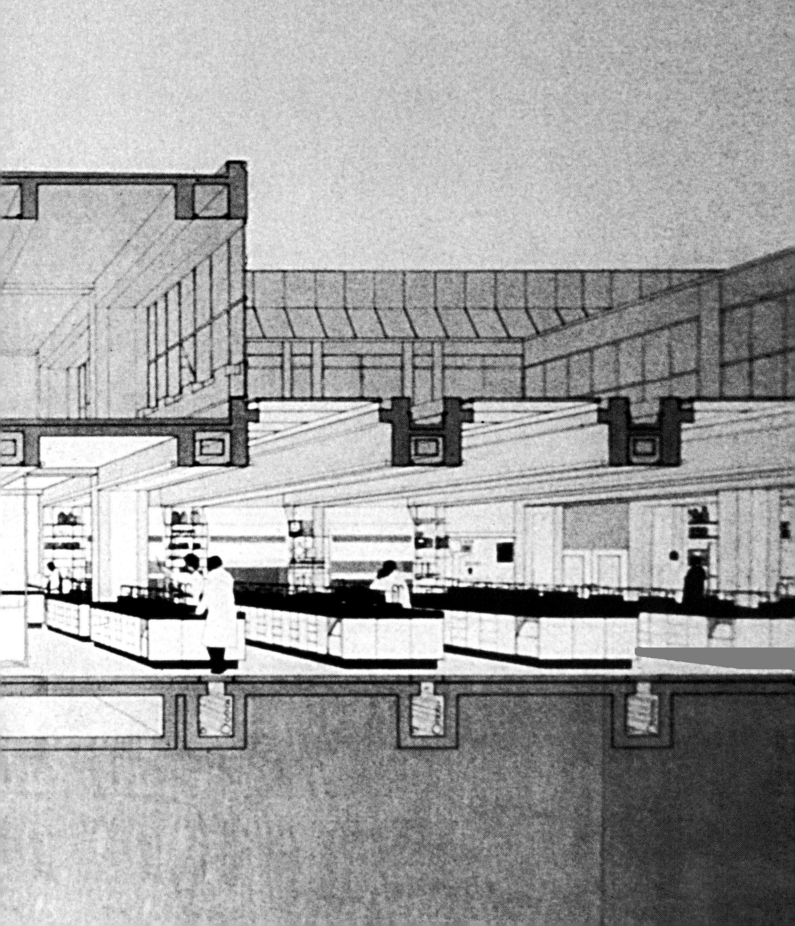

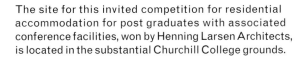

1986

CHURCHILL COLLEGE
Cambridge University
Colquhoun + Miller

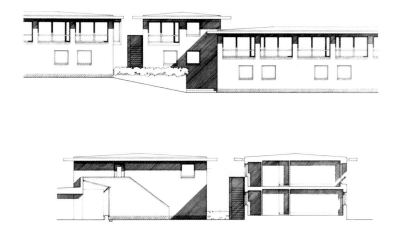

The site for this invited competition for residential accommodation for post graduates with associated conference facilities, won by Henning Larsen Architects, is located in the substantial Churchill College grounds.

The Colquhoun + Miller entry is organised around a gently ramping covered walk running longitudinally east–west in response to the sloping site. It is open to three two-storey residential courts on the southern side. These open onto smaller semi-open courts that in turn give access to the College grounds. The upper floors of the two easterly residences span the walk and thus associates it with its adjacent space. The residence to the west terminates the walk. A band of car parking is contained at eastern and western ends by building. Pedestrian entries through the parking strip relate to the courts beyond. A further band of parking is located to the north of the service road. Social accommodation including a lecture hall, common room and dining hall is located at the easterly end.

The intention is to provide a sense of place without rhetorical gesture and the expression is deliberately modest, drawing on vernacular form. Upper windows of the hostels are enlarged to suggest an arcade and to disengage the roof from the masonry walls below. The lower square windows are paired, which provides a variation in the wall surface pattern.

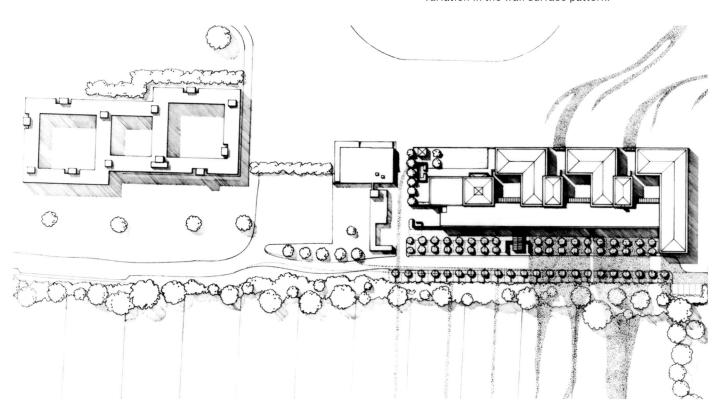

Opposite top to bottom Elevation and sectional studies; Site plan.

Top and bottom First floor; Ground floor.

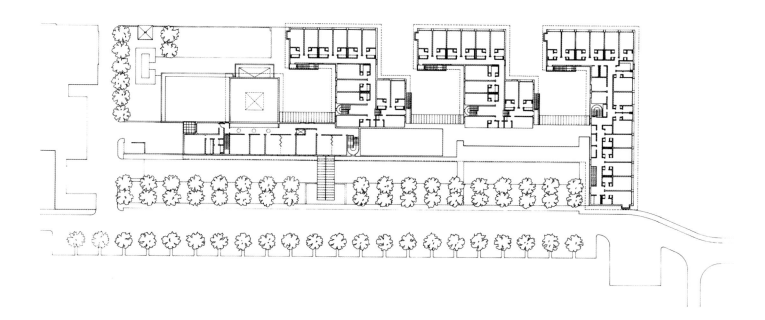

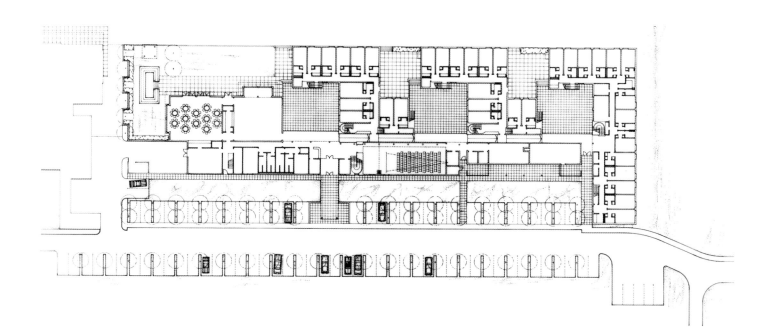

1991

STEVENS BUILDING
Royal College of Art
Colquhoun + Miller

In the mid-1980s, the Department of Education and Science, put pressure on the College to give up its satellite sites. Amongst the schools and departments affected were the Schools of Painting and Photography. Both had enjoyed an improvised existence: the painters and printmakers in a range of studios to the rear of the Victoria and Albert Museum, which had been their home since before the V&A existed; the photographers in a large villa in Cromwell Road.

The College was able to convert three houses on Queen's Gate and demolish the cottages on Jay Mews behind. It could then consolidate the remainder of its departments close to those of the main building on the Gore. The evacuation to the headquarters site on Kensington Gore and Queen's Gate was finally made in 1991.

The site is severely restricted and English Heritage had insisted that the height of the existing cottages should be respected. Although it had been accepted that the back of the three Queen's Gate houses could be demolished, the three nineteenth century stairs should be retained. The College in the meantime had elected to accommodate the Schools of Film and Television, Graphics, and a number of other departments in addition to the painters and photographers on the new site.

The Queen's Gate houses are Grade II Listed, restricting new building work to their backs and to a developable area extending to the Jay Mews frontage. The deep site requires a top-lit space at its centre and this divides the new Jay Mews accommodation from that in Queen's Gate. It provides a central exhibition area. The accommodation needs require six floors, two below ground and four above in the Jay Mews building, to be planned in the context of two- and three-storey cottages.

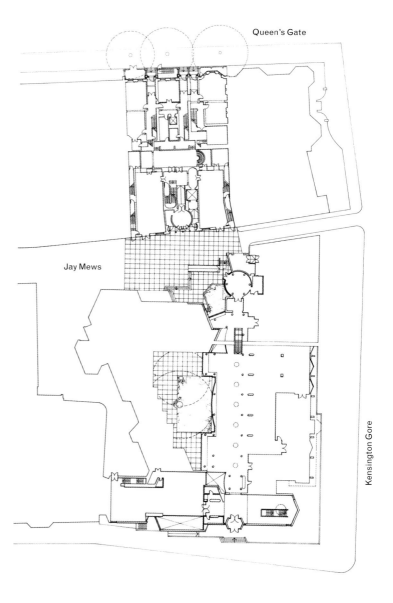

Queen's Gate

Jay Mews

Kensington Gore

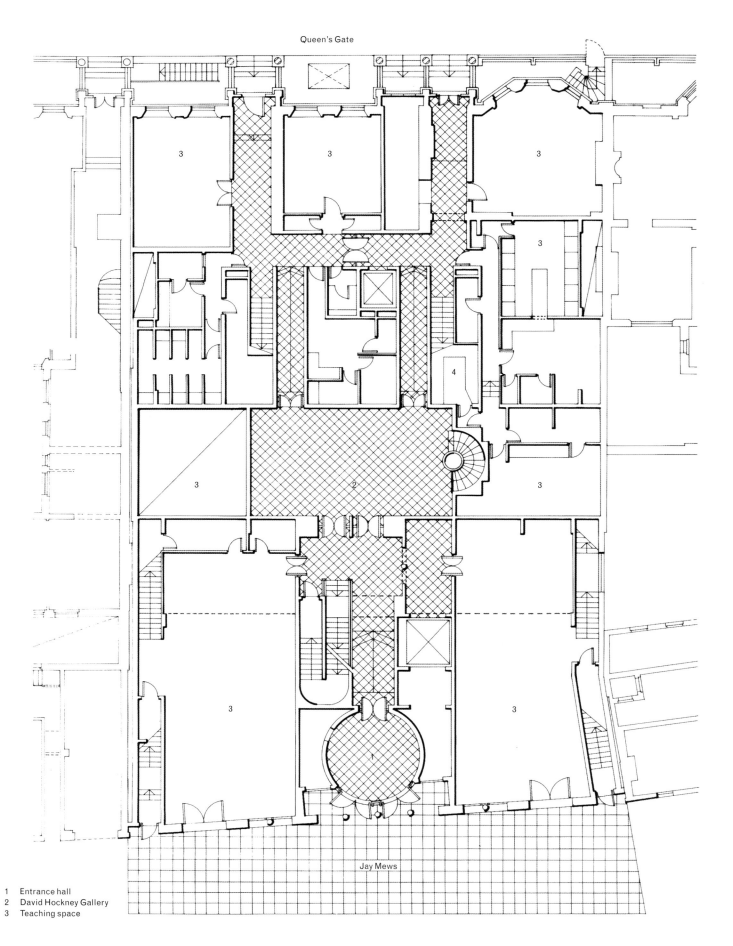

Queen's Gate

Jay Mews

1　Entrance hall
2　David Hockney Gallery
3　Teaching space

The Jay Mews elevation is conceived as a tripartite composition with a first floor parapet corresponding to the cornice heights of the adjacent properties; and an arcaded second floor set back from the plane of the elevation with an attic mansard above. This reduces the scale if not the bulk of the building. The elevation is rendered white with brick trim in the spirit of the existing cottages.

The new rear elevation of the Queen's Gate building is in a dark brick, corresponding to the adjacent houses. Internally, English Heritage have insisted that all three Queen's Gate staircases should be retained. This creates a labyrinth and an unclear circulation pattern. The request to demolish all three houses up to the back wall of their front rooms facing Queen's Gate has been refused, on the grounds that the three houses might be restored as entities sometime in the future.

The proposed departure of the Painting School to new studios in Battersea is an indication that the plan to accommodate so much in a constricted envelope was perhaps over ambitious.

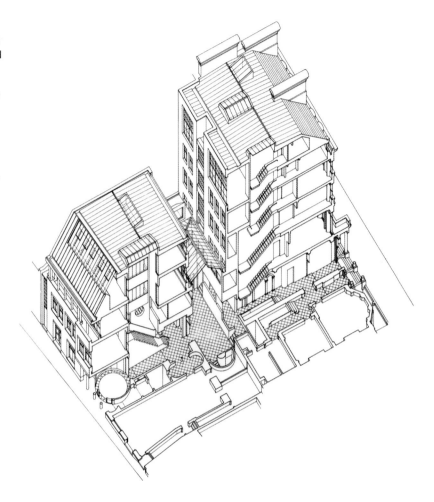

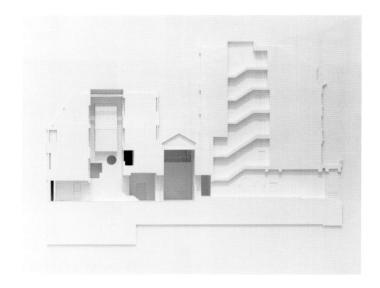

Top and bottom Photographic studio, © Martin Charles; Section through the Hockney Exhibition Gallery with the rear elevation of the Queen's Gate building behind.

Opposite Rear elevation of the Queen's Gate building and part of the flankwall of the Jay Mews block, © Martin Charles.

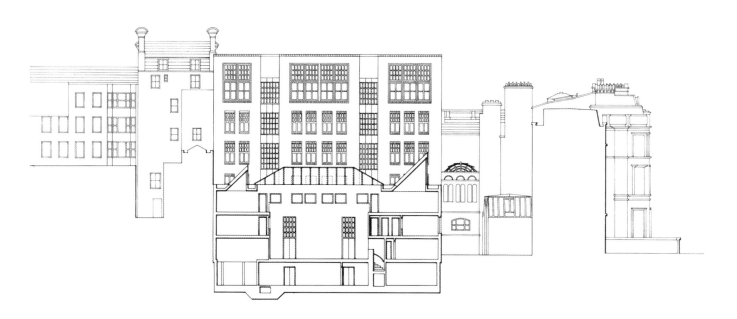

1992

NEW SCIENCE BUILDING
Portsmouth University
John Miller + Partners

Top to bottom Cross-section through the offices; Elevation of the entrance ramp to the laboratory building; Rear elevation; Elevation to King Richard the First Street; Long section.

Opposite top and bottom Axonometrics from the north and south.

This limited competition is for a New Science Building for the University of Portsmouth, known as the St Michaels Building. The brief implies that Portsmouth City Council anticipate developing the adjoining site for a multi-storey car park and offices.

The triangular laboratory building is an extension to an existing building. It faces southeast, southwest and west. It benefits from a passive solar system for thermal storage and delivery. This makes use of a void between two skins, the outer one glass and the inner one masonry with a narrow space between them. This is known as a "trombe wall".

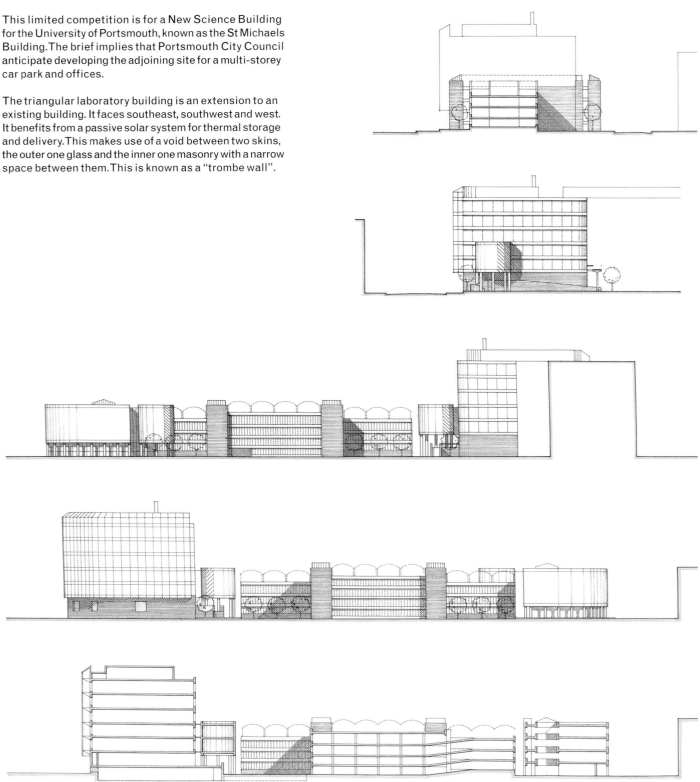

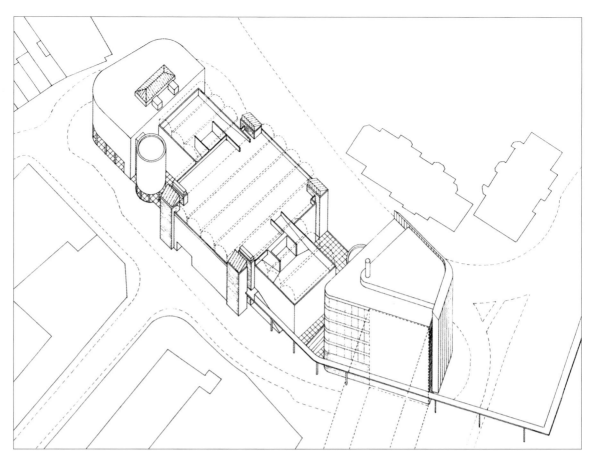

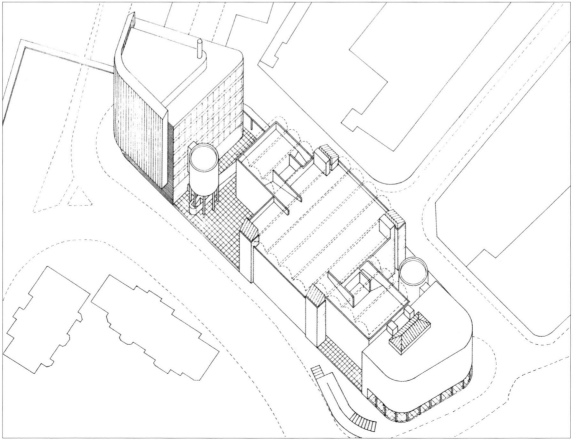

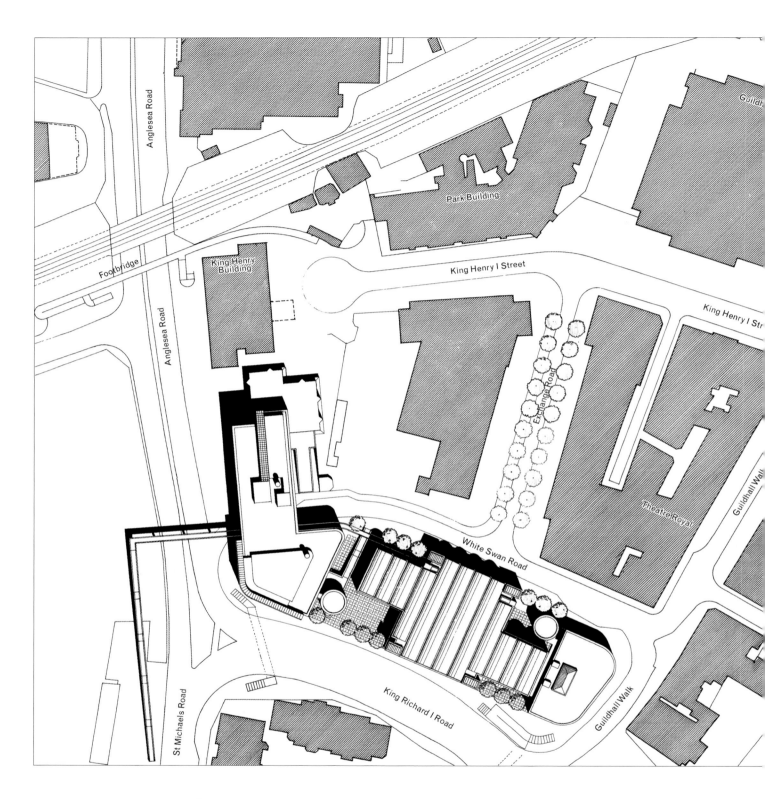

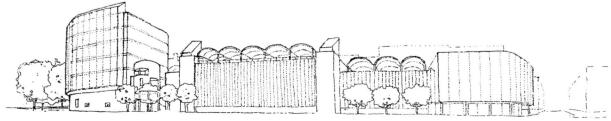

Opposite top and bottom Site plan; Perspective sketch of the south elevation.

Clockwise from top Views from White Swan Road; Perspective sketch of the southeast corner.

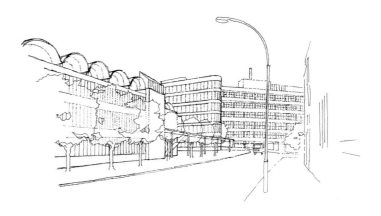

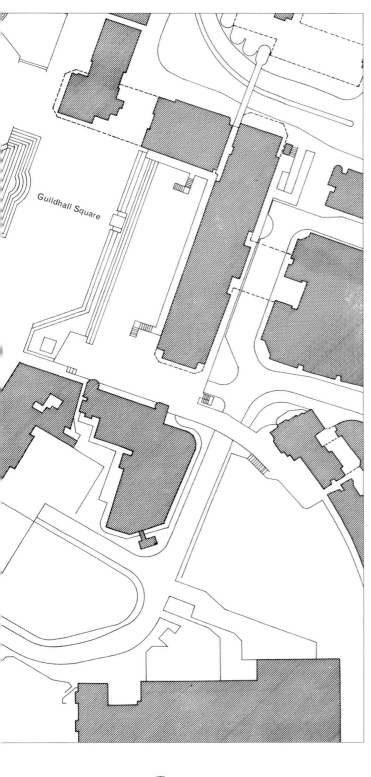

Guildhall Square

QUEEN'S BUILDING (OTP)
University of East Anglia
John Miller + Partners

In the late 1980s, the University of East Anglia was encouraged to provide a programme of health related academic subjects and agreed with the Regional Health Authority that it should build on the University of East Anglia site. The Queen's Building for Occupational Therapy and Physiotherapy OTP is the result of this enterprise.

The adjacent Lasdun Science Building captures the view of open Norfolk landscape and does not anticipate future development other than by extrusion. This had created an area of backland, given over to a number of temporary buildings and greenhouses. The recent masterplan has humanised this area with planting and new building work. It has set the scene for the design of the Queen's Building, or OTP as it is also known.

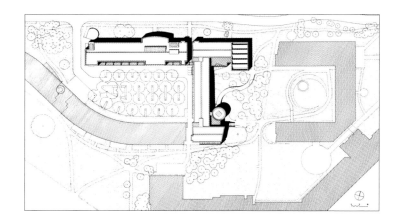

It seems that John Miller makes it a point of honour that everything should share in the design, that designed quality should be evident at all levels.
Architecture Today, April 2004

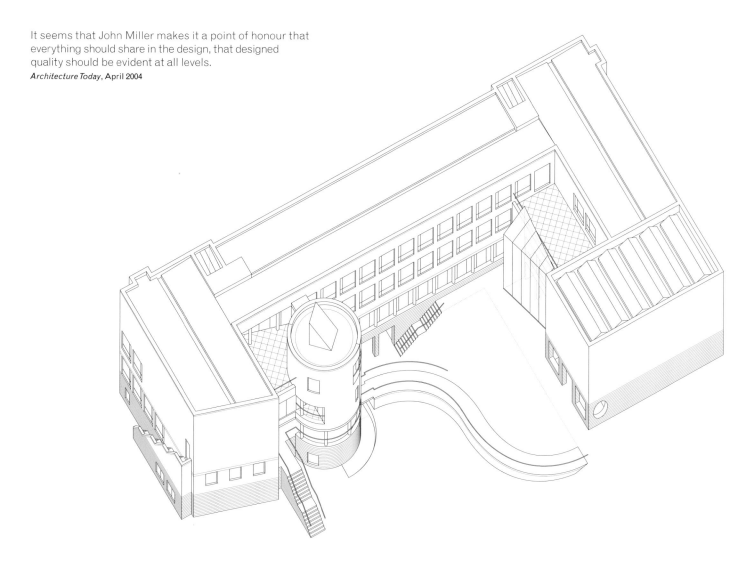

Opposite top Site plan.

Opposite bottom Axonometric of the Queen's Building, drawing by John Hewitt.

Top and bottom First floor; Ground floor.

<table>
<tr><td>1</td><td>Entrance foyer</td><td>9</td><td>Academic office</td></tr>
<tr><td>2</td><td>Administration office</td><td>10</td><td>Plant</td></tr>
<tr><td>3</td><td>Store</td><td>11</td><td>Gymnasium</td></tr>
<tr><td>4</td><td>Teaching classroom</td><td>12</td><td>Common room</td></tr>
<tr><td>5</td><td>Resources</td><td>13</td><td>Lecture theatre</td></tr>
<tr><td>6</td><td>Anatomy suite</td><td>14</td><td>Control/projection</td></tr>
<tr><td>7</td><td>Changing/lockers</td><td>15</td><td>Terrace</td></tr>
<tr><td>8</td><td>Seminar</td><td></td><td></td></tr>
</table>

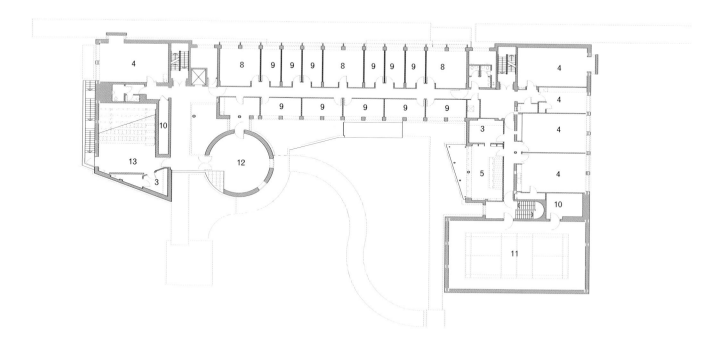

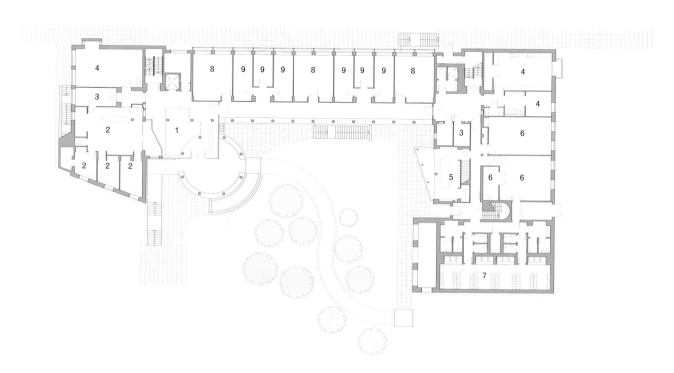

Below Sketch showing the entrance sequence.

Opposite top and bottom Photograph of model; Second floor.

Overleaf Queen's Building, entrance elevation from the birch grove,
© Dennis Gilbert/View.

1 Entrance foyer
2 Administration office
3 Store
4 Teaching classroom
5 Resources
6 Anatomy suite
7 Changing/lockers
8 Seminar
9 Academic office
10 Plant
11 Gymnasium
12 Common room
13 Lecture theatre
14 Control/projection
15 Terrace

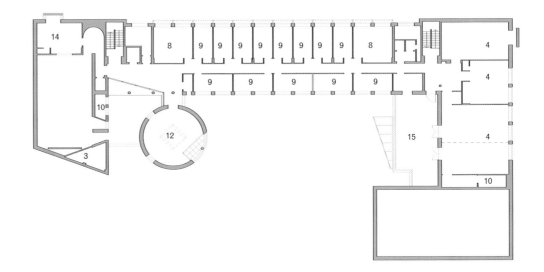

It is a credit to the clear thinking of the client, and to the
capacity of the architect to listen, that the building
manifestly satisfies every aspect of its brief to produce a
work of architecture that captures in some extraordinary
way the ethos and aspirations of the institution.

Sensitively planned and meticulously detailed, the
building was clearly constructed with an exceptional
degree of care and attention. The result of this is that,
after its first year of occupation, it looks in perfect
condition and well able to stand the rigours of student use.
Comment by the jury for the RIBA Award 1995

OTP is planned as an open U, and offers partial closure to the courtyard of the adjacent Computing Services building. It encloses a grove of silver birches. The entry drum refers to the cylindrical form of the small extension to the faculty of science located on the easterly approach.

The fall across the site provides complexity at the entry drum. The change in level allows the serpentine approach to cross over a lower pedestrian access which is reconciled formally with the ground floor entry above. The crossing of the two routes is celebrated by a timber 'bridge'. The approach and the circular entry space are paved; although the bridge is fixed, it suggests the mobility of a draw bridge. The drum's entry space prepares the visitor for the point of entry.

A small library is embraced and expressed in the 'elbow' opposite the drum. It is glazed and is given a formal value to contrast with the band of adjacent normative offices and classrooms.

Because of the fall, the arcaded ground floor has the characteristics of a *piano nobile*. It connects the gymnasium and the 120 seat lecture theatre planned at its two extremities. Faculty offices and classrooms on three floors are located between these two communal functions.

The building is designed to be energy efficient using the thermal mass of the structure and a high level of insulation. It incorporates low E glazing, and energy saving artificial light.

The structure is a reinforced concrete frame with reinforced concrete ribbed floors forming shallow vaults. The vaults act as reflectors for fluorescent up lighters. Dry partitioning maximises the internal spaces.

External materials are engineering brick and reconstructed stone block for the base, with string courses and parapets in engineering brick. The infill panels are rendered. Windows and rooflights are in coated metal.

ELIZABETH FRY BUILDING
University of East Anglia
John Miller + Partners

The Elizabeth Fry Building or the New Academic Building (NAB) is a neighbour of the Queen's Building.

The section takes advantage of the fall across the site with four lecture theatres and two seminar rooms ranged at lower ground level. Teaching spaces for short courses are at an upper ground level, the formal entry level, with two storeys of tutorial offices and common rooms above.

The double-banked upper floor corridors are relieved by the slipped alignment of the two common rooms over the main entrance. This dislocation connects the entrance hall visually to the upper floors and celebrates the two common rooms on the elevation. The section anticipates a connection to a future building via a covered walkway at the rear of the building.

The building structure acts as an energy store. This combined with low pressure mechanical ventilation, heat recovery, and opening windows maximises ambient conditions. The airtight envelope is insulated. Windows are triple-glazed giving minimal solar gain.

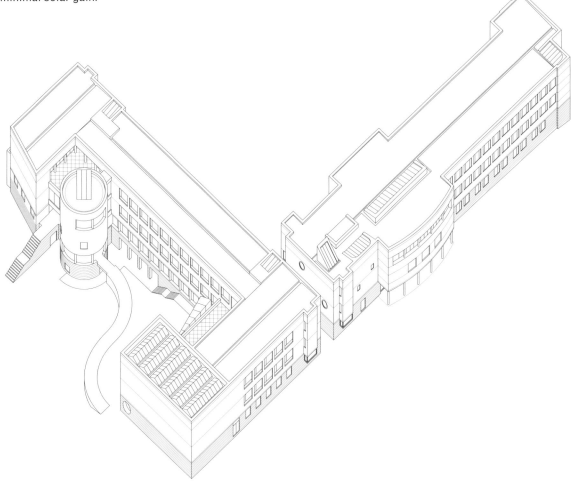

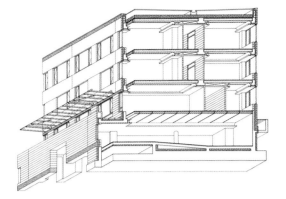

Opposite top and bottom Entrance elevation, © Anthony Weller/View; Axonometric showing the Queen's Building and Elizabeth Fry Building, drawing by John Hewitt.

Top to bottom Cross-section; Upper floor; Upper ground floor; Lower ground floor.

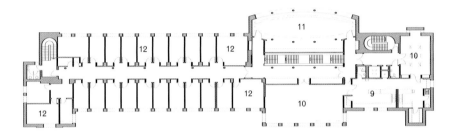

1	Lecture theatre
2	Seminar room
3	Plant
4	Entrance
5	Seminar room
6	Office
7	Arrival business centre
8	Postgraduate office
9	Kitchen
10	Dining/meeting room
11	Common resources room
12	Academic office

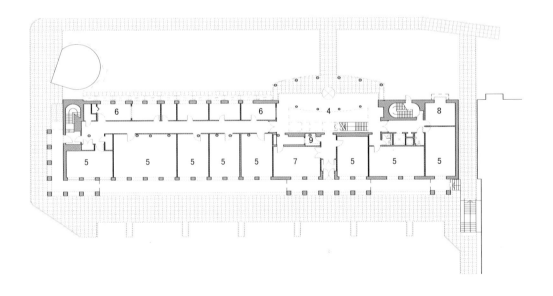

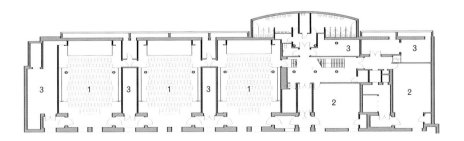

Top and bottom End elevation; Part of the north elevation,
© Anthony Weller/View.

Opposite top and bottom Part of the north elevation; South elevation
to the car park, © Anthony Weller/View.

A minimal heat demand of 24 kw is achieved with two domestic wall mounted boilers serving a building of 3,000 m^2 with a potential occupancy of 850 people. There is no mechanical cooling.

The building provides an opportunity to experiment with energy conservation techniques in line with University of East Anglia policy.

The materials, and expression of the building are in sympathy with the adjacent Queen's Building, with a base of stone-faced blockwork and white rendering to walls above.

Clockwise from top Main staircase from the second floor; Accomodation stair; View of the first floor from the main stair, © Anthony Weller/View.

Opposite Link canopy to the Queen's Building, © Anthony Weller/View.

A fitting response to the University of East Anglia's well-
publicised policy of procuring environmentally responsible
buildings... it represents a passive environmental response
which can cope with a potential 1,300 simultaneous users
in extremely varied accommodation.
The Architects' Journal

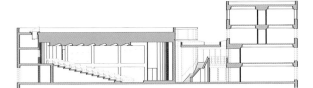

Clockwise from top left Cross-section; Entrance canopy; Entrance elevation, © James Morris/View.

Opposite top and bottom First floor; Ground floor.

1995

RAMPHAL BUILDING
University of Warwick
John Miller + Partners

The Ramphal Building meets the University's academic needs and is also available for conferences. It is conveniently close to the centre of the campus and to Gibbet Hill Road. A three-storey L-shaped block, containing seminar rooms and tutorial offices, embraces a cylindrical structure containing a 400 seat lecture theatre. The thrust of the theatre's rake is contained in this static form. Informal 'breakout' and refreshment areas are located to either side and back of the theatre.

There are four theatre entrances; two at first floor approached by bridges, and two from the foyer. Two staircases lead to the bridge connections. They lie on the diagonal and underpin the buildings geometry. The foyer is top-lit and is animated by the open galleries which overlook it. The theatre is fully equipped with AV projection and teaching aids.

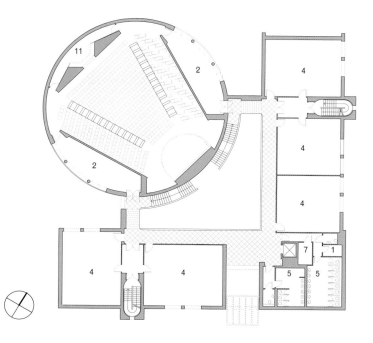

1 Lobby
2 Library
3 Administration
4 Book returns
5 Periodicals
6 Librarian's office
7 Computer room
8 Photocopier room
9 Archive office
10 Archive
11 Campus Road

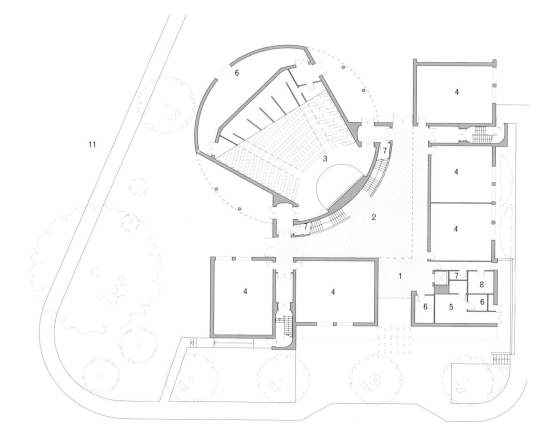

1998

SHACKLETON
MEMORIAL LIBRARY
Cambridge University
John Miller + Partners

The project is for a library extension for undergraduate and research use, together with archive storage and administration space. The existing complex consists of the 1934 Founders Building facing Lensfield Road, with a two-storey 1960s block behind linked to a three-storey rear block. The two-storey building provides the main entrance. This replaces the original in the Founders Building. The whole is Grade II Listed. Available land for development is limited.

The brief has called for additional space for both readers and books suitable for both undergraduates and research workers with space for archives and administration. The existing two-storey entrance block has been partially demolished to provide space for the new Library and an area for book stacks to be linked to existing ground, first and second floor levels, as well as to a new basement level, contiguous with the existing rear basement.

The chosen circular form acts as a foil to the existing rectilinear block, and mediates between the existing contrasting architectural styles. Reconstructed stone and stock bricks are used to match existing materials, in a series of alternating banded courses, to unify the circular 'tower' with the flanks of the existing building. The whole building is to be upgraded to provide access for the disabled including a new lift to all levels, and new WCs.

The structure is a reinforced concrete frame clad externally in brick and stone bands, with a lightweight steel panel attic storey over the existing structure at second floor level. The coffered plaster ceilings designed on a bookcase module accommodate purpose designed uplighters. They provide even lighting to book shelves. Internal finishes include oak block floors and plaster walls, in keeping with existing materials.

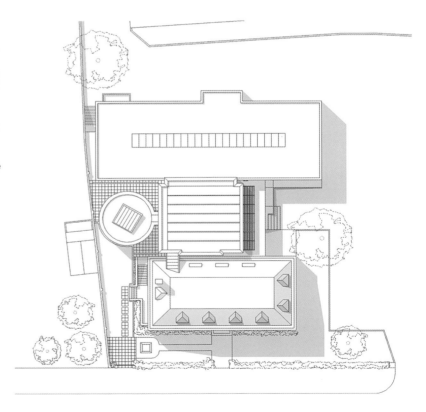

Top and bottom The building before the extension; Site plan showing relation to the existing building.

Opposite View of the library 'tower' from Lensfield Road, © Anthony Weller/View.

Clockwise from top left View of the entrance drum; Top floor of the drum; View showing the link to the existing building, © Anthony Weller/View.

Opposite View of the entrance drum at the top floor, © Anthony Weller/View.

2005

NEWNHAM COLLEGE LIBRARY
Cambridge University
John Miller + Partners

Top Site plan.

Bottom View of the east elevation with the Rare Books Library by van Heyningen and Haward in the foreground, © Dennis Gilbert/View.

Opposite top and bottom First floor; Ground floor.

Newnham College is an exclusively female college. The original buildings, by Basil Champneys, are in the English Free Style. They date from the 1870s to the early twentieth century. The college lines Sidgewick Avenue, terminating at its west end with The Thompson Library of 1879, with its double-height space graced with a single barrel vault painted pale blue. The Thompson Library has served the College well; but following a feasibility study it has been decided to develop the site between The Thompson Library and The Stevens Room of 1982 to provide space for expansion.

This reflects the growth of library book stock, archives and the increase in readers' needs. The new extension connects The Thompson Library to The Stevens Room and is attached to the corridor spine that runs the length of Champneys' building. The vault of The Thompson Library apse is retained and is the point of connection between old and new. The scale and character of the context is acknowledged with matching red brick and a plinth of blue engineering bricks. The interior has two storeys with a basement stack.

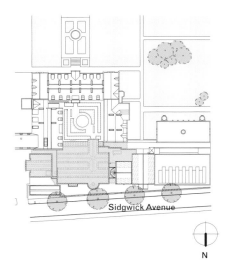

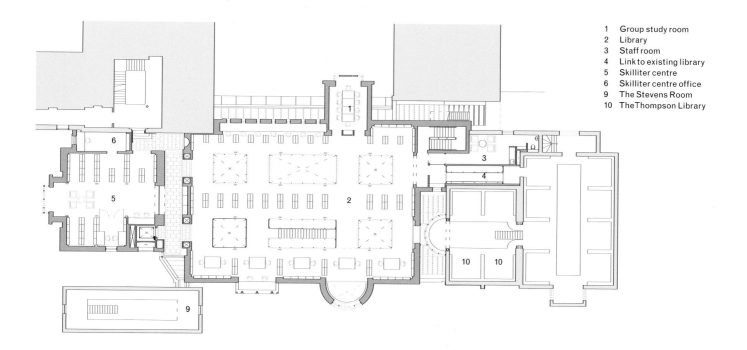

1 Group study room
2 Library
3 Staff room
4 Link to existing library
5 Skilliter centre
6 Skilliter centre office
9 The Stevens Room
10 The Thompson Library

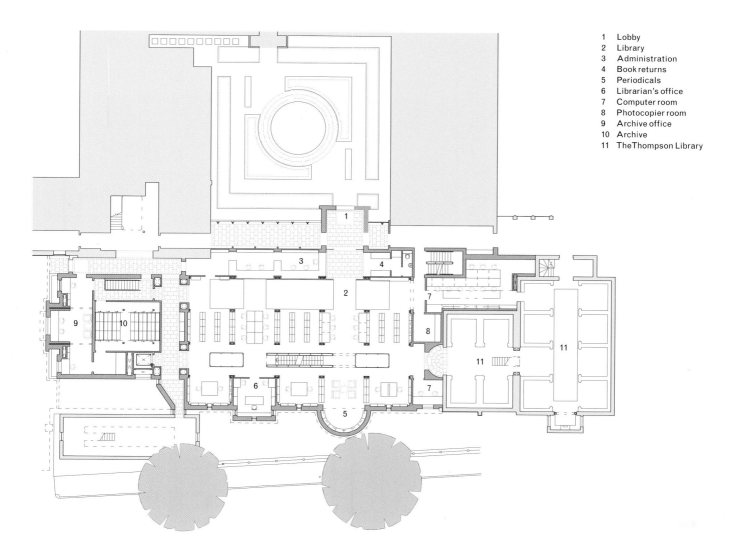

1 Lobby
2 Library
3 Administration
4 Book returns
5 Periodicals
6 Librarian's office
7 Computer room
8 Photocopier room
9 Archive office
10 Archive
11 The Thompson Library

Opposite top and bottom Existing Yates Thompson Library renovated; East elevation, © Dennis Gilbert/View.

Top and bottom Model showing the relationship to the existing College buildings by Basil Champneys, and the herb garden.

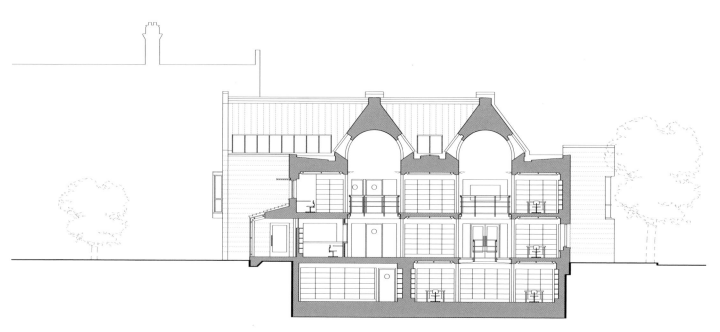

The top-lit extension is vaulted and has translucent glass floors and stair treads to distribute daylight to the lower floors via lightwells. The building is designed to perform to low energy standards and to achieve modulated lighting for readers in a naturally ventilated environment. South-facing rooflights and windows are shaded to minimise solar gain. Fresh air, supplied via low-velocity displacement diffusers, is tempered by the fabric or by regenerative heat exchange when the Library is occupied.

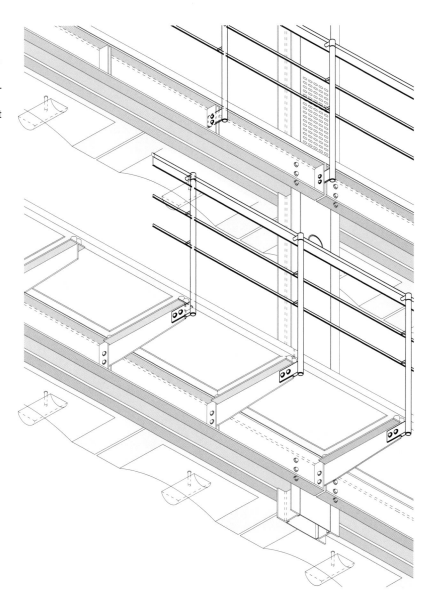

Above Detail of the walkway to the rooflights.

Opposite View of the triple-height lightwell, © Dennis Gilbert/View.

Overleaf View of the south elevation from Sidgwick Avenue, © Dennis Gilbert/View.

Clockwise from top right Site plan; Part elevation of Phase 1, © Ronen Numa; Phase 1, 2 and 3, © Paul Riddle; Detail of the elevation, © Paul Riddle.

1   Gibbet Hill Road
2   Ramphal Building
3   Business School

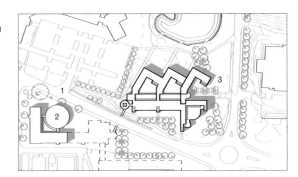

Top to bottom left Ground floor, Phase 3; Ground floor, Phase 2; Ground floor, Phase 1.

Bottom right Cross-section.

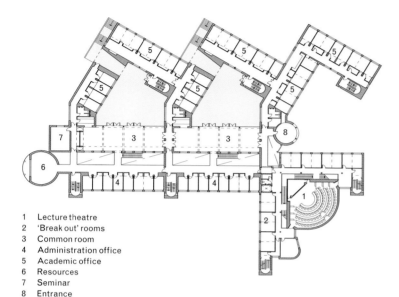

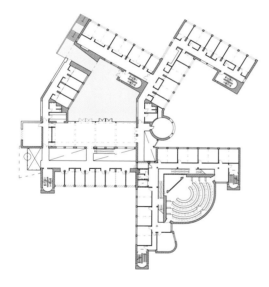

1 Lecture theatre
2 'Break out' rooms
3 Common room
4 Administration office
5 Academic office
6 Resources
7 Seminar
8 Entrance

2008

WARWICK UNIVERSITY BUSINESS SCHOOL
Faculty of Social Sciences
John Miller + Partners

Phase 1: 1999, Phase 2 : 2002, Phase 3 : 2008

The Business School is within the Warwickshire Green Belt. The Ramphal Building is on the Campus site. The two buildings are separated by Gibbet Hill Road. The proposed bridge to connect them has been abandoned to be replaced with a pedestrian crossing in a later phase of the development.

The Business School's first and second stages set a formal pattern for the future, with a continuous main circulation spine and follow the broad intentions of the masterplan.

Suites of single banked offices, grouped around intimate courts are attached to this spine. They benefit from views over the lake. Each phase accommodates the gently sloping site and contains both hard and soft landscape elements.

The first phase contains two stacked 70 seat theatres, associated seminar rooms, a business centre and common rooms. The second contains a 70 seat raked lecture theatre below the courtyard, associated seminar rooms, faculty and administration offices. The third contains an 80 seat raked lecture theatre under a courtyard with associated seminar rooms, offices and a postgraduate IT centre.

The four-storey envelope is highly insulated and the mass of exposed in-situ concrete coffers. Combined with night ventilation, this provides passive cooling. High occupancy spaces are provided with mechanical cooling.

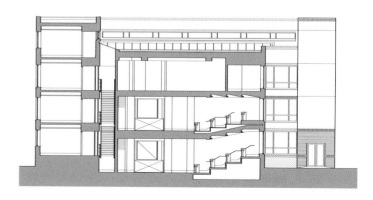

Clockwise from top left Staff common room courtyard; Entrance hall, Phase 1; Main circulation, © Ronen Numa.

Opposite Lecture theatre, © Ronen Numa.

Top and bottom Detail of the accomodation stair, © Ronen Numa; Main staircase, © Paul Riddle.

Opposite Main circulation within the atrium, © Paul Riddle.

INTO THE MODERN
Robert Maxwell

In the summer of 1954, I was young and recently married, living in a two-room basement, with one child delivered and two more on the way. I still found time to do an open competition, working with Alan Colquhoun, a friend whom I had met in India in 1946, when we were together in the Indian Army, and he was adjutant to the Depot Batallion at Roorkee, and my boss. It was a building for the offices of the Electricity Board in Kampala, Uganda. It turned out to be a five-storey cube, on stilts, with structural columns, vertical *brise-soleils* and window mullions all on different grids, which made for lively elevations. I enjoyed that work, and after due deliberation, which took longer than I intended, I approached Alan with the suggestion that we might form a partnership. "Oh, he said, I just signed up with John Miller."

That was the beginning of Colquhoun + Miller, although the partnership was only formalised in 1961, when the possibility of a commission for a high school arrived. It would not become famous until after they had worked together on the Whitechapel Art Gallery, in 1985. And this will no doubt explain why I have remained interested in their subsequent work and, after Alan Colquhoun retired in 1990, in the work of John Miller + Partners.

But that was to take some time. Their first project to be built was the Forest Gate High School, in West Ham, not completed until 1965. As in so many cases, it came to them by way of a recommendation from Lyons Israel and Ellis where both John and Alan had worked. It is remarkable for its clear formal structure.

The plan is compactly squeezed into a square, with an entrance on the central axis marked by a kind of triumphal arch into the playground space, beyond which an external stair leads up to the visitors' entrance on the *piano nobile*, the route used by parents attending school events. Within the perfectly square assembly hall, the distributed access stairs that lead up on each corner from the children's entrance and cloakroom on the ground floor are rationally disposed so that the steps up to the platform level take precedence. Yet, within this formality, the rest of the massing follows a pragmatic grouping offset by a certain diagonal symmetry generated by the assembly hall, with two major classroom blocks running out from a square classroom on the corner.

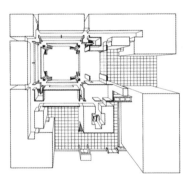

The composition is thus highly complex and full of fragmented views which nevertheless hold you by the power of the facades that face you. The block containing the visitors' entrance is conceived to make maximum use of the blank brickwork, and a similar effect is created on the last bay of the gymnasium block where windows of different sizes make a complex pattern. The careful grouping of windows of different sizes contrasts with the nearly total glazing of the classrooms, but it is enough to make us aware of a sensibility at work. For instance, the view across the back of the assembly hall comes to rest on a corner staircase where the cantilevered landing meets the line of the downstand beam above, creating a wonderful 'cubist' motif. A lay person would hardly notice this, but the architect goes "Hah!"

In short, the demanding requirements of a secondary school, deriving from accessibility and circulation, have been met without giving away the right of an architect to create some beauty, within the limitations of the job.

The next job to be completed was a small print and map shop for Weinreb + Douma, on the corner of Bloomsbury Street and Great Russell Street; it was neat and rational: that was about it. There were a few cylindrical columns in the small space, and that stood for 'architecture'. They did carry loads more elegantly than wall remnants. But the fact

Top Alan Colqhoun and John Miller.
Middle Forest Gate High School, 1962.
Bottom Weinreb + Douma Print Shop,
© Richard Einzig/arcaid.co.uk.

that the shop was situated halfway between the British Museum and the Architectural Association meant that it was not overlooked, so it added to the architects' prestige.

More impressive was the next job: laboratories for the Royal Holloway College at Egham, in Surrey, completed in 1971. A fairly large building, which resulted from a recommendation by Sir Leslie Martin. This building has been entirely rationalised to become an essay in typology. The larger laboratories evidently benefit from toplight, all other rooms from sidelight. So the laboratories occur in the middle as static entities, with toplighting, while the research labs and staff rooms are arranged in long sweeps around them. The whole is organised on a tartan grid, where double columns provide duct space for the ubiquitous pipe work. The result is clear and rational; but it is given life through the fact that the site is sloping, so that ground floors become first floors further on, and basements become ground floors. The lecture halls have been drawn out from the generality of spaces, and form a small group directly opposite the main entrance. The glazing, both for toplights and elevations, remains absolutely consistent.

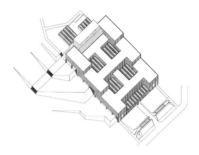

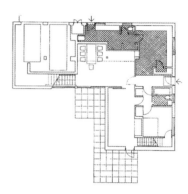

Yet, perhaps because of that consistency, certain parts stand out; the entrance sequence, for example, where the glazed sides of the entrance hall are angled, and the downhill terminations, to which one can only look up, as the hillside continues on downward. These aspects reveal a compositional quality in the proportions and confirm that a sensibility is at work. Those who report daily for work here may be blind to these qualities, but the visitor, if he is lucky to have a sunny day, will be aware of a certain lyrical distinction in an otherwise humdrum environment.

The next job was a small house in a remote part of Wales for a young farmer and his family, and it is a wonderful essay in the vernacular, apparently simple but complex in the allocation of space. Every inch counts in a marvelously compact plan, where family life focuses on a southwest-facing courtyard, protected from prevailing winds, on to which the dining room looks from the centre of the house. The windows (either square or horizontal rectangles) are disposed so as to make interesting patterns. The one-way pitched roof emphasises the form and makes it tell.

Pillwood was a family property on the mouth of the Fal near Falmouth, in Cornwall, just before it narrows to a small river, and was ideal for yachting holidays. A house for a family member was exactly the sort of project that young architects usually have to start their practice. But since the firm was founded in 1961, and had built a high school by 1965, this private commission came rather late!

The house at Pillwood was a vacation house for family, built by the architect. Being intended for family, it did not have to be so conventional, and it takes advantage of this. In a general way it is like the farmhouse project but, whereas that had been built of traditional materials, this house was built of the latest stuff. The structure is of tubular steel, painted bright green, with reinforced concrete floors; the walls are made of polyurethane-filled modular panels, coloured white; the windows are of greenhouse glass. The look is forthrightly high-tech but the form is vernacular, with a one-way pitched roof, not unlike the farmhouse.

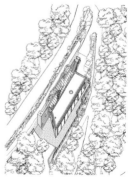

The layout is arranged to suit varying numbers of people living together for the weekend, with sliding panels that can make different bedroom arrangements, and a single bathroom. The result is decidedly informal, suggestive of a way of life that doesn't stand on ceremony. Yet, architecturally, this flexibility allows for an extreme formality in the organisation, with the central axis marked by two spiral staircases. The use of greenhouse glazing

Top to bottom Royal Holloway College Chemistry Building, axonometric, drawing by John Hewitt; Lower House Farm; Pillwood 1; Pillwood 2.

probably came from Stirling and Gowan's building for the Engineering Faculty at Leicester, completed three years earlier. Though tiny by comparison, this house is very modern in its immediacy.

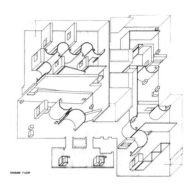

Another house at Pillwood for a graphic designer was not built. It was modern in form, but fairly conventional in that it had a long glazed facade facing south, terminating at the west end with a terrace slightly enclosed by the pointed end of the house, an unusual feature. The glazing is divided into four bays, not three or five, and is of an extreme elegance, since the unit of glazing is an exact square. The roof is flat, with roof glazing above the corridor. It reminds one in a general way of Le Corbusier's house for his parents on Lake Leman.

In 1978, the architects were asked to 'do' an exhibition, in this case an exhibition of Dada and Surrealist art at the Hayward Gallery. Between a dark ceiling and a wood floor come white walls. The exhibition consisted of 17 sections, each entered through an introductory space in the form of a half cylinder, white, like the main walls. Sometimes the half cylinders coagulate, sometimes they remain separate. Sometimes they invite you in; sometimes they are obstacles to walk around, making the space more interesting. The architects have intervened, but with discretion and, without calling attention to the framework they have provided, they have decisively framed the works of art. This exhibition design, although modest, was important, as they were working with Alan Bowness, Michael Compton, John Golding and Roland Penrose, with David Sylvester in the role of chief curator, so they gained a reputation in the art world, and this resulted, immediately, in the Whitechapel Gallery becoming interested. Architecturally, that would not bear fruit until 1985.

In 1979, the Millbank Housing Competition, for a stupendous site just upstream from Lambeth Bridge, was approached in a playful spirit. The flats were to be arranged in three separate buildings, one square in plan, one triangular, and one circular. As a group, they would have been less obstructive than a single block. They share an open terrace facing southwest. The use of exact geometrical forms stemmed from the then current interest in the rationalist approach in Europe. Rationalism was given prestige by the work of Aldo Rossi, and was used empirically, with verve, by Mario Botta in the Ticino district of Switzerland. Its use here puts me in mind of a project by James Stirling for housing at Canary Wharf, not designed until 1988, which places volumes of quite different configuration on top of each other, in a spirit that declares itself free of empirical constraints but wants to show that, all the same, it can get by. Until 1975, the doctrine of functionalism insisted that architectural form emerged from the programme; now this seemed like an arbitrary rule, and rules can be broken.

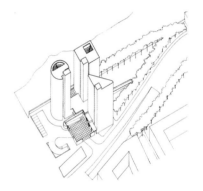

The housing at Fenny Stratford is a further exercise in the refreshing of vernacular forms. A run of two-storey houses is roofed in sections of one-way pitch, revealing the vertical wall that rises to the top of the pitch in big masses of what I characterise as "high blankness", a most expressive use of brickwork. In addition, small windows are placed close to the corners, in a way reminiscent of the architecture of Andrea Palladio, which further increases the extent of the blank brickwork, and confers a certain nobility on what is otherwise fairly humdrum housing. The odd house at the corner of the site is dealt with consistently, so as to bring it into line with the others, and car parking is put firmly at the rear.

In 1979, the architects were asked to provide some housing for a couple of sites in Kentish Town, in adjoining Caversham Street and Gaisford Street, pretty well opposite each

Top Dada and Surrealism Reviewed, Hayward Gallery. **Middle** Millbank Housing, axonometric. **Bottom** Fenny Stratford, © Martin Charles.

other. The problem was to replace demolished parts of existing houses. On Gaisford Street the space of three terrace houses was filled with five duplex apartments, with a modern flat roof. On Caversham Street the missing half of a large semi-detached villa was filled with two duplex apartments, and the pitched roof of the other half was extended over the new. In both cases, an imitation of the traditional walk-up external stairs provided access from the street. The original brief called for a community centre between the two sites, but this was later abandoned.

What strikes one here is the discretion with which the new has been added to the old, without giving up any of its entitlement to be modern. The Italianate roof of the half villa has been extended but the new building below it is uncompromisingly modern. The wall above the top storey windows in the other block has been carried up to the height of its neighbour, but there is no trace of a cornice and, because the windows are slightly lower (and horizontal rather than vertical rectangles) one gets a glimpse of the high blankness that we have met before; while the external stairs, which in Caversham imitate the old, here run straight up into the building behind a glazed screen. The walls are stucco throughout. The proportions are in both cases exactly determined and, in the case of, Caversham especially, produce a striking effect.

Another exhibition intervenes: The Arts of Bengal, at the Whitechapel. The work was a whole range of both religious and secular art from the twelfth century to the twentieth. Using cheap partitions, the wide space of the gallery was subdivided into different sections, creating two kinds of space: shrine-like for the display of religious sculpture, and ambulatory for secular paintings and craftwork.

Back to public housing, this time a nine-storey block of small flats in the London Borough of Hornsey: at four per floor, a total of 34. Each flat has two rooms, kitchen and bathroom. The bedrooms function like bed-sitting rooms, so the accommodation suits young people who may or may not be living together, may or may not be beginning a family. In addition, the building contains a caretaker's flat; also a common room and a laundry, both of these being places where one might meet one's future partner while living one's own life. The building is made of load-bearing brickwork, with concrete floor slabs, and is faced with red brick. Unusually, the space under the main windows is filled with glass blocks, which gives the equivalent light of full floor-to-ceiling windows while maintaining privacy: undoubtedly, a building on the side of new life.

Next year, the Hayward Gallery came back to ask for a layout for their exhibition of Picasso's Picassos. In the broad extent of the main spaces, small rooms and angled screens provide an assortment of situations, while the sculpture was displayed on freestanding plinths; again, sufficient variety is created by the simplest of means.

The Whitechapel also came back this year, 1982, to ask for a layout for their exhibition of the work of Sir Christopher Wren, a great architect. The result was magnificently architectural. A series of cross walls divides the gallery, each one pierced by two doors decorated in a simplified baroque style. These doors define the circulation, but also echo the idea of baroqueness, as demonstrated in St Paul's and all the city churches, and in this way they frame the work.

From 1975 onwards, Britain entered a period generally known as "Po-Mo", or "postmodern". Architecture is now into 'references' and 'historical allusions', including outright pastiche and, to an extent, gradually culminating, with the Canadian Frank Gehry, also into fragmentation and even deconstruction.

Top Hornsey Lane, © Martin Charles.
Bottom Sir Christopher Wren exhibition at the Whitechapel Gallery.

Architectural forms are, to a greater extent than those of the other arts, governed by certain functional considerations, and to treat them otherwise calls for a certain bravado. In Britain, it is not so easy to display such nerve; there is rather a tendency to attempt to hide one's light under a bushel, so to speak, by proclaiming oneself high-tech. The high-tech architect can be just as devoted to an architecture of art, but aims rather to be seen and judged as a scientist, bent on functional and structural rectitude. Foster and Rogers have led the way in this, followed by Hopkins and Grimshaw, the architect who made his name with the first Eurostar station at Waterloo. In Britain, Zada Hadid is the only one who has shown the necessary nerve. It is worth a moment's diversion to take a closer look.

All the other arts had taken a postmodern slant from the beginning: think what James Joyce's *Ulysses* would have been without fragmentation, allusions, historical or otherwise; or without distortion and fragmentation T S Eliot's *The Waste Land*; or Picasso's *Demoiselles d'Avignon*. Only in architecture did functionalism, with its devotion to the programme, put a straitjacket on the search for new forms. Only at the end of the twentieth century did architecture finally escape from these constraints. But in the case of Colquhoun + Miller the situation is somewhat different, since I believe they were not so much searching for new forms as looking for ways to retrieve old forms from impotency, and give them new life. Their method never lacks in discretion, in a sense of propriety.

One does not expect to find sweeping differences in their work after 1975. There is nevertheless, a difference. The family house at Pillwood is clearly in the high-tech tradition, while following vernacular forms. Perhaps one becomes aware of a new perspective with the housing in Kentish Town, particularly the block in Caversham Street. The extension of the Italianate roof over the new half of a semi-detached building certainly suggests an awareness of a change in the framework. Yet the character of that building remains 'modern', and it is exactly that gentle contrast that makes the building so enjoyable. So, one does not expect extremes in their work, but rather an increased awareness of the background.

The housing at the Oldbrook Estate, known as Oldbrook II, at Milton Keynes, of 1982, certainly shows this. The brief was for a layout for 152 dwellings, for families of two to seven people. Around this time most architects would have seen this as an invitation to play with the idea of the village, with an apparently picturesque composition broken down into accidental patterns: what my architect daughter calls "institutionalised nook-and-cranny". Colquhoun + Miller had another idea: the idea of a town. Some of the most enjoyable vernacular building that remains is in the form of three- and four-storey town houses, built in a row. So their work follows an exact formality, with houses that present a common front to the street. Looking to renew an idea of urban structure, they would have preferred them all to be of three storeys, but the local authority insisted on a proportion of two-storey houses. Their response has been to group the two-storey and three-storey houses together, in two distinct situations. The result is orderly, but judicious.

The increased awareness of background shows in another way, in the architecture of these houses. The use of brick is hardly surprising, but here the general brickwork of buff-coloured facings is framed by the use of lines of a darker brick, and this provides a method of creating different proportions. Allied to the enjoyment of high blankness is the increased area of plain brickwork achieved in the three-storey frontages, again aided by the Palladian trick of pushing the windows close to the corners. The beam facings above the openings echo the brick-on-edge plinth. Balconies under the pitched roof overhangs make another variation. Three-storey houses face one another across

Top Oldbrook II, elevation.
Bottom Casa Cogollo, Vicenza.

quite narrow streets, and the two-storey houses that face and terminate these streets create the impression of a courtyard. The ends of the three-storey blocks are particularly carefully thought about, with two protruding windows joining to give a strong vertical motif whose square pattern fenestration is echoed in the pattern on all the garage doors. The result is a housing estate that confers individuality on its inhabitants, and therefore dignity.

Two years later, the success of Oldbrook II brought the architects a whole swathe of commissions for public housing. The Shrubland Road and Albion Drive housing, on two streets in Dalston, is unusual in the way they have latched on to the character of the existing houses, a series of Neo-Classical pairs dating from 1840. The architects have produced a similar series of pairs, each pair sharing a pedimental gable, the entrances in a recess behind a single cylindrical column, the universal sign for 'architecture'. The entrance floor remains on exactly the same level as in the old houses, with stairs up to the front door and down behind railings to a basement.

The Church Crescent scheme is just four houses, in pairs on the curve of a crescent in another part of Dalston. Because of being approached from the outside of the curve, the masses are rather detached so, by making the entrances on the side, the architects have been able to provide two three-storey houses in each 'villa'.

With the Two Mile Ash Housing and the Willen Park Housing at Milton Keynes the architects were able to re-run some of their ideas from the earlier schemes. Two Mile Ash has 54 houses for families of two to five people, this time for sale, and this explains why the clients preferred the semi-detached format. The constructional system was left to the builder who, for speed, chose dry construction on timber frames, with brick facings. Willen Park has 48 houses for families of two to six people. At Two Mile Ash the near pyramidal pitched roofs with strong overhangs clearly derive from Caversham Street, while the exposed gable fronts at Willen Park come from Shrubland Road. By now the architects have worked out a whole vocabulary to deal with public housing in a consistent way.

In the same year, as if to remind us that there are other things in the world as well as kitchen/dining rooms, the architects were asked to do an exhibition on Adolf Loos: but this time to travel. What has been provided is a kit of parts, made of prefabricated units that can be assembled quickly in different locations. When assembled they define a set of rhythmically linked volumes based on the geometry of the cube. The interest has to focus on the furniture and objects from Adolf Loos' world, generally dark in colour, so there is nothing to distract from that prime aim.

We are now in the year 1985, and the Whitechapel Gallery is looking for an architect to extend and refurbish its own premises. The committee chose Colquhoun + Miller, whom they already knew from their work at the Hayward Gallery, and had themselves used for two exhibitions.

What they needed was an upgrading of the viewing environment, with air-conditioning and sun control, and new lighting; improvement of the staircases, and a new small gallery, and generally, an improvement in the services and public requirements. Nowadays no gallery is complete without a cafe and book shop: a modest enough assignment, but one that the architects were to make the most of. The process of finding a solution that was satisfactory to all was long and tedious, but finally led to an outcome. No modern architect can afford to bypass this process.

Top Albion, Shrubland and Brownlow Road, Hackney, © Martin Charles. **Middle** Church Crescent, Hackney, © Dennis Gilbert/View. **Bottom** Two Mile Ash, © Martin Charles.

The final scheme provides additional volume without losing the character of the original building, which was a Grade II Listed building, a supreme example of the English Arts and Crafts style at the turn of the twentieth century. The architect, CH Townsend, was a designer of originality, and his bold placing of the entrance doors off-centre in the street facade, otherwise marked with symmetrical corner turrets, made a memorable image, effective because of the expressive blankness achieved through the asymmetry. The brief required the renovation and upgrading of the existing galleries to today's standards, together with the provision of a new small gallery, lecture theatre, audio-visual space, cafe, education room, bookshop, offices, storage and plant space. The principle changes affecting the galleries are to the public stairs, and circulation. These are carried out so as to preserve the integrity of the two original galleries. The new elements are sympathetic to the existing fabric, without imitating it. Fortunately, the finishes of the interior were of extreme simplicity and this allowed the architects to design with the simplicity of the modern minimalist style, with no need to compromise. The result seemed to embody the spirit of the original idea, which was to bring art to a deprived section of London, and so it was received with enthusiasm.

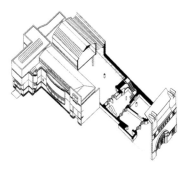

Working on public housing had not only provided useful experience of dealing with the public realm, it had also, as we have seen, brought into play a vocabulary of preferred forms. The square grid pattern of the fenestration used at Oldbrook reappears, now with a Secessionist flavour, tying the modern detailing effortlessly to a *fin-de-siècle* period evocation. The opening from the reception space into the main gallery is marked by a central pier, rounded so that it appears to be a column, reminiscent of the column used for the porches at Shrubland Street, and the tympanum above is glazed with a square grid. A new volume is created on the west side to contain the lecture room and cafe, approached on the outside beyond the adjoining building by a small passage, which leads into a tiny space known as Angel Alley. This new volume is marked by two projections: a small semi-circular one which provides a window to a staircase landing, and a large bow-fronted one which gives an expansive shape to the cafe and, above it, to the Education Room. The way these projections have been handled, in conjunction with darker brick bands, is of extreme suavity, and suggests a capability far beyond the scope of this tiny courtyard. So this job brought the architects much wider recognition than their work on housing estates, and set them up for a wider role as architects of well-loved spaces. Among many other awards, it received an RIBA Regional Award and was shortlisted for the Mies van der Rohe Pavilion Award in Barcelona. Colquhoun + Miller had at last become famous.

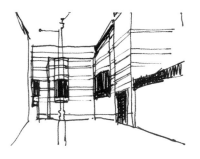

After the favourable reaction to Whitechapel, the architects were selected to enter the competition for a major extension to the National Gallery in Trafalgar Square. Their design is remarkable for the straightforward way the building is made to front onto Pall Mall East, the continuation of the north side of Trafalgar Square. Other designs, notably that of James Stirling, agonised about inflecting it towards the main entrance, while Venturi, whose design was selected and built, made do with a corner entrance. In addition, the Colquhoun + Miller design is quite Italianate in seeking to make an axial emphasis to its entrance, by using cylindrical columns in a pair at the entrance, in a row of five bays above the entrance, and in a further row of five bays with the columns in pairs under the eaves. Together with vertical grooves that divide the facade into three, a broader central portion corresponding to the colonnade, with a pavilion either side, results in the unification of the whole facade in a traditional way. The internal planning is straight-forward, the mezzanine contains the cafe restaurant, with windows behind the lower row of columns; the auditorium, which doesn't require natural lighting, is in the basement; and the bookshop, adjoining the main entrance, with its own entrance

Top Whitechapel Art Gallery, axonometric, drawing by John Hewitt. **Middle** Whitechapel Art Gallery from Angel Alley. **Bottom** National Gallery Extension.

from the street, is dignified with a column and arch, *à la* Whitechapel. In all, a design much to my own taste, which would have been very effective when built.

Another invitation to enter a competition arrived in 1986, for extensions to the Staedel Institute of Art in Frankfurt. The programme asked for a new permanent gallery on the second floor, to be connected by a bridge to the main gallery of the existing building, and a gallery for changing exhibitions to be installed on the ground floor. The design used a similar language to that used for the National Gallery, with a new entrance behind a cylindrical column, in this case given extra weight by a projection in the floor above. A projecting bay window on the corner nearest the existing gallery and a corner window with a single column on the corner are brought in to enliven facades that otherwise proclaim all too clearly the presence of top-lit spaces, an excess of blankness that ceases to be expressive! The design won second prize, which at least was an honourable outcome.

A further case of museum design was to arrive in 1987, when they were invited to enter a competition for refurbishment of the Messepalast in Vienna. This was a delicate problem dominated by the presence of existing buildings by Fischer von Erlach and Gottfried Semper. A long range of low buildings had to be retained, and the new spaces contrived behind them. The original building was too constricted to be used for display, so it remained as the centre of administration and to dominate the formal axis. Behind it an enclosed courtyard divides the new accommodation into two separate parts, and provides the focus for the cafe-restaurant. It was a tough problem to solve, complicated by the language difficulty.

Language must have also been a problem in dealing with another invitation to a competition for housing for IBA—the Internationale Bauausstellung—on a large site covering two city blocks in Berlin. The elevations that resulted were based on cutting the accommodation into smaller entities, but the result is still somewhat unresolved, with an extensive use made of 'rationalist' facades, based on repeating rows of small square windows. In the background there persists an image of Adolf Loos' Looshaus.

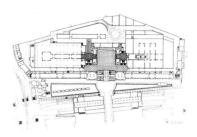

In the same year came an invitation to prepare a masterplan for the Tate Gallery in London. After all the bilingual effort put in on the National Gallery, then on Staedel, then on Vienna, then on Berlin, that must have caused a sigh of relief! The masterplan is much valued by architects because, if it is accepted, they have a good chance of being invited to put up some buildings. In due course, this happened to John Miller + Partners, but there was a long process of planning and adjustment before work finally began, in December 1997, on the ground on a big section of Tate Britain, virtually a quarter of the gallery space, on the south side, with a new entrance directly into their work. By now Alan Colquhoun had retired from the practice, having become a full-time Professor at Princeton University.

The next major project was to provide additional accommodation for the Royal College of Art, in Kensington. This was the construction of the Stevens Building, in a mews courtyard behind the building designed by Cadbury-Brown and Casson on Kensington Gore, together with some modifications to the adjoining houses behind in Queen's Gate. The programme called for new studios and workspaces for the departments of Video and Film, Painting, Graphics, Illustration, Computer Studies and Photography. The deep site required the incorporation of a top-lit space to provide daylight to the centre, forming an exhibition area for the whole new faculty building. All this is managed within the limitations of a restricted site, in a modest way, with just the occasional cylindrical column to declare the

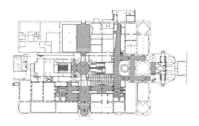

Top Staedel Institute of Art Extension.
Middle Messelpalast competition, Vienna.
Bottom Tate Gallery, masterplan.

architectural stakes. Externally, separate windows are kept for the ground and first floor, but under the eaves there reappears a colonnade of columns, with some pairs declaring the existence of a division of the facade into three parts, as we saw with the National Gallery design. It is as if, behind the constraints of functional planning, and the will to end up with satisfied clients, a yearning for 'real' architecture is constantly reappearing.

The years following the reconstitution of the firm as John Miller + Partners saw an unprecedented flurry of try-outs. Designs were done for urban housing in Alcoy, Spain; an entry was prepared for the Churchill Competition for post-graduate accommodation at Cambridge; schemes were made for the Tate Gallery at St Ives, the Geffrye Museum, a School of Midwifery. The firm was invited to enter limited competitions for an Art Gallery in Hanover and an Art Gallery in Manchester. None of these projects resulted in a building.

However, John Miller + Partners are now clearly in the window of university planners, a privileged group of clients, who may be sympathetic to real architecture. The next opportunity came from the University of East Anglia, which had recently employed Rick Mather Architects to provide a masterplan. The occupational Therapy and Physiotherapy Building (known as the Queen's Building) was the next commission. It occupies the site next to Rick Mather's Education Building, and takes its cue from that. Mather's building is a three-sided rectangular courtyard, open at one side, and Miller's building completes this courtyard. It also adopts a similar system of white wall panels, but not the roof overhangs. Instead, courses of brick-on-edge provide crisp trims to the wall surfaces, one-and-a-half bricks at cornice level, and one brick deep at first floor level. The site is steeply sloping, and this has been exploited to make two separate entrances, the lower one for the gym, which can thus be used when the main building is shut. The main entrance is marked by a circular tower, and is approached by a bridge crossing the path to the lower entrance. This provides a certain drama, as well as being reminiscent of a game played by Le Corbusier in his Salvation Army Hostel in Paris. The cylinder also refers to a similar cylinder employed by Mather in his nearby Climate Research Unit. The search for real architecture is thus well in hand; but nothing results that is deleterious to the client's use of the building, which indeed is marked by a close attention to function. An example of this is the way that a store at the entrance to the theatre is used to create a thick wall, through which the light from two windows above makes a dramatic impact. Another is the way that a small balcony is cut out of the top storey of the cylinder, to allow smokers access to the open air. The fact is that Miller has found a discretion that allows function to be well satisfied, while also making certain connections that lift the building out of its everyday uses and give it a higher profile.

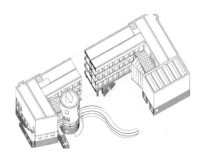

The next year, the University of East Anglia commissioned the Elizabeth Fry Building on an adjacent site. This is an academic building for the department of Social Studies with some seminar rooms, a multitude of staff/tutorial rooms and three lecture theatres. Inevitably, it takes the form of a bar, with rooms either side of a central corridor. However, the bar is enlivened with a shallow projection above the entrance, here given the same segmental curve used for the education room at the Whitechapel, and a slight projection on the other side. This expansion gives enough space for a dramatic staircase that rises continuously in four half-storey flights under a toplight, dramatised by large circular windows from the adjoining offices at either end. The 'bulge' also allows space for a generous computer room on each level. Externally, brick-on-edge bands civilise a wall panel system similar to that used in the Queen's (OTP) Building. On the other side of the site, the landscape takes over, with Lasdun's stepping terraces and Foster's Sainsbury Centre dominating, whereas this building is close to and continues the road frontage of the gymnasium wing of the Queen's Building, so the two buildings work together to make an 'urban' environment. The Elizabeth Fry Building was completed in 1995.

Top to bottom Stevens Building, Jay Mews, Royal College of Art, © Martin Charles; Alcoy Villa sketches; Queen's Building, University of East Anglia, axonometric, drawing by John Hewitt; Elizabeth Fry Building, University of East Anglia, © Anthony Weller/View.

In 1996, the firm completed a competition design for an Art Gallery for the city of Dundee. The design took the form of an L-shaped block, with an entrance marked by a circular porch, on columns, clearly repeating the success of the entrance at the Queen's Building, UEA. The lecture halls are in the basement, which because of the slope on the site becomes ground level on the downhill side. The winning design followed the same layout, but was less successful in dealing with the site's slope, downhill to the right, which Miller had dealt with very elegantly by a series of regular terraces.

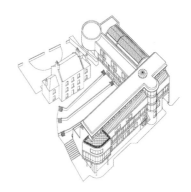

The next client to come forward was the University of Warwick, near Birmingham, which had already distinguished itself by employing the architects Yorke Rosenberg and Mardall. It wanted a conference centre with seminar rooms, to be known as the Ramphal Building. The triangular site formed an important threshold completing a line of existing buildings leading from the main campus. The accommodation consisted of a 400-seat raked auditorium fully equipped with AV presentation systems, with projection facilities and teaching aids.

The result is a very clear scheme with the auditorium enclosed in an exact circle, placed within the arms of a simple L-shaped block containing the teaching rooms and toilets. The arm facing the access road is penetrated by the entrance, which breaks through as a double-height space, leading to a spacious foyer defined by the auditorium and teaching blocks. Ever since the pre-war Impington Village College by Maxwell Fry, the awkward shape that an auditorium causes on the outside has plagued modern architecture. Placing it into a circle not only idealises it, but also provides two useful foyers giving access to the back, at first floor level, from which the seats descend towards the platform. The curve projects into the main foyer, heralding the performance to follow, and gives a graceful form to the staircases that rise to first-floor level. The upper corridors serving the seminar rooms look down into the foyer through a set of cylindrical columns finished in dark blue, again suggesting an audience interested in what is going on inside it. Without doing anything spectacular, without making use of unusual forms, this design is deeply original in redefining basic architectural meanings.

Next up was work on the Serpentine Gallery in Hyde Park. This project was funded by the Arts Council via its Lottery Fund. The brief asked for a new entrance, a coherent gallery sequence, a new bookshop, new offices and improved environmental conditions.

The Serpentine gallery is unique. It is one of only a few publically funded contemporary art galleries in central London that is free of charge and open seven days a week during exhibitions. Its director, Julia Peyton-Jones, is energetic and outward looking, and has commissioned a series of temporary pavilions that have attracted world-famous architects and have caught the public imagination. She has succeeded in bringing contemporary art to the people, rather in the spirit of the Whitechapel. So naturally John Miller has really worked at giving her the best facilities possible within the confines of a rather lumpish building designed in 1934 by J Gray West, architect to the Office of Works, and Grade II Listed. Extension above ground was not permitted, so increased space for plant, workshops and storage had to be obtained by excavation. Now, the galleries have increased natural lighting, augmented with daylight-compatible artificial lighting, which compensates for the fact that the central dome does not provide toplight. Consistently white walls and grey floor tiles form a background, which allows the art to stand out and provide the stimulus. The impression given as you go through these galleries is that you are in a coherent modern space.

Top Dundee City Art Gallery, drawing by John Hewitt. **Middle** Ramphal Building for Social Sciences, University of Warwick. **Bottom** Serpentine Gallery, © Peter Durrant/ archblue.com.

While working on such a restricted programme the firm found some relief by doing a design for an Art Gallery at Gotenburg, in Sweden, also set in a park. The scheme, not to be realised, contained a rectangular range of galleries offset by a horse-shoe shaped cross-axis providing other facilities, and distinguished by a dramatic open-air entrance sequence which mounts the inside of the horse-shoe.

In the same year, 1998, Cambridge University asked for a design for the Shackleton Memorial Library. This was really a library extension for undergraduate and research use, with some archive and administration space. Again, this meant working within the confines of a Grade II Listed building , on a very limited site. The extension, behind the existing building, is constructed in a matching brick banded with stone courses, between it and an existing 1960s extension. But part of the accommodation has been put into a perfect cylinder, of similar construction, and partly visible from the front on Lensfield Road. It provides a working library at three levels, linked by an elegant staircase that sweeps up behind a large window, supplemented by a square rooflight set at an apparently arbitrary angle. The result is perfectly conducive to long periods of solid working, head down, but provides light-hearted relief the minute you raise your head. It gained an RIBA Regional Award in 1999. The judges particularly appreciated the glass lift. "It has the appearance of a shaft of ice that has plunged down through the building", an appropriate note for a building that commemorates polar exploration.

The University of Warwick, for whom they had designed the Ramphal Building in 1996, now asked for a design for a Business School, or at least, a major extension to the existing Business School. The architects provided a masterplan, with two buildings organised in a phased development. The first of these, now partly built, has a spine with entrance at one end and three raked auditoria for 70 at the other, piled one on top of the other. The two ends are joined by a spacious corridor with, on one side, staff rooms, and on the other, a series of patio terraces overlooking courtyards. The three courtyards are closed by a series of three teaching blocks arranged in echelon, overlooking a lake. Stage two of this phased development was completed in 2001 with Stage three completed in 2007.

The most ambitious of all John Miller's recent projects has been his work at Tate Britain. He had produced a masterplan as far back as 1987, but only in 1997 was the site handed over to a project manager, and only in 2002 were their new galleries opened to the public.

It had never been intended to implement the masterplan in a linear sequence. Areas were described and priced as packages, and funders were sought to match them. The northwest quadrant was the most ambitious package in the plan, but when two principal funders—the Linbury and the Manton Foundations—were brought together, and matched with Lottery money, the scheme was off to a good start. The needs were for new gallery space for the permanent collection, and the need to deal with large numbers during blockbuster exhibitions.

There was some deliberation as to whether a separate entrance should be provided from Atterbury Street, on the west perimeter of the Tate, but this was finally agreed. It is located on the central cross-axis below Gallery 9. The architects had to argue for the large entrance space they proposed, but it has proved to be a great success, allowing Friday night concerts and informal talks, as well as dealing satisfactorily with unprecedented numbers of visitors. It gives immediate access to the temporary exhibition space, and from it a monumental stone staircase connects to the main axis of the Tate at first floor level, which compensates for the situation of the entrance being slightly below ground level, and restores us to the grandiloquence of the original building. With wide treads and shallow risers it is quite comfortable to walk up. The walls are finished in a type of Venetian plaster that blends with the stonework on the upper floor.

Top to bottom Museum of World Culture, Gotenburg; Shackleton Memorial Library, University of Cambridge, © Anthony Weller/View; Business School, University of Warwick, © Paul Riddle; Tate Gallery, Manton stairs, © Richard Bryant/arcaid.co.uk.

The new galleries are remarkable for their discretion. Simply detailed and modern in spirit, they nevertheless repeat the vaulted form of the old and become an integral part of the museum. Daylighting is taken care of without any fuss. The round column, a universal sign of architecture, reappears in some places, often finished in gloss black, which has the odd effect of making it virtually vanish.

In 2002, the firm prepared a project for an Art Gallery at Woking. The site was a constricted one on the canal, and so it took the form of a square administration building attached to a tail of galleries, of different heights, all with top light, and all serviced by a glazed loggia of diminishing height along the canal side.

In 2003, the firm were asked to arrange an exhibition of Matisse Picasso at the Tate. Of this Henry Meyric Hughes wrote in the *Times Higher Educational Supplement*: "Any misgivings about the suitability of the spaces for temporary exhibitions... were dispelled by John Miller's designs for a sequence of variable spaces, alternating openness with enclosure, natural with artificial light... and grand sweeps and perspectives, with pauses for intimacy and reflection".

This was also the year when the firm designed a major library extension for the Bedford Library at Royal Holloway College. Although not realised, it was an interesting design. The new contrasts decisively with the old by being contained in a curving, glass-walled extension, three storeys high, which adapts, by the use of two curves, to an irregular site. The structure, however, is a regular square grid of concrete columns that simply stops where it has to.

Another major job of fitting in: the Library for Newnham College, Cambridge. This involved a major extension of the very beautiful Yates-Thompson Library, designed by Basil Champneys in 1897. A building of 1962, which had become structurally unsound had to be demolished, and both the demolition and the new building were difficult on this very constricted site.

The new architecture reflects the college's existing character in scale and materials, with red brick matching the surrounding buildings and a plinth of blue engineering bricks making reference to the adjoining Rare Books Library by van Heyningen and Haward. It also reflects and completes the spatial divisions already marked out by the old structures. The central bay, a continuation of the axis of the Yates-Thompson Library, extends a staircase hall the whole length of the new building, with glass bridges at intervals connecting the accommodation on either side. This is an impressive barrel-vaulted space with high clerestorys bringing in plenty of daylight. At the end, the archive, which is impenetrable to the public, allows the axis to jump a bay to one side, with the inner suite of accommodation providing an external projection to terminate the sequence. The projecting element in this side in fact gives expression to the Skilliter Centre for Ottoman Studies on the ground floor, and by shifting the emphasis towards the south avoids crowding the Rare Books Library to the north. The entrance comes from within the college, from a courtyard on the south side, forming a cross-axis which comes through to the outside as a semi-circular projection facing Sidgewick Avenue. A high gable emphasises the main entrance, a motif that is repeated, with three gables, at the eastern termination. The new building is thus given a clear identity, while at the same time it results in knitting together a complex set of connections.

The next work of importance was a commission to work for the Fitzwilliam Museum, also in Cambridge. Colquhoun + Miller had already responded to a request from Michael Jaffe

Top Woking Galleries. **Middle** Bedford Library, site plan. **Bottom** Newnham College Library, University of Cambridge, © Dennis Gilbert/View.

to design an extension fronting Trumpington Street, but that had been abandoned, as had a proposal to extend the museum towards the north, which was in line with the original architect George Basevi's expectation. However, this made some difficulties with the adjoining Peterhouse College. Finally, it was decided to extend the southern wing, which was just one room wide, around three sides of a square; it was obvious that the ring of rooms thus begun could be completed, and a common entrance hall placed in the middle. A toplight, creating an atrium, could light the middle space, this being now the preferred means of dealing with public buildings. All this was in due course carried out. But owing to an unexpected reduction in the Lottery funding available, it did not happen until 2004. It gives the opportunity for improved access for the general public, in line with University policy. The resulting ambiance seems relaxed and modern in comparison with the old building, still very much in evidence. Touches like the steel and glass spiral staircase reveal the modern sensibility underlying the continuing discretion.

With the Playfair Project, for the National Galleries of Scotland, the yearning for 'real' architecture was at last satisfied. This was not tucked away in a mews, it was out there for all to see: a world heritage site. The restoration of the Royal Scottish Academy Building and the creation of the underground link to the National Gallery would provide world-class exhibition space and visitor facilities in the heart of Scotland's capital city. John Miller + Partners won this commission through a limited competition. Work began in 1999, and the new facility was completed in 2004.

It was a complex operation, which could not begin until engineers had satisfied themselves that the structural stability of the Scottish Academy had been restored. Built on a raft of wooden piles, most of them now rotted, in the soft earth taken from the New Town, it was in danger of subsidence: a trench had to be dug along its east side and concrete forced into the voids, before work could begin on the new Weston Link, which would give visitors' facilities and access to both the Academy and the National Gallery.

The new building is at the level below both museums, and provides access to them with new lifts and staircases, the lifts wrapped by the staircases, in a compact and elegant way, using Pouilleney limestone and etched glass. The quite extensive area of the entrance hall is supported on a square grid of cylindrical columns, forming in effect a veritable hypostyle hall, more spacious than the Egyptian original. Two vaulted extensions of this grid give an identity to the Information Technology space and the shop. As you enter, the information desk is straight in front of you, occupying one bay of the grid, with top light coming down from a stepped pyramid in the pedestrian square above. To the left is the cloak room, to the right is the restaurant, which has windows towards the park to the east. The restaurant has been made at three levels, joined by three steps and a gentle ramp, so that the inside tables still have a view of the gardens.

What is the basis of John Miller's success? His competition-winning design for the Playfair Project was judged by the jury to have already solved the problem. Other entrants to the competition tried various eye-catching ideas, to no avail. This suggests that in all his projects he has adopted a way of working that really does get down to the functional problems. Yet the result seems painless at the nitty-gritty level, it is all about 'real' architecture, meaning idealised forms. So attention is given to both horizons: the way a building will work, the way it will look.

So, how does he fare when he faces a straight-forward new build, on a suitable site, with lots of spare space?

Top Courtyard Development, Fitzwilliam Museum, © Dennis Gilbert/View. **Bottom** Playfair Project, National Galleries of Scotland, © Keith Hunter.

The Brindley Arts Centre, of 2005, is just that. It is an ambitious new Arts Centre for Halton Borough Council, near Runcorn. The site, just north of the Bridgewater Canal, looks down across the town centre towards the bridge and beyond across countryside to the Mersey.

There are three primary functions: the main auditorium seating 420, which is intended for speech, drama, music and dance, with proscenium, deep stage and a full height fly tower; a smaller multi-functional flat floor studio, with retractable raking seats for 120, intended for a variety of performing options including theatre, dance, cinema, conference and group activities; finally, an exhibition space with education workroom. These functions are expressed as separate elements, linked together by a top-lit curving foyer, with seating alcoves and a bar, and giving access at first-floor level to a cafe and restaurant with a south-facing terrace overlooking the canal. The project benefits from a passive energy strategy for the cooling and ventilating of the theatre by using the structure as a thermal store. So the building is generated from its uses and is also technologically up to date.

As with the Ramphal Building, for the University of Warwick, the auditorium with its fan-shaped seating is enclosed in a smooth circular plan, and the curve it generates gives animation and a sense of anticipation to the foyer that surrounds it. The curve also gives a sense of direction to the restaurant with its wide views over the countryside. So the functions have been put together with a ready sense of their physical and social implications. All this went through without a hitch, and "The Brindley" opened in July 2004.

It appears therefore that we are really dealing here with a prime case of form following function: function understood not simply as physical enablement, but with all the psychological ramifications added; plus, we must by now have become aware, a devotion to 'real' architecture and with it, an eye for beauty.

Should one feel bad about this? Most architects struggle in the same direction, they don't all have similar success. In Miller's work there must be a genuine love of architecture, a sense of its potential, which keeps him at the difficult problems until they 'come out'; yet they don't come out for him until he has also achieved something at the highest level.

In discussing this with John I have found that we are agreed about certain aspects of architectural design. It is to do with having a complex goal that wants to both innovate and retrieve at the same time. His description of this syndrome is *Custom and Innovation*, which he has chosen as the title for this book. I like the phrase *Ancient Wisdom and Modern Knowhow*, which is the title for a book I have not yet written. In Britain, most architects want only to innovate, and a glamour of always being innovative attaches to the high-tech school, and gives a goal to many practices.

But there are two things that can be said about this: within the high-tech way of approaching architecture, certain solutions come to be preferred, come to have a fixed meaning, and so are always followed; so that within the high-tech school there can still be a division made between what is genuinely innovative and what is routinely innovative. Every mode of design soon begins to have its own tradition, so it's almost impossible to start from a *tabula rasa* every time.

The second thing is to do with continuity, particularly the idea of continuity at the cultural level. Our culture is cumulative, yes, but this does not prevent us from still enjoying things that were once new, and have now become well known, such as The

Top Brindley Arts Centre, preliminary scheme, Runcorn. **Bottom** Brindley Arts Centre, Runcorn, © Dennis Gilbert/View.

Beatles or, in my own case, Fats Waller. Fats is fixed by his position in time, within early jazz up to the beginning of the "swing era". The Beatles are also fixed in time, from their success in the swinging London of the 60s. Music is a case in point: every form of music is fixed by its origins. There is clearly a spirit of the times, that is the result of what applies *now* and that always moves on. Yet, no one is suggesting that we should stop listening to Bach or Mozart. In architecture, no one is suggesting that Paris would be better without the Eiffel tower, vastly innovative at its inception; or that London would be better without St Pauls and Westminster Abbey, both built in the tradition that reigned at their inception. As James Stirling said, a city without monuments would be no kind of a place. The continuity of the city, within which every new building must take its place, provides one very strong reason why architecture must always keep one eye on the past, without stopping to look towards the future. The fact that the city bears the record of history is what makes it a city.

There is a general problem in the visual arts about innovation in our society, which has to do with the nineteenth century concept of the avant-garde. Since Walter Benjamin idealised the role of the avant-garde, since Duchamp in the twentieth century idealised the role of the conceptual artist, no artist today wants to be regarded as *not* avant-garde. As with our first point about innovation, above, this fails to deal with the statistical fact that if everyone is avant-garde, we are being led from behind. The very concept of innovation becomes humdrum. It has always struck me that the great success of IKEA results from a clearly considered policy of combining slick (and cheap) modern design, eminently suitable for young people setting up house for the first time, with a readiness to provide traditional (and decorative) fabrics and rugs, craft objects, cane chairs and so on, which young people also enjoy equally. Everybody, it seems, wants to be up-to-date without losing the enjoyment of familiar things.

I have suggested that in enclosing his auditoria in circular plan forms, John Miller was both idealising and innovating. In other words, innovation is not a one-dimensional thing, it does not necessarily imply simply being at the edge of technology. To appreciate the innovative aspects of this work requires that you consider it in a wide framework, that you are not just looking for the 'innovative' and that which proclaims itself as innovative. I believe that to see what is genuinely innovative in this work requires that you see it as a whole.

Before the end of the film, there is a period called retirement. The French call it *La Retraite*, the retreat. You draw back from the world, but you continue to enjoy your family and meet old friends. John and Su have bought an old house in France—La Batterie—north of Toulon, on a hilltop near Evenos. It looks out south across wild, unwalkable country, towards a view of the sea, where Japanese freighters make their stately way towards Marseille. To attract the grandchildren, the first year was spent building the swimming pool: small, rectangular, but with an 'infinite' edge, and surrounded by wood decking. When that was complete, they tackled the house. Instead of going up and down, they put in a level floor throughout. The garden, on the other hand, continues to go up and down. The house is ancient, but inside it is thoroughly modern. The kitchen, like the cooking, is supremely modern. Because, in the end, whatever our feelings for the past, we all are part of the present. John Miller + Partners is a firm of modern architects, and their work is a just summation of what modern architecture can do.

Top La Batterie, view along the terrace, © Martin Morrell. **Middle** La Batterie, swimming pool with the sea beyond, © Martin Morrell. **Bottom** La Batterie, view toward the sea, © Sandra Lousada. **Opposite** La Batterie, interior, © Martin Morrell.

HOUSING

1975

PILLWOOD
Cornwall
Colquhoun + Miller

This holiday house is located on Pill Creek, Feock Cornwall. The site lines the Creek shore.

The house is designed for summer vacations and sits in a rectangular clearing surrounded by thick oak woodland, providing privacy. The form, materials, and colour scheme refer to the tankers moored in the Fal estuary and to the natural colours of the site. The living areas are at first floor in order to take advantage of the view of the estuary. The two internal staircases and sliding screen walls do away with the need for a corridor.

It has a tubular steel frame structure, with reinforced concrete floors. The exterior is clad in 100mm thick, GRP panels, with neoprene joints. The frame is painted green. The flooring is in ochre coloured plastic sheet. The sloping glazing has retractable pale blue blinds to reduce solar gain. The house has opening glass louvres at high and low level. Cool air is drawn from the creek by a venturi affect.

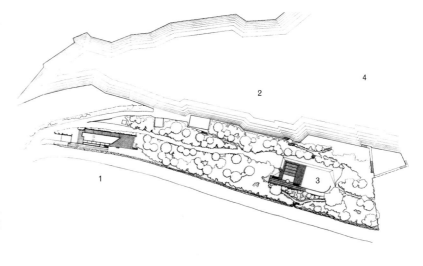

1   Pillwood 2
2   Boathouse
3   Pillwood 1
4   Pill Creek

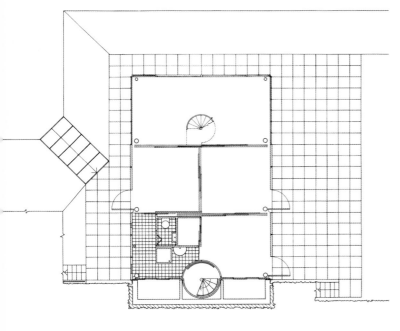

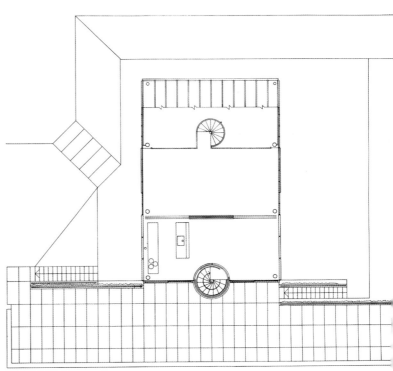

Previous page Pillwood 1, view of the side elevation and terrace from the wood above.

Opposite clockwise from top Site plan showing Pillwood 1 and 2; First floor; Ground floor.

Below View from the garden.

In 1974, a project for a second house on part of the Pillwood site was submitted for planning approval. Sadly the client decided the design was too remote from his workplace. The site was bought back and reworked as a permanent family home. Foundations were laid. Approvals received and subject to funding, construction can start.

Where Pillwood 1 is an essay in industrial technology, Pillwood 2 returns to more conventional construction. The technology of Pillwood 1 is restricting. The installation of service distribution is complicated. Inner faces of the GRP panels are unfriendly to picture hanging, fittings, etc., and the design does not readily accept change through use.

Pillwood 2 has a long plan with bedrooms at one end and a terrace at the other, with living room, kitchen and dining room between.

Externally it has a turf roof, white rendered walls, triple glazed metal coated windows, a dark grey slate plinth and wall cappings.

Internally, the principal materials are a grey slate floor, plastered and tiled walls.

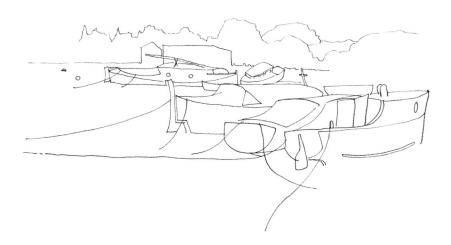

Opposite Sketch of Pill Creek.

Below Interior of the first floor of Pillwood 1 with view of Pill Creek.

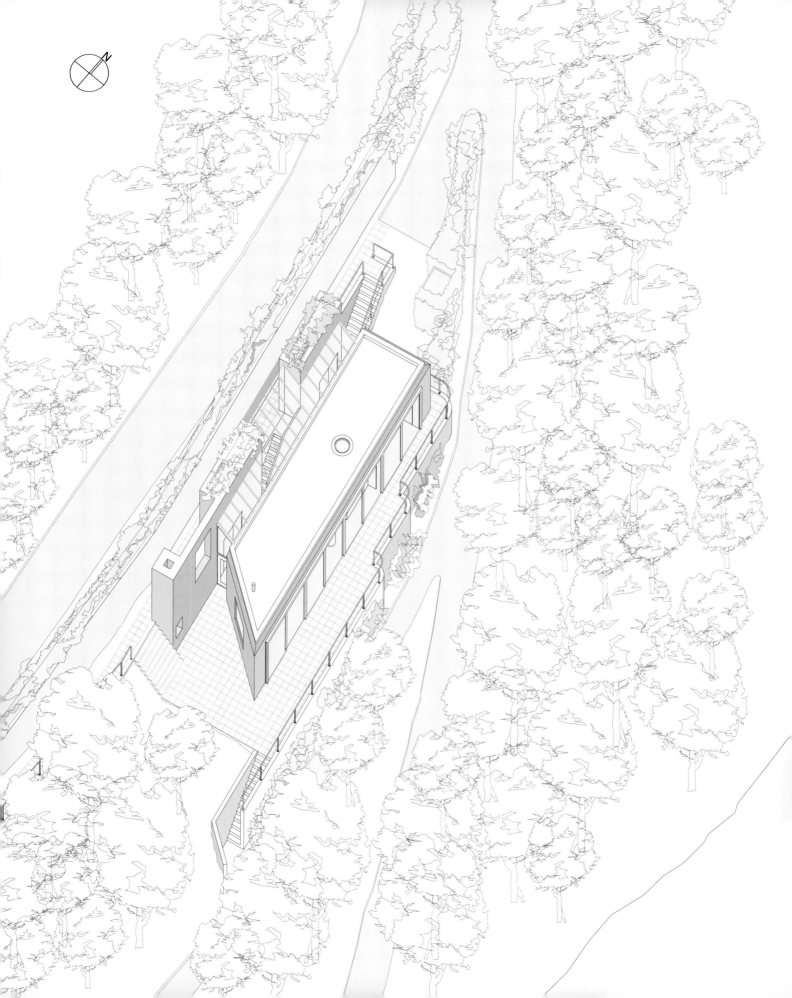

Opposite Axonometric of Pillwood 2.

Top to bottom Section through the site; Elevation from the east; Plan.

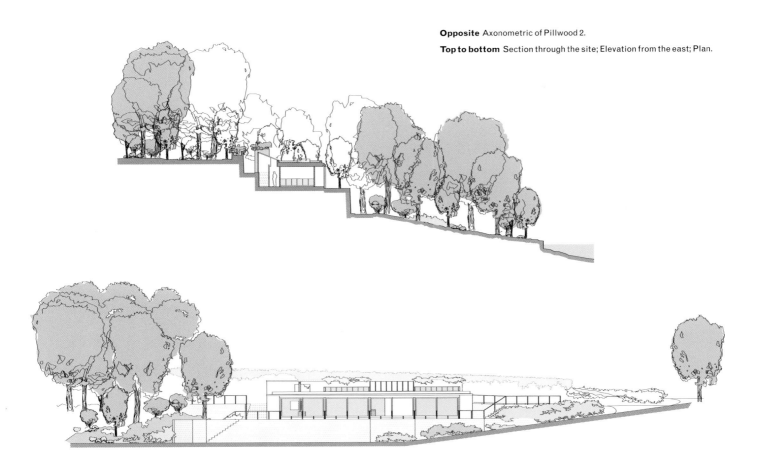

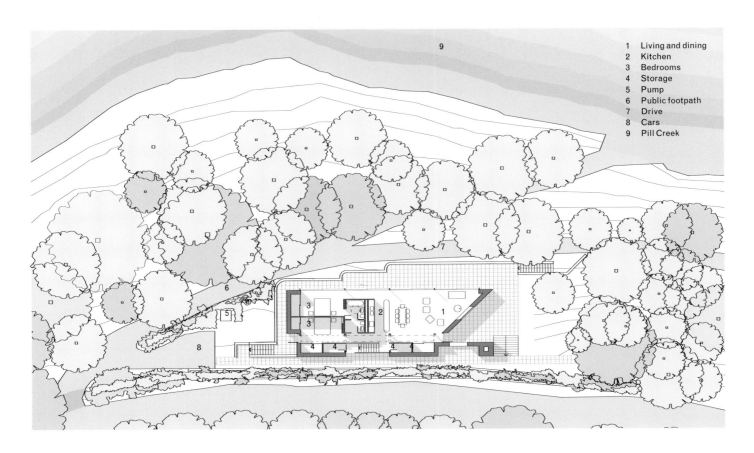

1 Living and dining
2 Kitchen
3 Bedrooms
4 Storage
5 Pump
6 Public footpath
7 Drive
8 Cars
9 Pill Creek

1978

VERNACULAR HOUSING, FENNY STRATFORD
Milton Keynes
Colquhoun + Miller

Fenny Stratford is part of the Milton Keynes Development Plan. The corner site is the first of Colquhoun + Miller's projects for the new city. It is located at a busy crossroads in the old village. The brief called for a group of houses with small gardens, to reinforce the existing fabric. The building datum is approximately one metre higher than the adjacent pavement and this, and the alternating house plans with enclosed gardens, gives protection from the noisy street. Parking for seven cars is provided at the rear of the site. Although the configuration is uneconomical, the simple plans and the stacking of adjacent bathrooms and kitchens help to contain costs.

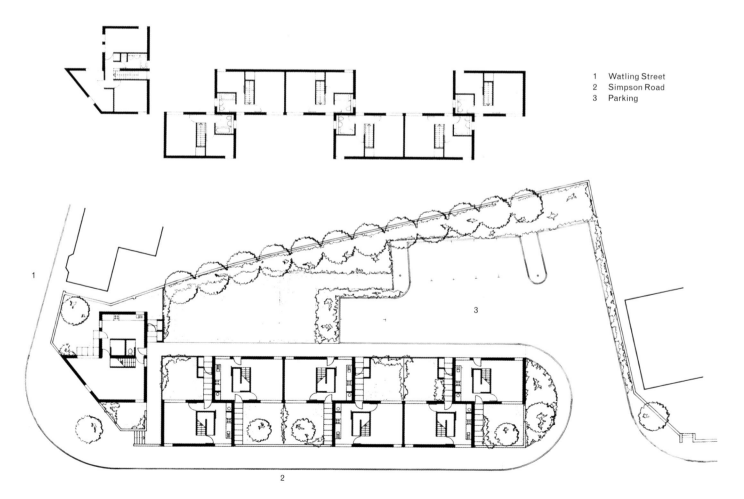

1   Watling Street
2   Simpson Road
3   Parking

Opposite top to bottom Model, ©MKDC; First floor; Ground floor.

Above Elevation from Simpson Road, © Martin Charles.

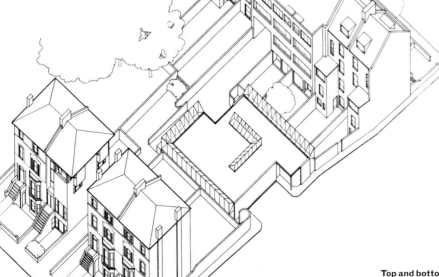

1979

HOUSING, CAVERSHAM ROAD AND GAISFORD STREET
London
Colquhoun + Miller

The site runs between the terraced Gaisford Street and Caversham Road, which is lined with semi-detached houses.

The Caversham site requires the completion of the missing half of a semi-detached villa. The challenge is a problem of scale; accommodating two maisonettes in a single villa type. The blank wall at first floor and the distribution of window openings are arranged to suggest one occupancy under a projecting hipped roof. The expression is deliberately ambiguous. This typology draws from the precedent of eighteenth and nineteenth century London villas that are often sub-divided in this way.

The Gaisford Street terrace requires a different approach. Five duplex apartments are provided with direct access from the street. Their entrances are similar in scale to those of the adjacent terraces. The lower apartments of both have back gardens while balconies are provided for the upper apartments. Both buildings are finished in stucco.

The brief called for a community building to be set between the two buildings in part of the back gardens. This was not realised.

Top and bottom Axonometric of the house on Caversham Road, drawing by John Hewitt; Axonometric showing Caversham Road and Gaisford Street.

Opposite Corner house from Caversham Road, © Martin Charles.

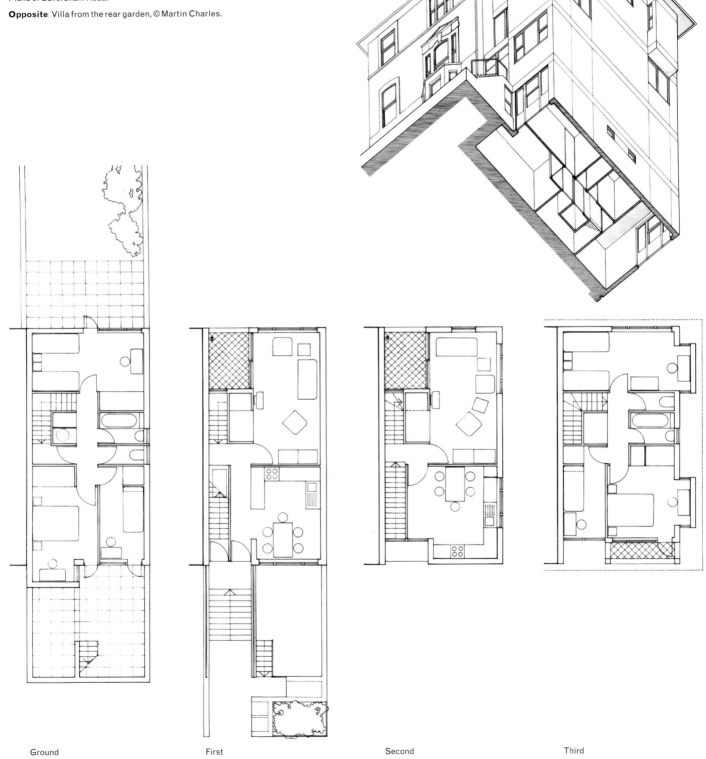

Top and bottom Worm's-eye view of Caversham Road house; Plans of Caversham Road.

Opposite Villa from the rear garden, © Martin Charles.

Ground   First   Second   Third

Clockwise from left Detail showing the entrance stairs on Gaisford Street; View of the Gaisford Street access; Gaisford Street elevation, © Martin Charles.

Opposite top and bottom Gaisford Street elevation, © Martin Charles; Plans of Gaisford Street.

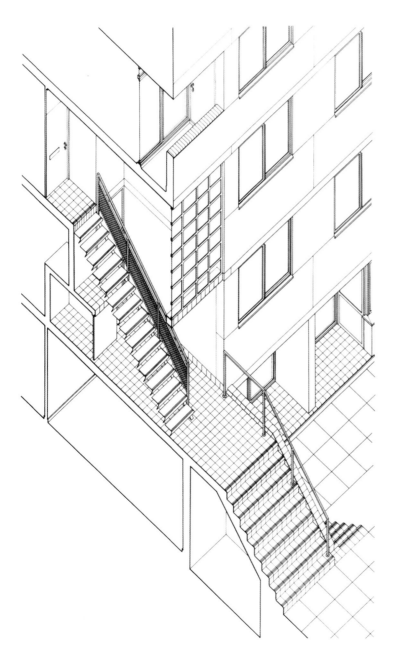

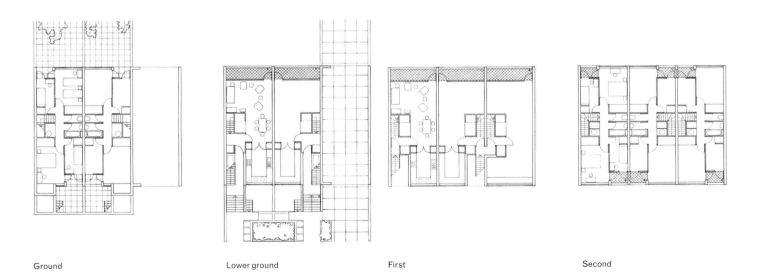

Ground

Lower ground

First

Second

1980

HOUSING, HORNSEY LANE
London
Colquhoun + Miller

Hornsey Lane is lined with medium-rise apartment blocks similar in height to the new building.

The brief called for a nine-storey building with 34 suites of paired single bed sitting rooms with shared bathrooms and kitchens. There is a caretaker's flat, a laundry and common rooms opening on to a communal garden. The new building is set back from the street with a planted paved parking area. Many suites are now used as small flats for couples.

The materials used are calculated load bearing brickwork with warm red facings and matching soldier and string courses.

The windows are fully glazed with high performance timber opening lights above glass block panels.

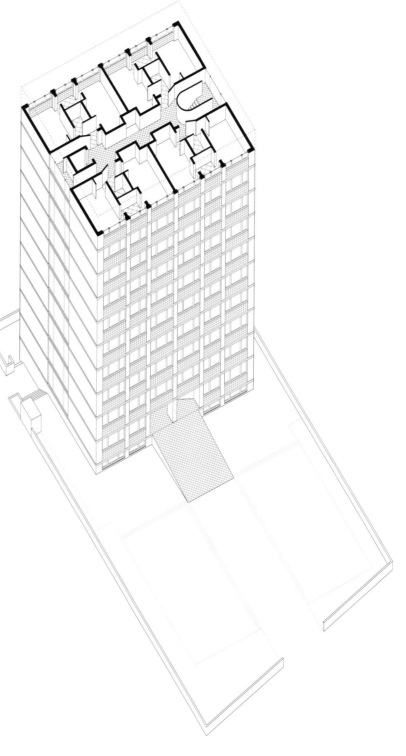

Left and above Oblique view showing the front and side elevations, © Martin Charles; Axonometric showing a typical floor plan, drawing by John Hewitt.

Opposite Entrance elevation, © Martin Charles.

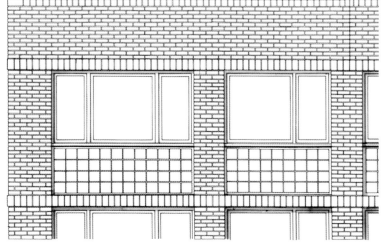

Top and bottom Typical interior, © Martin Charles; Detail of elevation.

Opposite clockwise from left Detail of the staircase, © Martin Charles; Axonometric showing typical flat; Entrance floor plan.

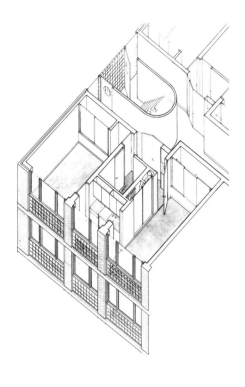

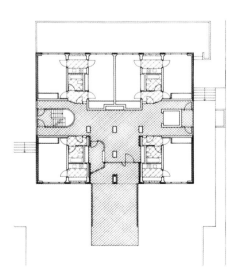

1982

HOUSING, OLDBROOK II
Milton Keynes
Colquhoun + Miller

As with the many other housing projects in Milton Keynes, Oldbrook's name is associated with a local feature, suggesting rural continuity in the context of the kilometre square city planning grid derived from a Californian model. The emphasis on road grid and roundabout is intended to allow its residents to move around easily. The catchword being "community without propinquity". The City has been planned as a 'forest city' and its landscaping and tree planting is its major triumph.

Oldbrook II is part of a grid square close to Central Milton Keynes. It provides 152 homes for families of two to seven people. The layout is intended to be urban with three streets of two- and three-storey terrace houses. The majority have integral garages with private gardens at the back. The gardens open onto communal play spaces or open public space. The scheme illustrates the difficulty of establishing an urban environment within a context that is fundamentally suburban.

The layout creates an urban scale by stressing the street as the locus of the *res publica* and contrasting this to the *res privata* of gardens and children's play spaces.

Each pair of three-storey terrace houses has a cranked dividing party wall containing the staircase. This innovation has two virtues. It allows ground floor corridors to connect front doors to gardens without obstruction and it provides some limited variety in the house plans.

Opposite Garden elevation showing 'crinkly crankly wall', © Martin Charles.

Above Elevation of the three-storey units, © Martin Charles.

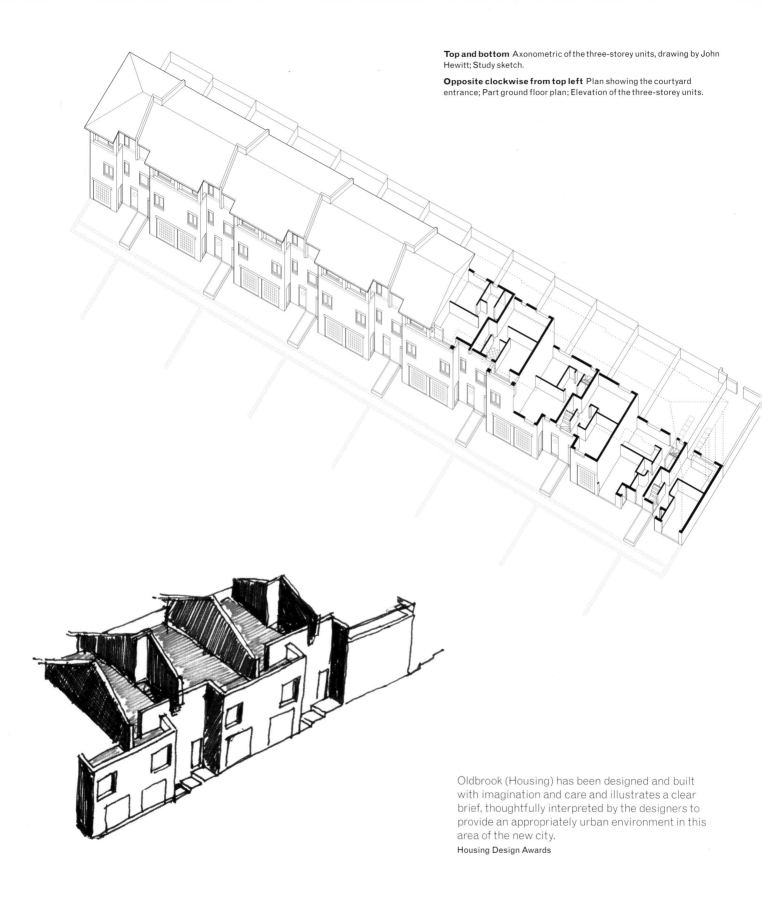

Top and bottom Axonometric of the three-storey units, drawing by John Hewitt; Study sketch.

Opposite clockwise from top left Plan showing the courtyard entrance; Part ground floor plan; Elevation of the three-storey units.

Oldbrook (Housing) has been designed and built with imagination and care and illustrates a clear brief, thoughtfully interpreted by the designers to provide an appropriately urban environment in this area of the new city.
Housing Design Awards

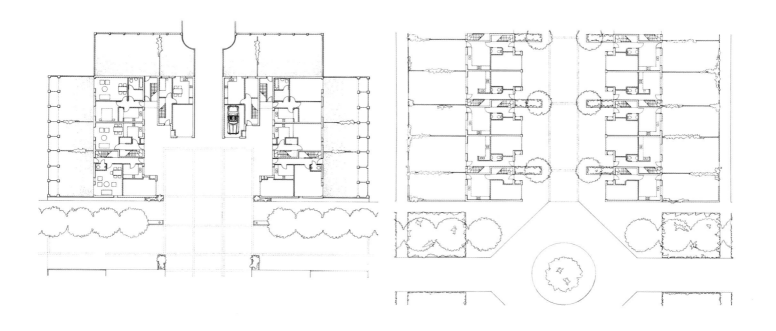

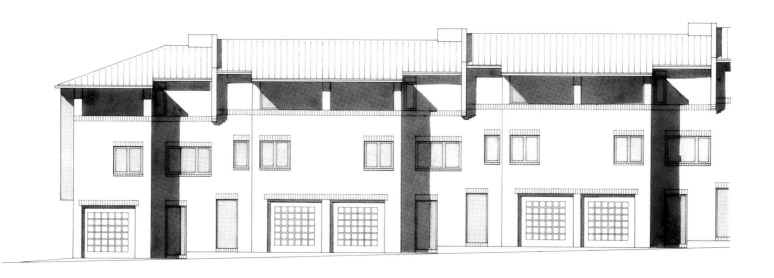

Clockwise from top left Site plan;Courtyard elevation; Street elevation
of the three-storey units, © Martin Charles.

Opposite clockwise from top left Garden elevation, © Martin Charles;
Plan of the two-storey units; Street elevation of the two-storey units,
© Martin Charles.

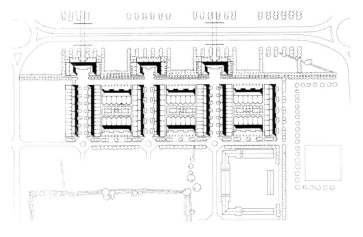

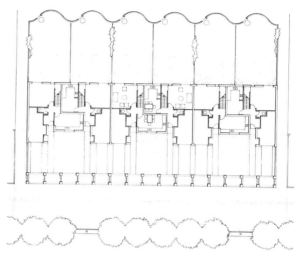

1990

HOUSING, ALCOY
Spain
Colquhoun + Miller

Alcoy is situated in the mountains to the north of Alicante on a high plateau, cut by a number of deep river gorges, requiring bridges to unite the many quarters of the town. It is densely built but the bottoms of the gorges have a rural character. The Riba site, close to the centre, is located in one of the quarters.

The Generalitat of Valencia commissioned six European practices to take part in a programme of urban reconstruction. Each was allocated an individual site.

The Riba overlooks a gorge and requires the completion of a quarter of the town behind the busy Carrer Saint Nicolau. The brief calls for 135 large apartments in buildings of four- and five-storeys with basement car parking for 242 cars. A small pedestrian shopping arcade with offices over connects the site to the Carrer and to a public square. Two ranges of apartment buildings, forming a fan shape with characteristic miradors, address the landscaped plaza, the focal space of the scheme with a view across the gorge.

Opposite top and bottom Aerial view of the city; General plan at level 5.

Top and bottom Site plan showing steep contours; Typical elevation.

Generic apartment plans, mostly duplexes, have a central living room with enclosing en-suite bedrooms. A 'public' space with supporting 'private' spaces, a city plan in miniature. The miradors face the public space and are a traditional building element arising in part from climatic necessity and in part from social decorum. They allow free passage of air while providing security, and visual contact with the street below.

External walls are rendered, with a continuous local stone plinth. Windows and balustrades are in metal. Roofs are generally tiled using local materials.

Clockwise from top left Model of a typical facade; Floor plans.

Opposite top and bottom View of the backs of existing houses on Caller St Nicolas; Axonometric showing integration of the old with the new.

1 Living
2 Kitchen
3 Bedroom
4 Mirador
5 Study
6 Gallery

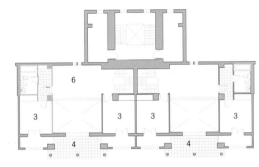

Plan at level four, duplex

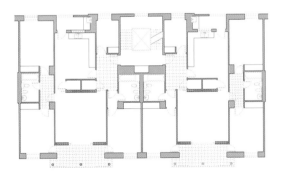

Plan at level two, apartments 3

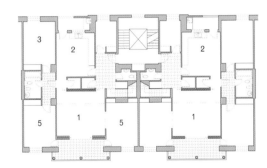

Plan at level three, duplex

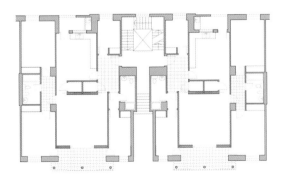

Plan at level zero, apartments 1

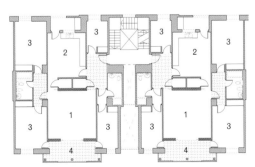

Plan at level one, apartments 2

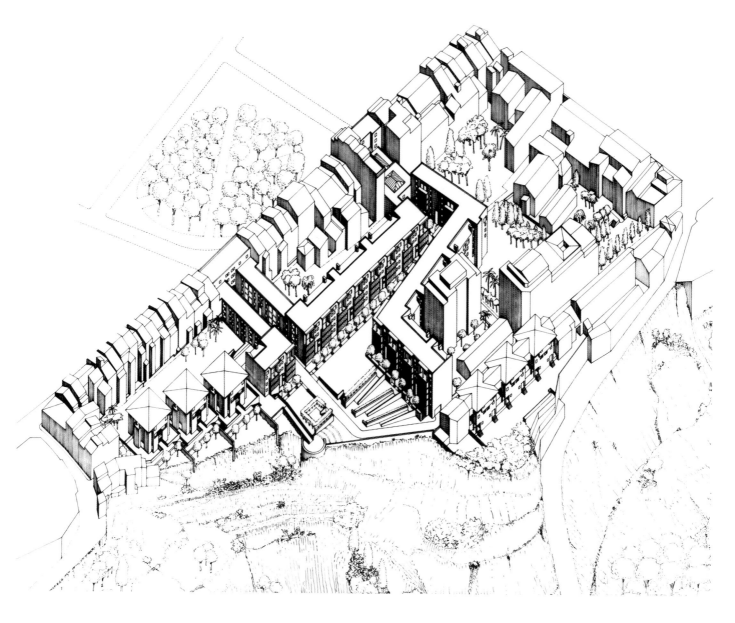

Clockwise from top Detail of kitchen with stair beyond, © Sandra Lousada; Mezzanine floor plan; Fifth (main) floor plan.

Opposite View of the library with mezzanine above, © Sandra Lousada.

2008

BEAUCHAMP BUILDING
London
John Miller + Partners

In the early 1990s, the existing office building was converted to provide nine duplex apartments with a penthouse. The top floor of the office building became the entrance floor of a triplex penthouse. The conversion accepts the earlier layout. The challenge was to simplify and to free the space of stylistic details.

The upper two floors and a principal floor (living, dining and kitchen area) with a gallery over, have a balcony around their perimeter. The envelope of these two upper floors is constructed in a lightweight panel system with a shallow vaulted roof.

One side of the gallery engages the external panel wall. The remaining three walls are free giving a double-height on three sides. The balcony is contained by partitions running from gallery floor to ceiling. They have three 'windows', one glazed to the bathroom and the remaining two open to the living and dining areas below. The gallery can be enjoyed as a 'house within a house'.

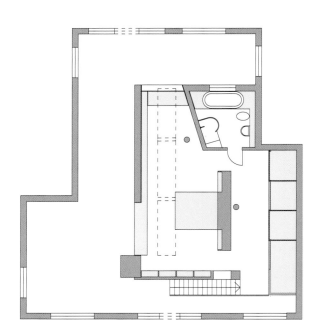

Clockwise from top right Details of the entrance stair; Enclosing wall to the mezzanine; Details of column to the mezzanine, © Sandra Lousada.

Opposite Stair from the fifth floor to the mezzanine, © Sandra Lousada.

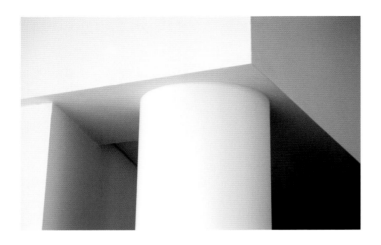

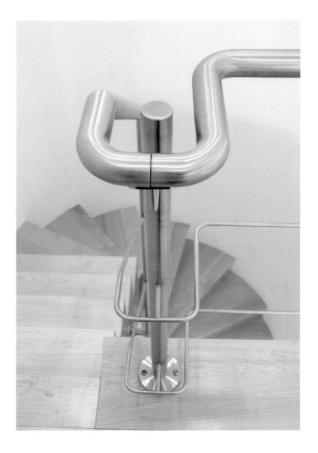

Below View of the kitchen from the dining area, © Sandra Lousada.

Opposite View looking towards the dining area from the living room, © Sandra Lousada.

JOHN MILLER: DESIGNING FOR ART
Nicholas Serota

In an age in which architects have sought to make or embellish their name with signature galleries, John Miller has created a series of quiet, purposeful, elegant spaces in which art, rather than architecture, captures the eye.

Building on an admired sequence of new buildings in the fields of education and public housing, Miller has produced some exemplary renovations and extensions. Starting with the Whitechapel Art Gallery in the early 1980s, these now include the Royal College of Art, the Serpentine Gallery, National Portrait Gallery, National Galleries of Scotland, Tate Britain, and the Fitzwilliam Museum. The length of this list testifies to his ability to work with demanding clients and to overcome the challenges of confined sites with planning and listing constraints.

In each of these buildings John Miller and his colleagues have generated intelligent and convincing answers to the perennial challenges of such projects. What should we retain, where do we better renew, where should we add and what should be the language of new additions—do we mimic, echo, or contrast with the original? Miller provides thoughtful and enduring answers to all these questions. The hallmark of his practice has been to create chambers in which the eye is contained and therefore settles on the painting, sculpture or installation on display. Miller's galleries, unlike so many, are grounded by his preference for walls which meet floors, for using daylight wherever possible to flood the space, and for sensitive and original detail which is deliberate and conscious, rather than suppressed. We feel the weight and gravity of a volume that makes a firm container for the encounter with the work of art. He encourages the eye to confront the work, rather than to slide off into nebulous space. The understated skirtings, the doors and seating depend on an aesthetic which has its roots in the precursors of modernism touched by a Corbusian feeling for proportion and the human scale. Like a well cut suit, the elegance of his architectural language has an ease which conceals the rigour and determination of his practice.

The current name of the company, John Miller + Partners, perfectly describes his preferred method of developing ideas through dialogue with a close associate or a client. Miller habitually works through a long series of drawings and overlays that test options and solutions until one emerges that feels completely unforced. He has been perceptive and fortunate in his choice of associates. For more than 25 years Alan Colquhoun encouraged the rigour that is the armature for the best of the Colquhoun + Miller schemes. Colquhoun's search for a simple expression of need in developing different typologies helped to purge Colquhoun + Miller designs of any unnecessary complications and thereby gave the built form a grace in its plan, section and elevation. Su Rogers, a partner in architecture and life, has continued that tradition in her insistence on the fundamental importance of clarity and practicality in the design and this commitment has been reinforced by the work of the other partner of longstanding, Richard Brearley. Together members of the practice have completed a succession of impressive, quietly spoken museum projects.

Looking back over the past 20 years it may now seem natural that a cultured architect with many connections to the art world should turn to designing spaces for art. However, Colquhoun + Miller were already in their 50s when work in the field of shop and exhibition design evolved into full scale gallery architecture with the commission to renovate and extend Charles Harrison Townsend's Whitechapel Art Gallery. Their scheme for that building discloses an approach, solutions and qualities, which have been developed in later museum projects. The challenge at the Whitechapel was to retain and enhance the character of the exhibition spaces so loved by artists and visitors, to introduce new facilities including a bookshop and cafe, spaces for learning and offices, and to dramatically improve access to the hidden upper gallery. All this had to be achieved within a site only slightly enlarged to the west by the addition of a narrow former school building. Unlike most other entrants to the competition, Colquhoun + Miller found a solution to the vertical circulation without intruding on the primary exhibition galleries. They resisted the temptation to use the beautiful northeast corner of the original gallery as a location for a new stair (since transformed into a vestibule in the 2009 Robbrecht and Daem scheme and now lost as part of the gallery) and designed a straight, naturally lit flight, a *scala regia* stair, to replace the dark hidden service stair. At the front a sweeping terrazzo stair (now demolished), carefully inserted in a small lightwell, encouraged ascent with a flood of light from a lay light above.

The architects made one bold move in the original ground floor gallery, inserting a new wall to create a reception area. This had the benefit of creating an additional buffer between the street and the gallery without interrupting the flow, while also giving a greater sense of definition and containment to the exhibition space itself. The detail of the new wall, with its simple generous arch window and small paned doors, echoed the original barrel vault of the entrance vestibule (both arch and door have also now been demolished and replaced by new elements). The new extension to the west, with its nod to Adolf Loos in the modest but strong facade in Angel Alley, packs an astonishing amount of accommodation into a small volume, but would have been improved if the Trustees of the Gallery had been able to purchase some additional land in the northwest corner of the site that would have allowed a larger gallery at the top of the stair and more adequate meeting rooms below.

The language and materials developed in the Whitechapel project, such as light oak and terrazzo floors, have featured in many of Miller's later buildings, notably at the Royal College of Art and Serpentine Galleries, but also in a more weighty form at the more complex projects for the National Portrait Gallery, National Galleries of Scotland and Tate Britain. In each of these later schemes Miller and Rogers have demonstrated a continuing ability to craft or adapt finely proportioned rooms. Spaces are often linked in a sequence which subtly modifies the insistent rule of the enfilade or are connected vertically by finely wrought stairs which ascend with ease from one floor to another. Few architects can now match John Miller's distinguished record in designing classically proportioned spaces in which all kinds of art can find a sympathetic home.

DESIGNING FOR ART

· WHITECHAPEL ART GALLERY ·
IN COURSE OF ERECTION AT THE EXPENSE OF
HARRISON TOWNSEND ARCHT · Mr J · PASSMORE EDWARDS

· SCALE ·

1985

WHITECHAPEL ART GALLERY
London
Colquhoun + Miller

The commission to extend and renovate the Whitechapel Gallery, Harrison Townsend's masterwork, followed a limited competition in the early 1980s. This pre-dated lottery funding. The gallery was closed until 1984 when sufficient private donations became available and when work could start in earnest. By this time, the Trustees had acquired a strip of land to the rear of the building and the old school building in Angel Alley, which abutted the Gallery's flank wall. Townsend's interior was minimalist, and the absence of ornament suited modern sensibilities, even if some the interior work did not match the brilliance of the Art Nouveau facade.

The principal 'moves' were to be an improvement to the promenade through the galleries, the creation of a bookshop, an education room, a cafe, administration offices, a meetings room and an art store. Additionally, environmental services and gallery lighting were primitive and needed renewal.

The hidden rear dogleg staircase had to be replaced, as visitors were often unaware of the existence of the upper gallery. Its replacement, with a modest version of Sangallo's *Scala Regia* gave the opportunity for a cafe and a small audio visual room on a mezzanine *en route* to the first floor gallery above.

Previously, a circuit through the upper gallery required a visitor to return via the same rear dogleg stairs (an older service stairs immediately behind the facade was not used). A new staircase in an old lightwell was built in a new entrance foyer formed by a new screen wall placed between foyer and main gallery, to permit independent gallery use. The foyer allowed the front doors to remain open to the street while the visitor could enjoy the calm of the main gallery without the bustle around an enquiry counter.

Much of this has been destroyed. The front stairs have gone to make a connection to the library next door. As has the screen which carried the 'imprint' of the barrel vault of the entry lobby. Sadly the peace of the main gallery has been affected by a further connection to the library in its far corner, a place favoured for exhibiting work.

When Colquhoun + Miller completed the renovation of the Whitechapel in 1985, no one could have anticipated that much of their work would be destroyed within the architects' lifetime. Now after some 20 years much has gone; this despite the Grade II Listing, the National and Regional RIBA Awards, a Civic Trust Award, the European sponsored International prize for Architecture, a finalist for the Mies Van de Rohe Barcelona Prize of 1988, and despite the plaudits of art and architectural critics. These talismans have given no protection and, as is so often the case, architecture has been treated as a resource and not something to be valued for itself.

Previous page Front elevation showing design for the unrealised frieze by Walter Crane, drawing by Harrison Townsend.

Opposite The entrance on Whitechapel High Street, © Martin Charles.

Below Axonometric showing the interior layout.

Opposite Foyer and new screen to the main gallery, © Peter Cook/View.

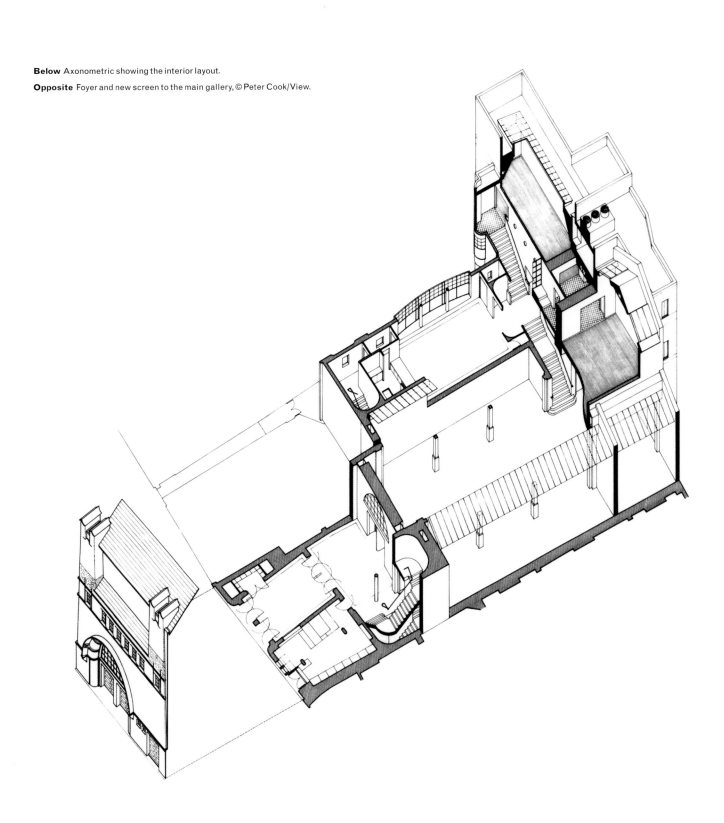

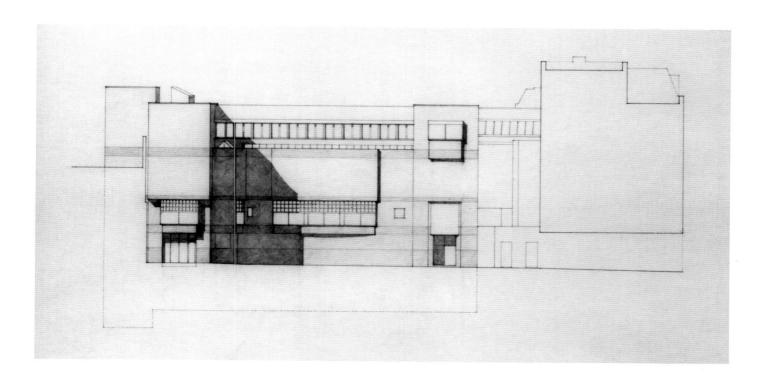

Opposite View along Angel Alley showing the cafe window to the right, © Martin Charles.

Top and bottom Elevation to Angel Alley; Study of Angel Alley.

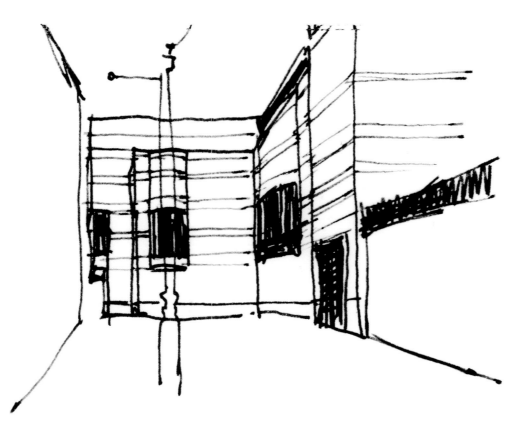

Clockwise from top Cross-section showing the integration of the services in the roof void; View of the ground floor gallery showing the moveable partitions, © Peter Cook/View; View of the ground floor gallery looking towards the foyer, © Martin Charles.

Opposite View of the entrance to the gallery, © Peter Cook/View.

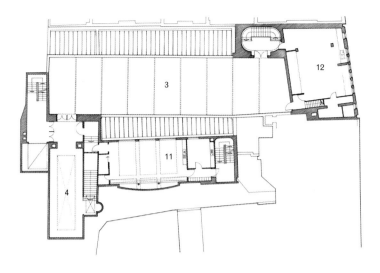

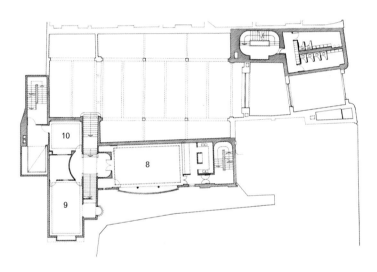

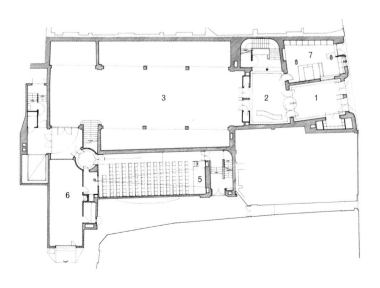

1   Entrance
2   Foyer
3   Existing gallery
4   New gallery
5   Lecture theatre
6   Loading/storage
7   Bookshop
8   Cafe
9   Meeting room
10 AV room
11 Education
12 Workshop

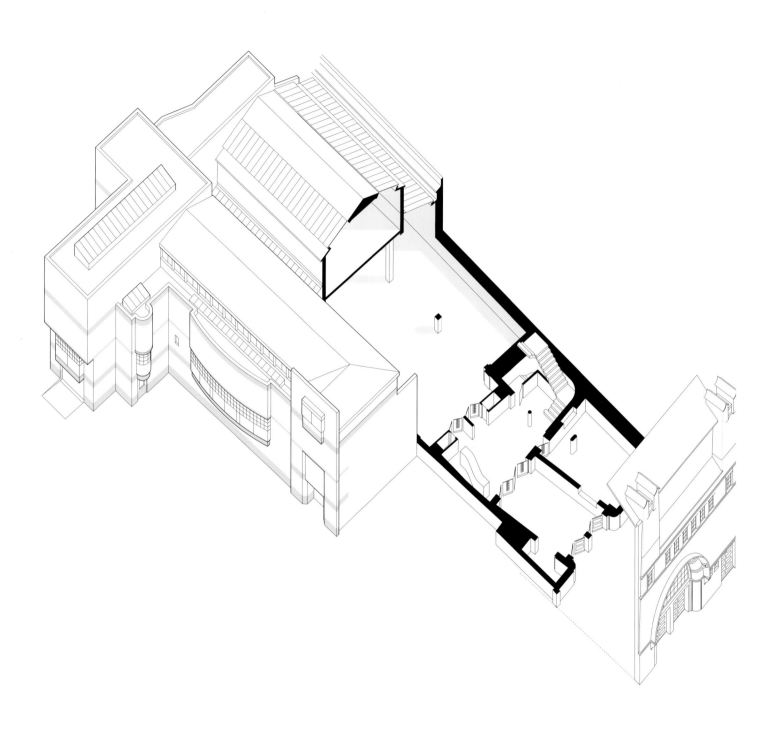

Opposite top to bottom First floor; Mezzanine; Ground floor.

Above Axonometric showing the front and side elevations, drawing by John Hewitt.

Top and bottom View of the first floor gallery, © Peter Cook/View; View from the new gallery to the existing first floor gallery, © Martin Charles.

Opposite Detail of the front stair, © Peter Cook/View.

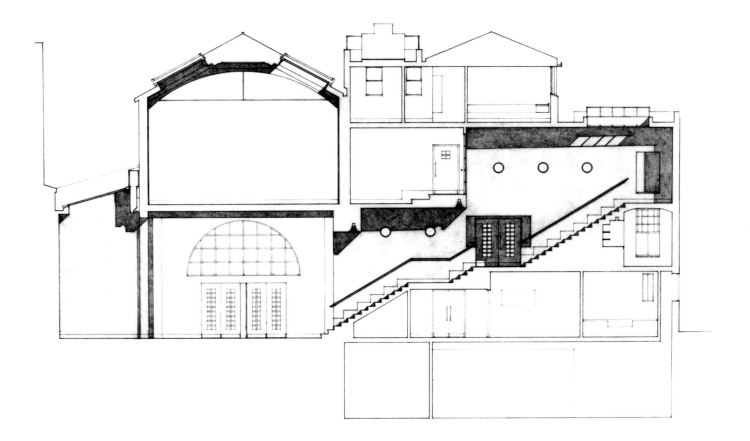

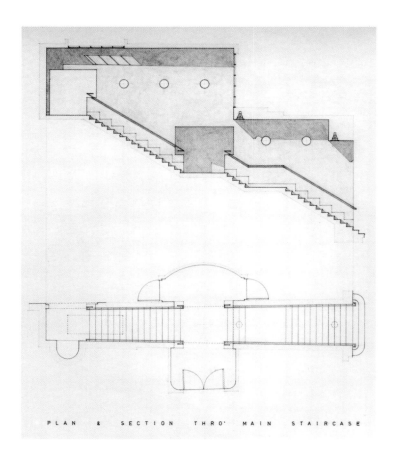

PLAN & SECTION THRO' MAIN STAIRCASE

Top and bottom Cross-section showing the entrance to the cafe on the mezzanine and the *scala regia* stairs; Plan and section showing the *scala regia* stairs.

Opposite View of the *scala regia* stairs, © Dennis Gilbert/View.

Jacqueline Poncelet

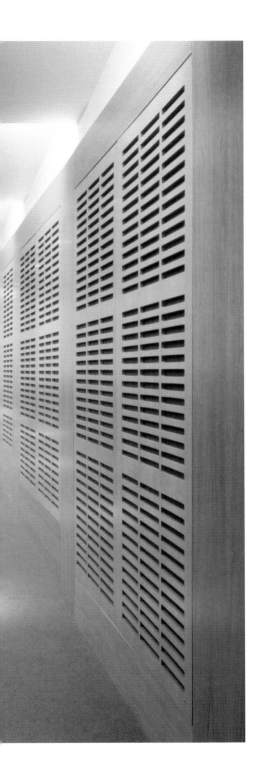

The ultimate success of a gallery may not depend on the style, wit and ingenuity of its interior design and planning but if it has these advantages—as does the Whitechapel—then it certainly makes it easier to display, to see and to appreciate the works on show. Colquhoun + Miller have done their bit in relaunching the Whitechapel and it is now up to the Director and Trustees to make the best use of the outstanding building they now possess.

Dan Cruickshank, *The Architectural Review*, November 1985

View of the lecture theatre, © Anthony Weller/View.

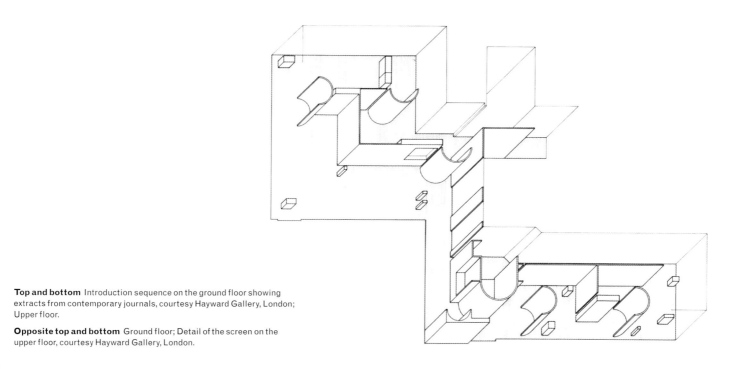

Top and bottom Introduction sequence on the ground floor showing extracts from contemporary journals, courtesy Hayward Gallery, London; Upper floor.

Opposite top and bottom Ground floor; Detail of the screen on the upper floor, courtesy Hayward Gallery, London.

1978

DADA AND
SURREALISM REVIEWED

Hayward Gallery

Colquhoun + Miller

The pleasure of exhibition design centres around the casual contact with works that otherwise are only known from books or visits to exhibitions. They are made accessible in a way that differs from a gallery encounter.

The Hayward Gallery's two floor plans, split by a lengthy dogleg staircase, and by half level changes, are a notorious challenge and one to stimulate a solution.

The generating ideas for the layout are the journals and magazines associated with selected works. A number of half cylinders, some two and a half metres high, introduce each section and are 'fly posted' with copies of these documents on their concave surfaces by the graphic designer Edward Wright. The density of the exhibition varies between cabinets for small objects to large works that need space.

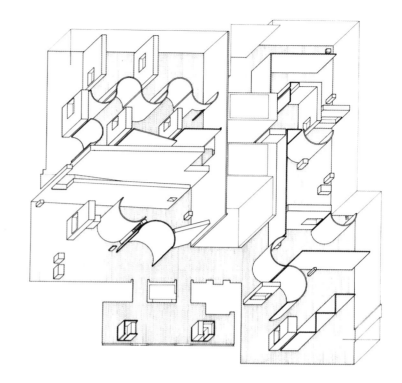

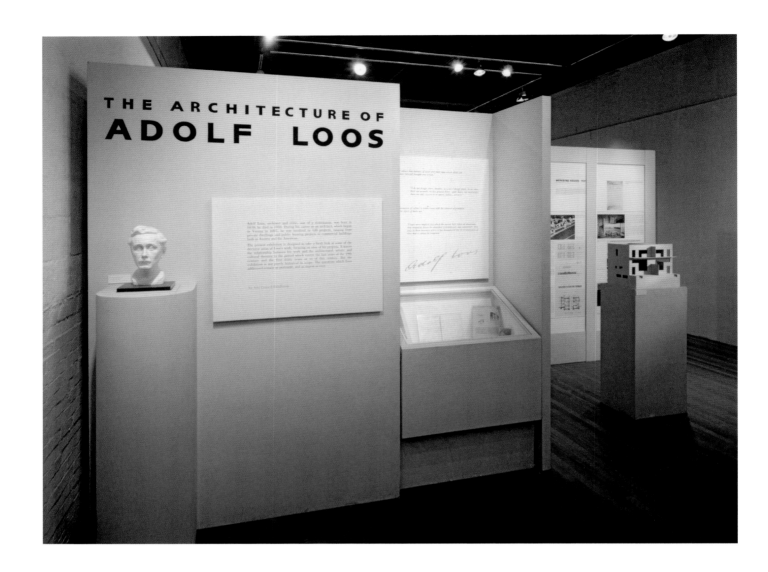

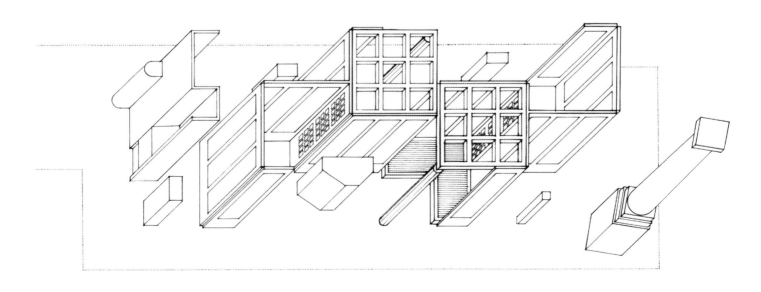

1984

ADOLF LOOS
Travelling Exhibition
Colquhoun + Miller

Designed to be dismountable, the exhibition travelled around Britain and abroad. Four rooms evoke Loos' interiors, exhibiting his furniture preferences together with examples of his architectural work, including the competition entry for the Chicago Tribune Tower of 1922.

Opposite top and bottom Introductory section to the exhibition; Axonometric of the exhibition, © Dennis Gilbert/View.

Top and bottom Exhibition spaces, © Dennis Gilbert/View.

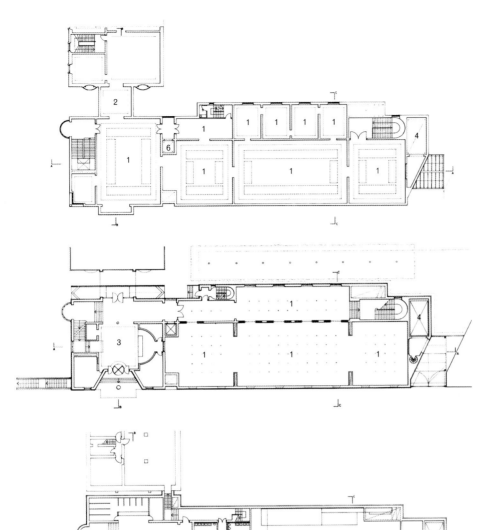

1 Galleries
2 Bridge to existing building
3 Entrance hall
4 Picture lift
5 Storage and packing
6 Lecture theatre

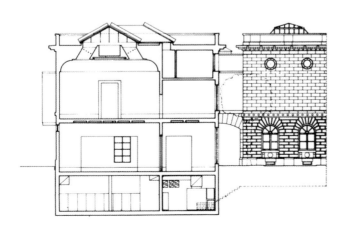

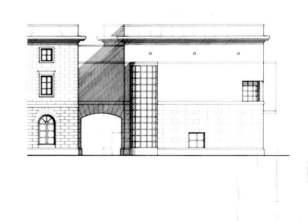

Opposite top to bottom Upper floor; Ground floor; Lower ground floor; Cross-section and end elevation.

Top and bottom Axonometric; Front elevation to Holbeinstrasse.

1986

STAEDEL ART GALLERY EXTENSION
Frankfurt, Invited Competition
Colquhoun + Miller

The existing gallery faces the River Main. The extension is sited between the gallery and the Staedelschule, facing one side of a sculpture garden and is at right angles to the main building. The *parti* of the winning scheme and the Colquhoun + Miller second prize entry are very similar. The difference is found in their two characters. The winner preferring an expressionist *leitmotif*.

The two-storey Colquhoun + Miller scheme draws on modernism rinsed with references to the existing building and to classical precedent. This is particularly so in the case of the front elevation with its blank projecting bay and the single rhetorical column announcing the entrance. The frontal emphasis this produces is then challenged by the part erosion of the corner and the exposure of a round corner column. This device and the glazed double-height staircase window unites the two elevations, necessary to this corner site.

The ground floor, the generating plan, is organised around a long axis and a short cross-axis. The long axis runs the length of the building terminating at each end with the wide bottom flights of the two main staircases. The cross-axis, the entry axis, connects the entrance to the sculpture garden. A shorter long axis runs across the entrance hall terminating in the down flight of the basement stairs and suggests a place for a work of art in the far gallery. The extension is connected by the bridge to the main floor of the existing gallery. Accomodation includes permanent collection galleries, cabinetti, a temporary exhibition space and a lecture theatre.

Materials make reference to the existing building with a sandstone base, rendered elevations, stone parapets and cornices.

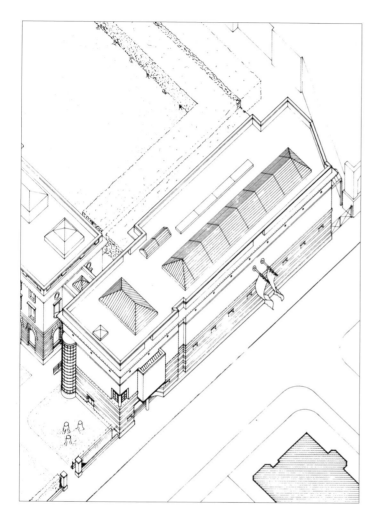

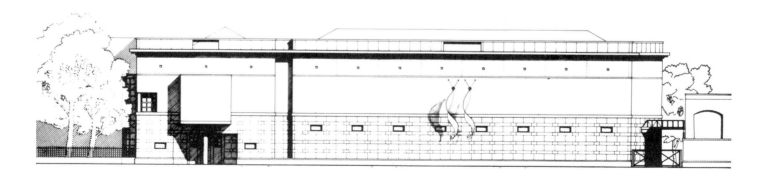

1987

MESSEPALAST
Vienna, Invited Competition
Colquhoun + Miller

The competition site is contained within a low range of buildings designed by Fischer von Erlach. This closes the prospect from the Hofburg complex on the other side of the Ringstrasse. The space to the front of the range is flanked by two museum buildings by Gottfried Semper.

The brief calls for a museum of modern art, an exhibition hall, museums for nineteenth century art and photography, and a special gallery to house the Leopold collection.

The nineteenth century galleries are planned at first floor on the Southeast side with large rooflights for the exhibition hall beneath.

The three-storey Museum of Modern Art is placed to the northwest. The Leopold Gallery connects the two buildings, forming three sides of the entrance court.

Service areas are at the rear of the site. Pedestrian access is provided via the *glacis* at the rear of the site and then via a series of ramps terminating below the Leopold Gallery.

A screen of housing lines the back of the site, interrupted by a semi-circular block of ateliers.

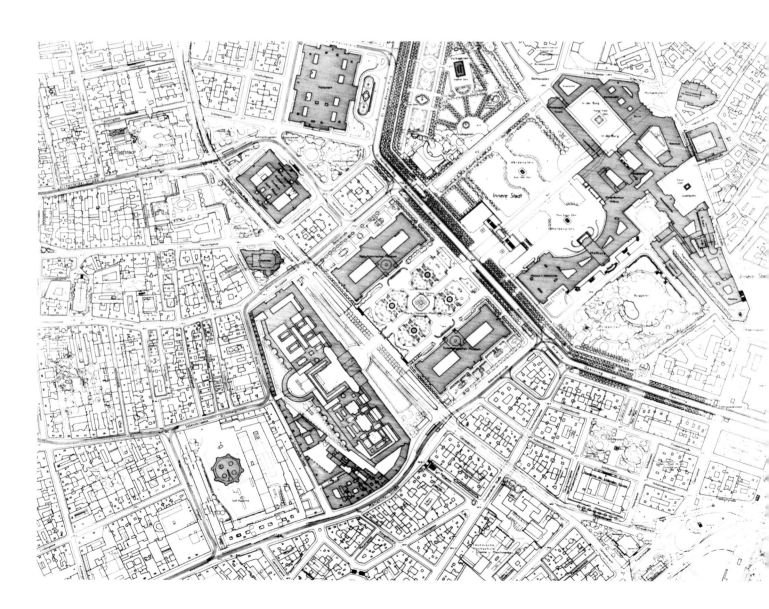

1 Entrance court
2 Entrance to museums
3 Historical museum
4 Museum of Modern Art
5 Service and parking
6 Existing building
7 Upper court
8 Leopold gallery
10 Underpass

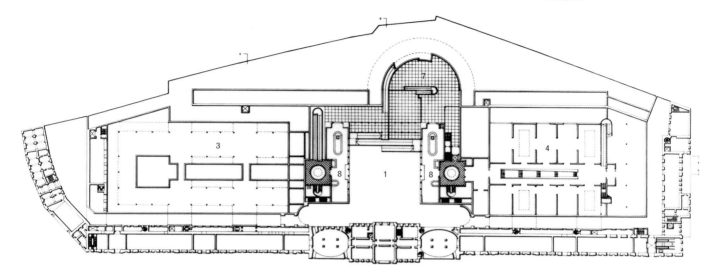

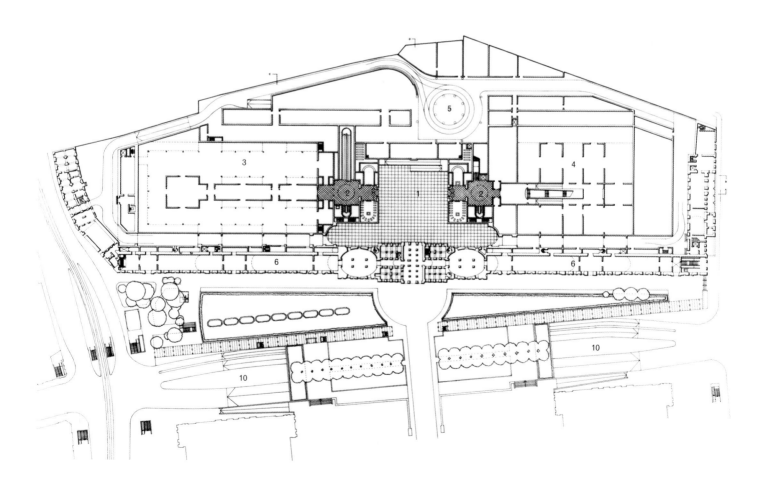

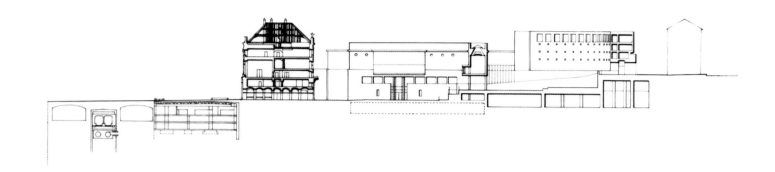

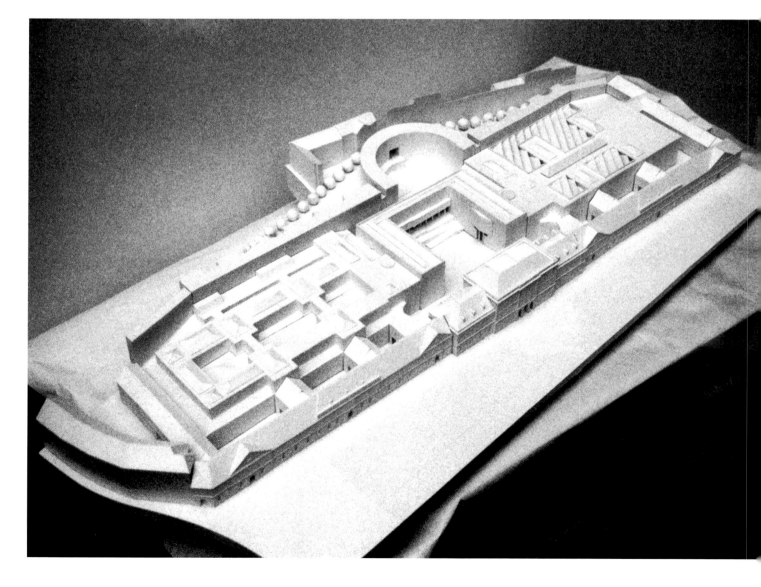

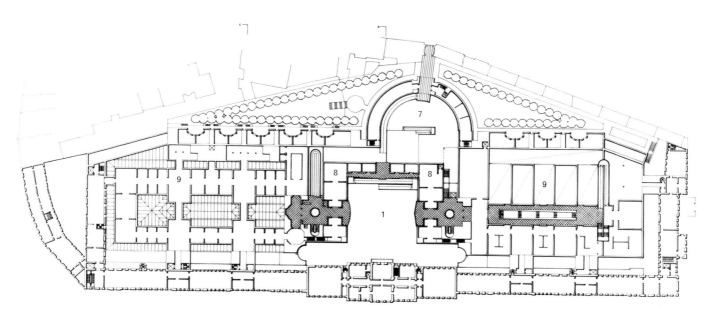

1 Entrance court
7 Upper court
8 Leopold Gallery
9 Upper floor gallery

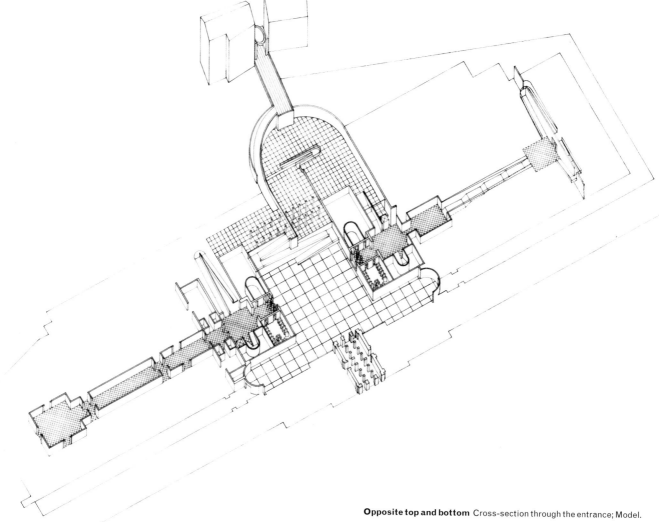

Opposite top and bottom Cross-section through the entrance; Model.

Top and bottom Second floor; Isometric showing the scheme's organisation.

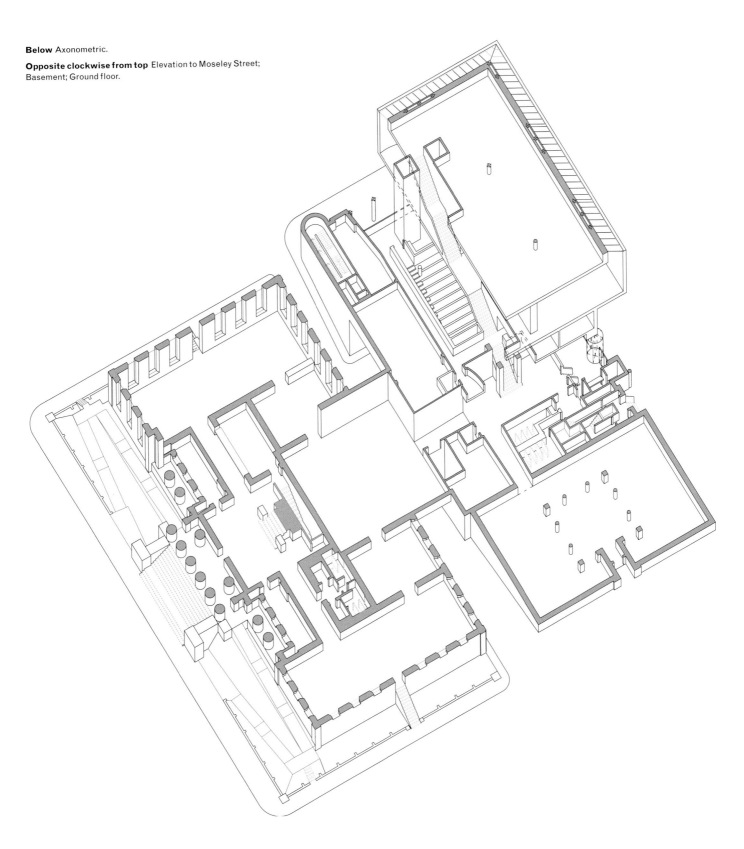

Below Axonometric.

Opposite clockwise from top Elevation to Moseley Street;
Basement; Ground floor.

1995

MANCHESTER CITY ART
GALLERY EXTENSION

John Miller + Partners

In 1992, John Miller + Partners were commissioned to undertake a scheme to extend Charles Barry's Neo-Classical City Art Gallery of 1884 and to connect it to Barry's adjacent Athenaeum of 1836. The proposal was three storeys high to align with the cornice of the existing gallery building. At that time no other funding seemed available other than that provided from the small amount of commercial space included in the scheme; and as a consequence the project slumbered.

In 1995, the Municipality introduced a limited competition for the project. Previously much had been made of the need to help fund the project through various integral commercial space. Now it was intimated that this should be substantial. Accordingly, the John Miller + Partners entry proposed six storeys of offices over the re-worked galleries. The jury seemed unaware of the need for a large commercial element and a scheme without it was awarded the commission. Lottery funding started in 1996.

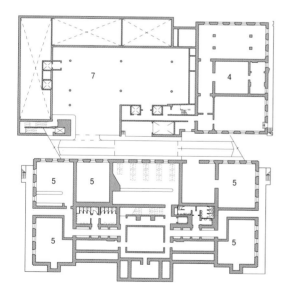

1   Existing galleries
2   Proposed cafe
3   Entrance to commercial offices
4   Athenaeum
5   Stores and offices
6   Entrance from George Street
7   Staff car parking
8   Moseley Street
9   George Street

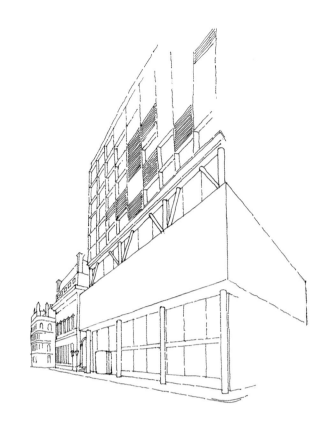

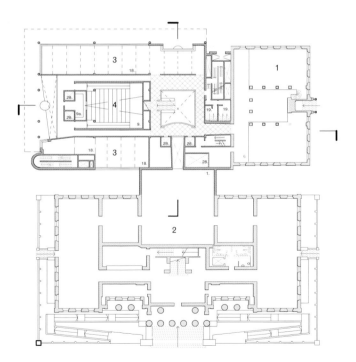

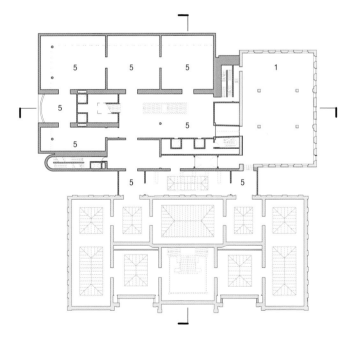

1 Athenaeum
2 Upper part, existing galleries
3 Storage
4 Lecture theatre
5 New permanent collection galleries
6 New exhibition hall
7 Lifts to commercial offices
8 Staircase commercial offices
9 Typical office floor

Opposite clockwise from top left View from Nicholas Street of the corner of George Street; View from George Street; First floor; Mezzanine.

Clockwise from top left Long section; Elevation to George Street; Typical floor of the office block; Second floor.

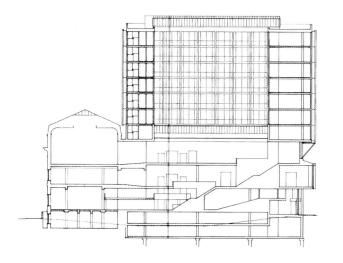

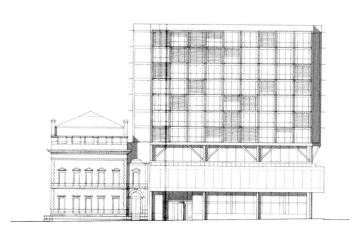

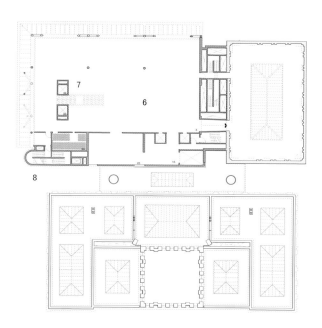

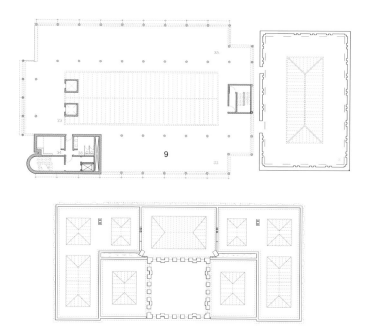

1996

DUNDEE CONTEMPORARY
ART CENTRE

John Miller + Partners

The Dundee Contemporary Art Centre is part of the plan to establish a fresh cultural identity for the City of Dundee. The site for the competition for the Centre is on Dundee's Nethergate, flanked on its west side by the Roman Catholic Cathedral and on its east by a substantial Georgian house. The site falls towards the Firth of Tay in the middle distance. The fall is three storeys high.

Competitors had the choice of retaining some or all of the existing warehouse and garage. The John Miller + Partners' proposal demolishes and provides a new building that meets user's needs. The accommodation includes galleries, a cinema, print workshops, a shop, research facilities, and cafe.

The idea for the *parti* is suggested by the view of the Firth and the steeply sloping site. An inviting two-storey *porte-cochère* leads to a promenade that starts at Nethergate and widens to terminate in a belvedere, where it is some three- to four-storeys higher than the road below. Social spaces line the promenade to one side and the promenade is open to a view of the intimate terraced garden on the other. The wing of the L-shaped plan is set at right angles to the promenade and contains the galleries, workshops and the other ancillaries.

1   Entrance hall
2   Shop
3   Cloakroom
4   Cafe/bar/performance
5   Kitchen
6   Meeting room
7   Sculpture gallery
8   Gallery
9   Activity room
10   Print workshop
11   Print service room
12   Studio flat
13   Office
14   Staff room
15   Terrace
16   Cinema
17   Research workshop/studio
18   Research service room
19   Art handling workshops
20   Loading bay/service yard
21   Plant
22   Store

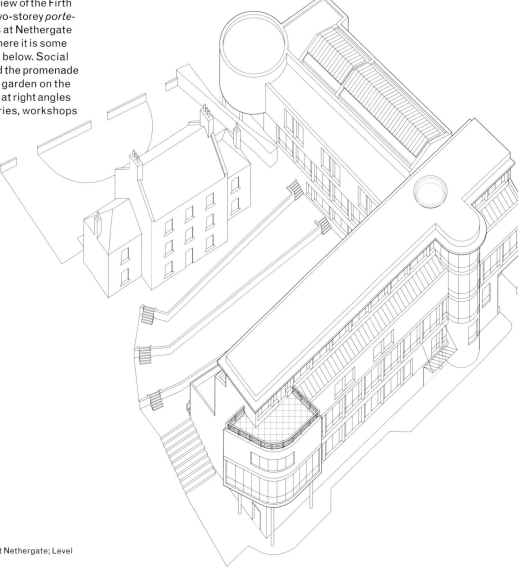

Right Axonometric, drawing by John Hewitt.

Opposite clockwise from top left Level 0 ground at Nethergate; Level 1; Level -1; Level -2 ground at rear.

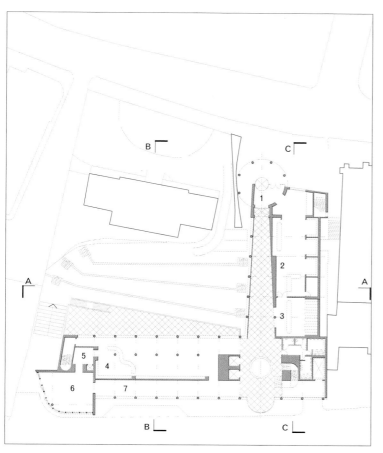

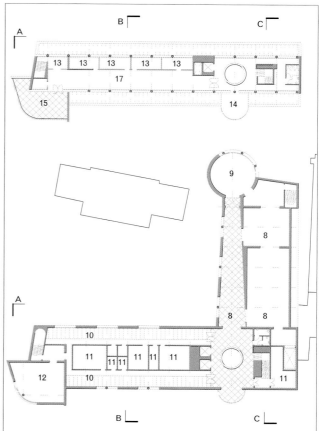

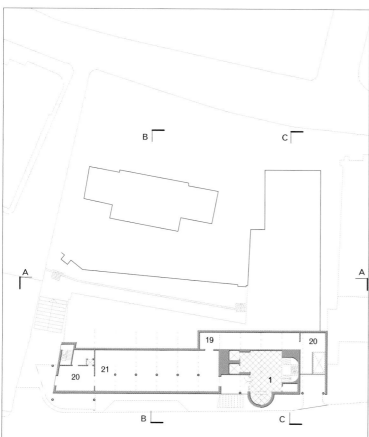

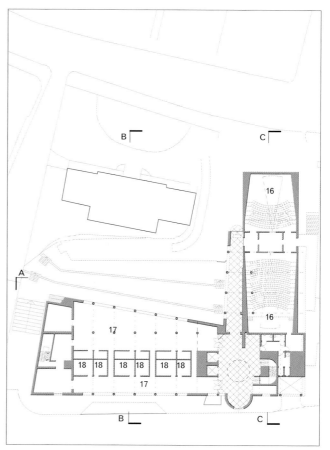

Opposite top to bottom View of the entrance on Nethergate; Elevation to Nethergate; Southwest elevation; Elevation to the Tay—southeast.

Top to bottom Section AA; Section BB; Section CC (long section).

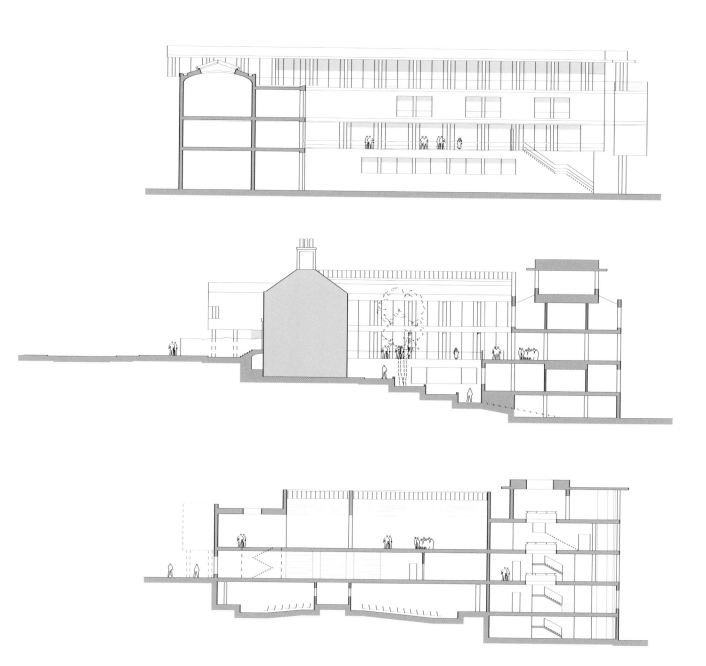

1997

QUEEN'S GALLERY
Buckingham Palace,
Limited Competition
John Miller + Partners

John Miller + Partners' proposal provides a new exhedra
as an entry forecourt on Buckingham Palace Road. This
leads to a top-lit barrel vaulted arcade with access to the
Gallery shop and to a wide flight of stairs and lift beyond.
The stairs lead to the new galleries via a small rotunda.
Five new galleries are arranged to provide two alternative
visitor circuits terminating with the existing Gallery.

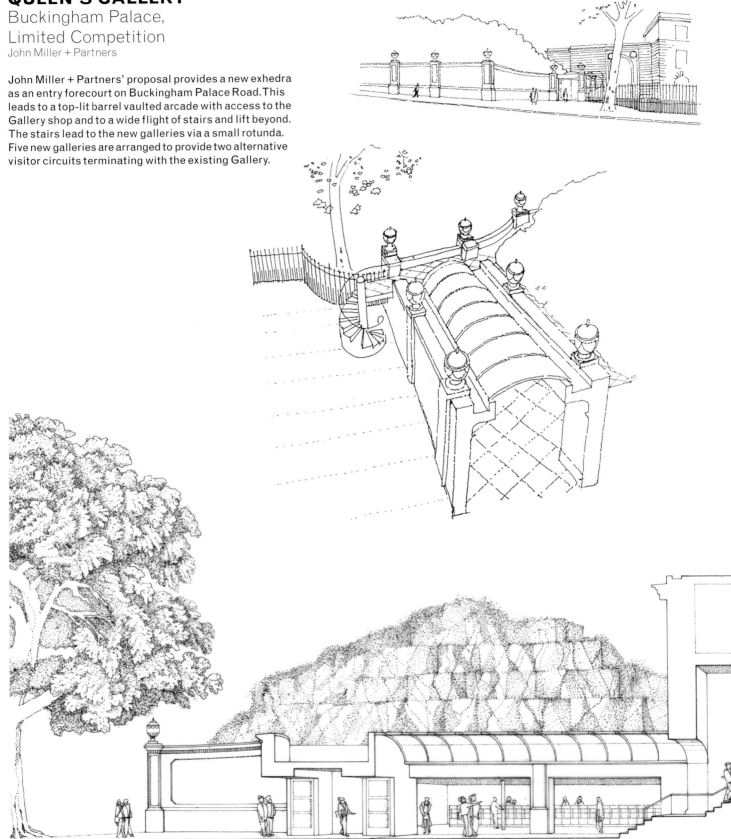

1 Entrance
2 Shop
3 Original Queen's Gallery
4 New gallery
5 Public lavatories
6 Cloaks
7 Office
8 Gallery/Shop stores
9 Passenger lift
10 Art handling lift
11 Plant
12 Police route
13 Garden

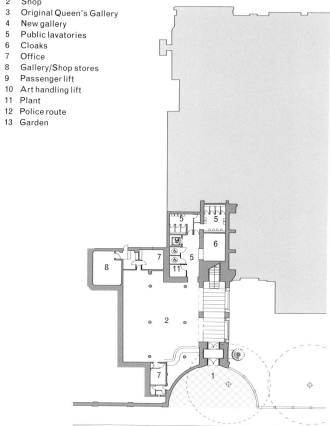

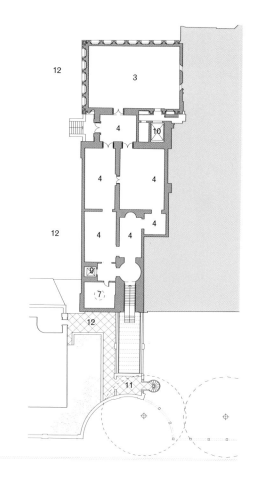

Opposite top to bottom View of the entrance on Buckingham Palace Road; Entrance canopy; Sectional perspective.

Top left and right Ground floor; Upper floor.

1998

SERPENTINE GALLERY
London
John Miller + Partners

The Grade II Listed Serpentine Gallery dating from 1908 was originally a tea pavilion. It occupies a dominant site in Royal Kensington Gardens, London. The Royal Parks and English Heritage required any changes to the exterior to be achieved within the existing building's footprint and any visible additions could only be of a modest scale. They should be of a character, and made with materials, compatible with the existing building.

John Miller + Partners were commissioned by the Trustees to find ways to improve the building's organisation and environment, in order to expand its range of activities and to improve its finishes.

The excavation of a new basement under the building footprint for stores and workshop allows space above ground level to be freed for primary uses. The main entrance migrates from the northern portico to what was the original service yard. The new main entrance in turn gives access to a hall, to which an enlarged bookshop, lavatories, personnel lift and stairs are directly related. Exhibitions can now be mounted and de-mounted uninterrupted by public access to the bookshop and enquiry counter in the entrance hall.

New offices are reached by lift and stairs and are connected to two existing and separate office suites located in the two pavilions. A roof terrace is provided for office use. A new education room is located in the old entry portico with access from the galleries.

An integrated landscaping design by Hal Moggeridge, with work by Ian Hamilton Finlay provides an entrance approach through Kensington Gardens, together with an outdoor display garden; this is used annually for the Serpentine Gallery pavilion constructions.

The Gallery re-opened in 1998. It now provides a flexible, environment for the display of international art. It was funded by the Arts Council and private donations.

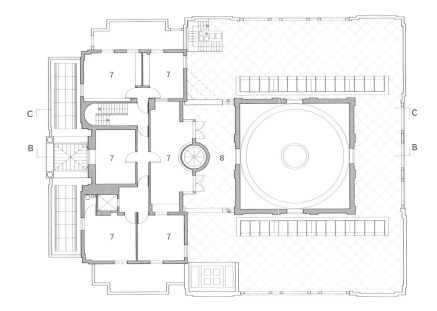

Top and bottom First floor; Elevation to Exhibition Road, © Peter Durrant/archblue.com.

Opposite Ground floor.

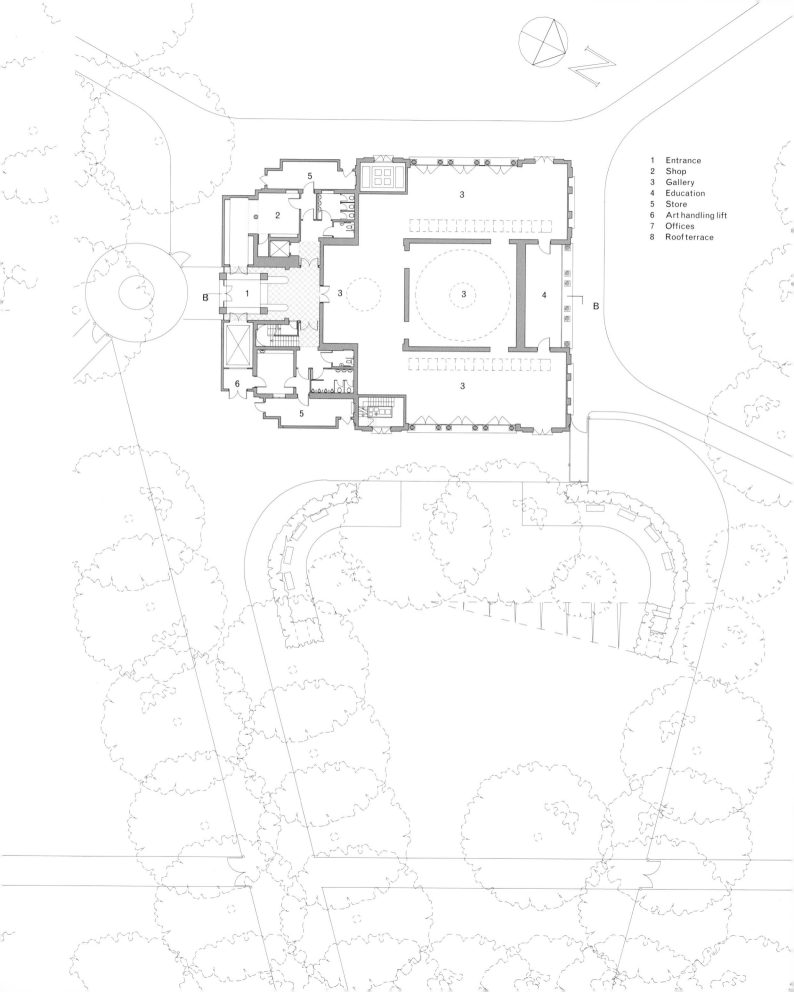

1 Entrance
2 Shop
3 Gallery
4 Education
5 Store
6 Art handling lift
7 Offices
8 Roof terrace

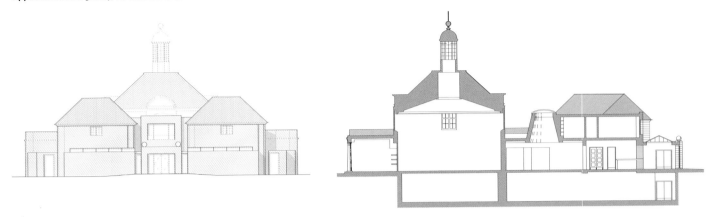

... the new Serpentine is a finely tuned instrument for the display of art which has been ingeniously wrought from the most limiting constraints. It is a wunderkammer, a crystal in the park, where a first impression of normality is followed by the alchemy of the interior.

The Architects' Journal

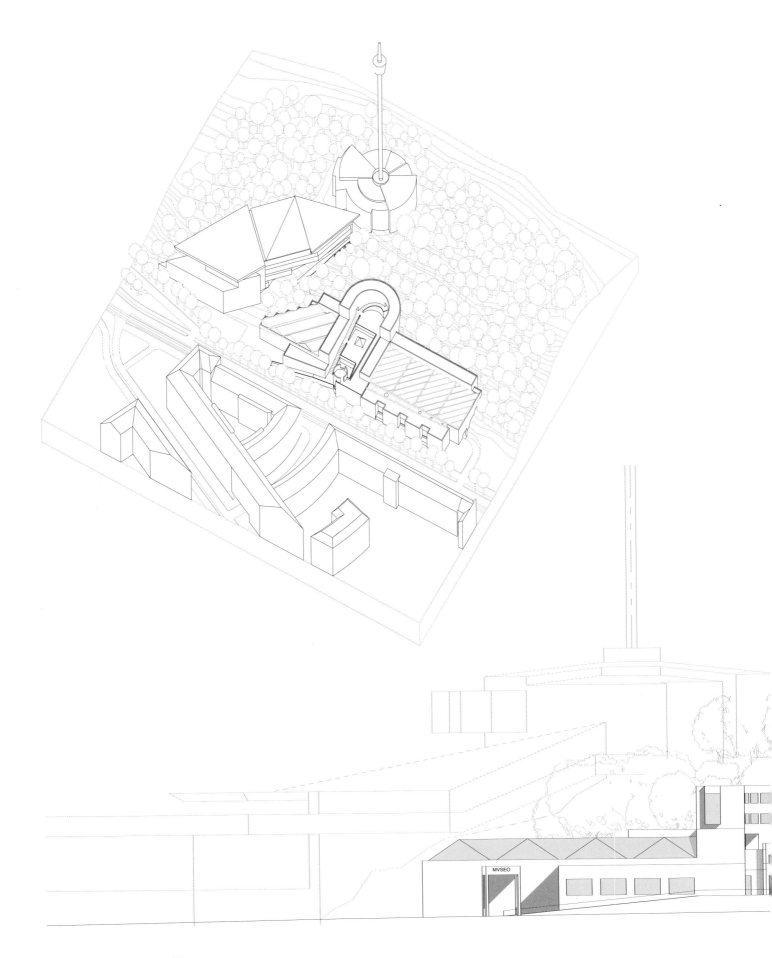

1998

MUSEUM OF WORLD CULTURE
Gotenburg
John Miller + Partners

The proposal for the Museum of World Culture has a similar *parti* to the competition for the Messepalast in Vienna. The site slopes from the Liseburg amusement park to the Sodra Vagen at its base. A semi-circular range of administrative office is in the centre of the composition, from which a cascade of terraces and ramps descend to the road below. These provide a pedestrian route through the site and space for displays.

Accommodation is organised with a small 'square' in the centre connected to the cascade and to the main entrance to the galleries. A temporary exhibition hall lies to the north of the central axis with the permanent collection to the south. Gallery service is in the rear and separated from visitors' circulation. Archives, Conservation and Workshops run along the back of the building. External materials include local dark red brick with dark green granite dressings.

Opposite Axonometric.

Top and bottom Entrance and terrace; Southwest elevation.

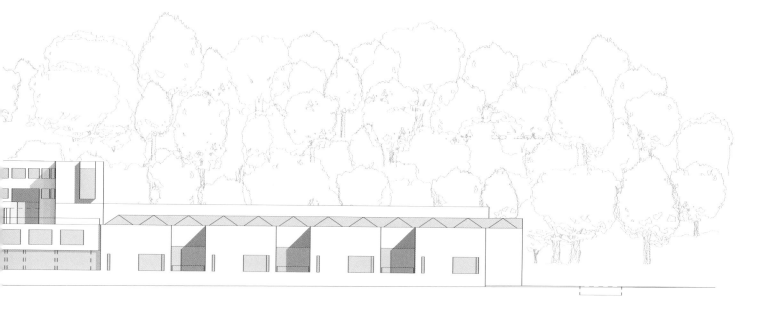

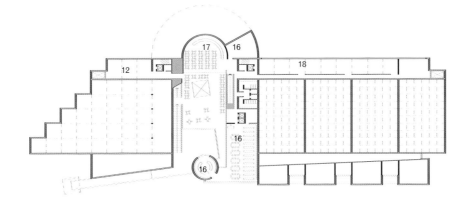

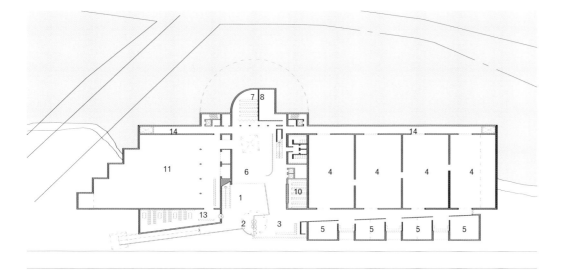

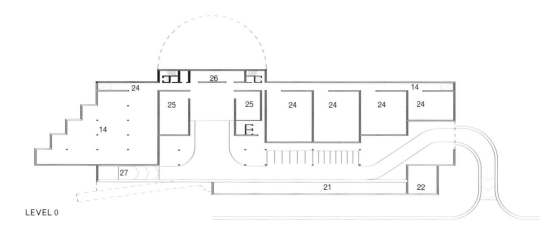

1   Terrace
2   Entrance
3   Reception
4   Gallery space
5   'Treasure' gallery
6   Small square
7   Auditorium
8   Conference room
9   WC
10 Cloakroom
11 Big square
12 Public workshop
13 Shop
14 Service corridor
15 Store
16 Library
17 Restaurant
18 Preservation rooms
19 Office
20 Personnel area
21 Plant room
22 Maintenance area
23 Delivery dock
24 Archive storage
25 Short term storage
26 Workshop
27 Route to the Science Museum

LEVEL 0

Opposite top to bottom Level 2; Level 1; Level 0.
Top to bottom Level 5; Level 4; Level 3.

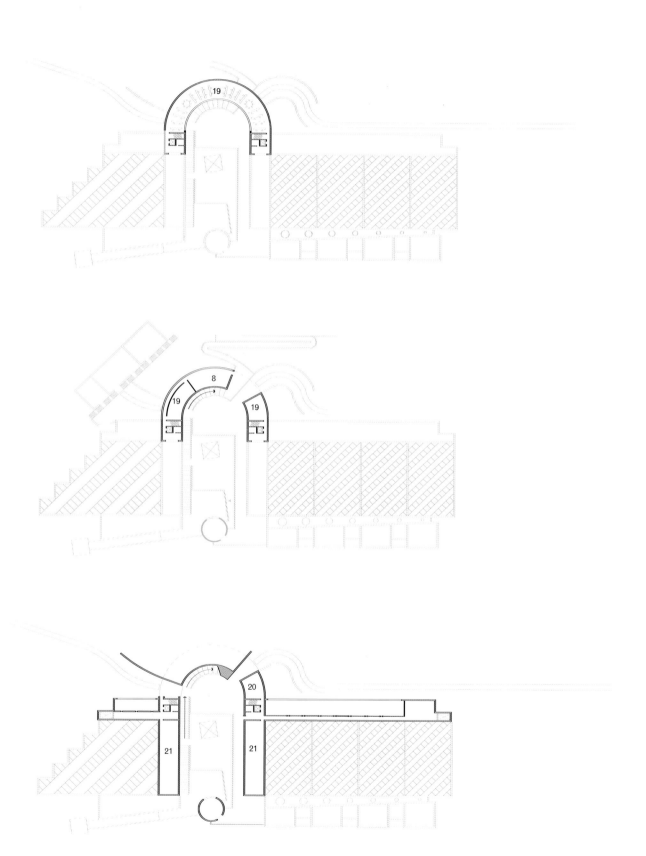

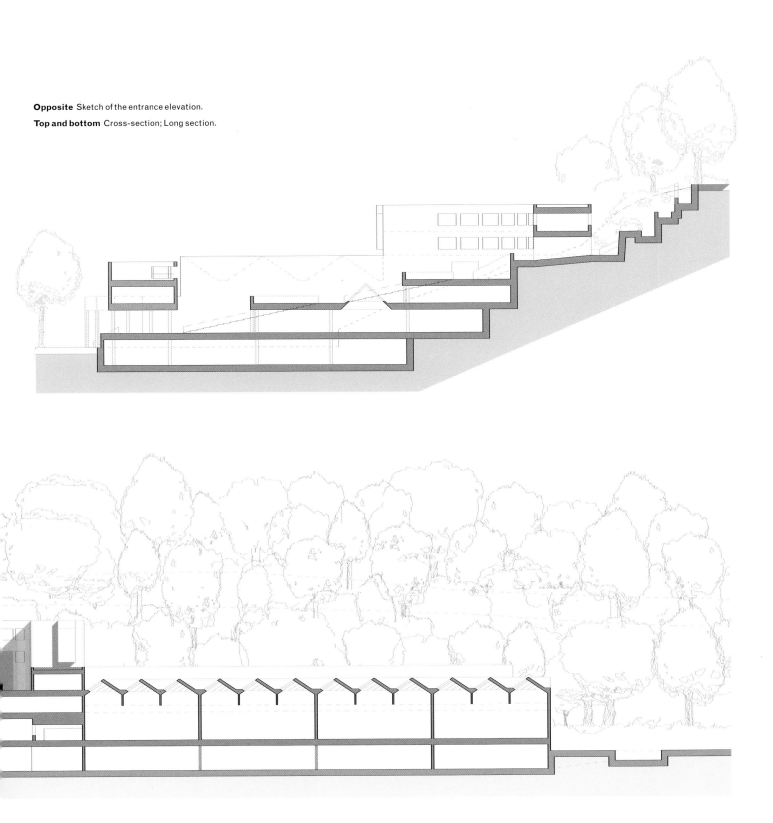

Opposite Sketch of the entrance elevation.

Top and bottom Cross-section; Long section.

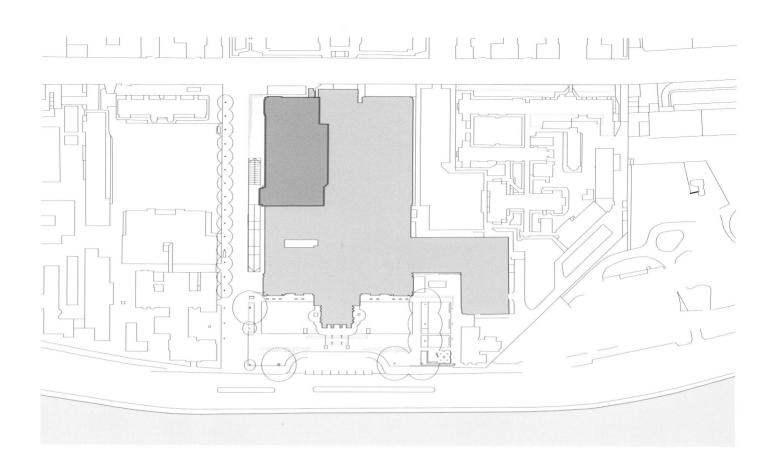

2001

TATE BRITAIN CENTENARY DEVELOPMENT
London
John Miller + Partners

The Gallery masterplan of 1987 was not designed to be implemented in a linear sequence. Nor was the empirical planning that followed required to meet a rigid list of requirements. A policy of "matching and making" to suit space availability was adopted. Areas were priced as packages. The northwest quadrant, was earmarked and donations from two principal benefactors, the Linbury and Manton Foundations, provided approximately half the funds needed. The remainder was to be matched by the Heritage Lottery Fund.

There were two principal requirements; gallery space and the need to tackle numbers when 'blockbuster' exhibitions were programmed.

The quadrant site, effectively a large yard, was open to the sky, contained by perimeter galleries fronting Atterbury Street and John Islip Street, the flank of Gallery 9 and the central Duveen axis.

There was doubt over duplicating entrances. Prompted by the needs of the disabled, access to the side of the portico steps was considered. But the route to the exhibition spaces at upper floor level was circuitous. An entrance on Atterbury Street, on the cross-axis, was accepted. It could provide a connection to the anticipated Stirling extension in the eastern courtyard. John Miller + Partners designed the new entrance sequence to be similar in scale to the Duveen sequence on the floor above.

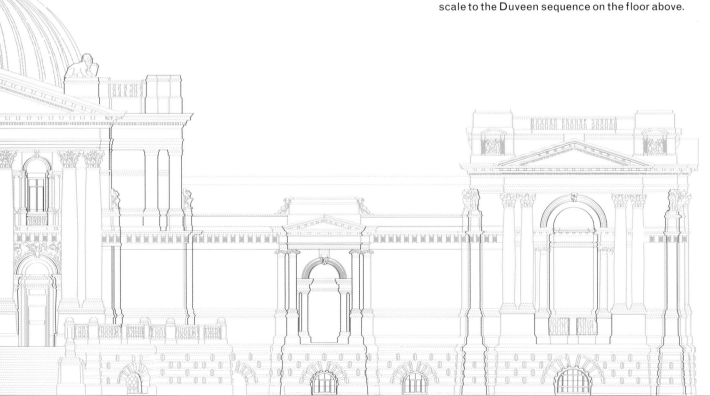

The hall now enjoys a number of functions, for example, informal concerts and talks. Visitor numbers, generated by temporary exhibitions, have justified the spatial generosity.

The Bookshop is accessed from the entrance hall as are the Temporary Exhibition Galleries. These are cellular following the footprint of the galleries above and contrast with the open exhibition space in the northeast quadrant.

New stairs in a triple-height space lead from the Entrance Hall to the gallery floor. A stepped skirting of the value of two treads increases the sense of monumentality.

The quadrant yields sufficient space for four equal bays. Three provide barrel vaulted galleries. The fourth bay accommodates the staircase well. The galleries are similar to the existing lateral galleries but are not replicas. Two thirds of the soffits are louvred with fluorescent lighting above to simulate daylight.

Gallery floors are in white oak; their wall surfaces are lined in proprietary board prepared to receive paint. Floors in the circulation areas are in limestone. Wall surfaces are in 'Venetian' plaster coloured to be sympathetic to the existing stone facings.

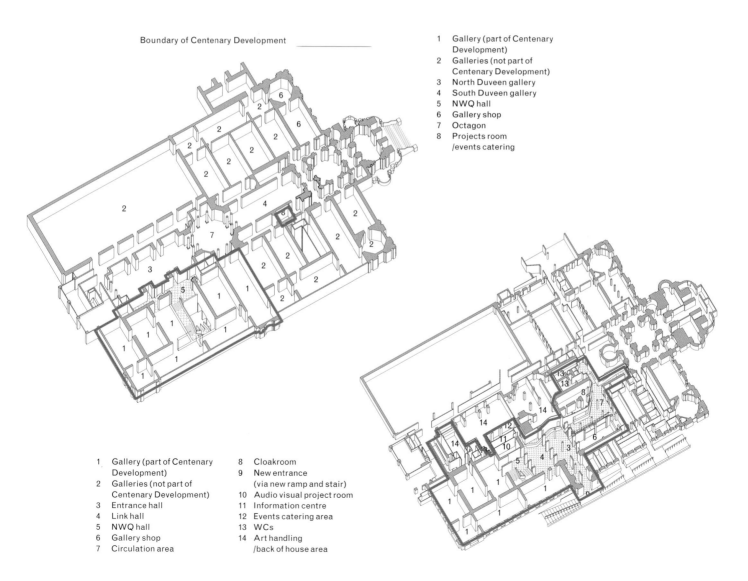

Boundary of Centenary Development _____

1 Gallery (part of Centenary Development)
2 Galleries (not part of Centenary Development)
3 North Duveen gallery
4 South Duveen gallery
5 NWQ hall
6 Gallery shop
7 Octagon
8 Projects room /events catering

1 Gallery (part of Centenary Development)
2 Galleries (not part of Centenary Development)
3 Entrance hall
4 Link hall
5 NWQ hall
6 Gallery shop
7 Circulation area
8 Cloakroom
9 New entrance (via new ramp and stair)
10 Audio visual project room
11 Information centre
12 Events catering area
13 WCs
14 Art handling /back of house area

Clockwise from top New upper level gallery; View of the new gallery from the Duveen axis; View of the Manton stairs from the Duveen axis, © Richard Bryant/arcaid.co.uk.

Opposite View looking back at the Manton stairs from the renovated perimeter gallery, © Richard Bryant/arcaid.co.uk.

The (Tate Gallery) Centenary Development exudes the wisdom that results from a good firm of architects building up a quiet confidence over years of practice… an extremely mature Englishness that permits us to relax gratefully.
Architecture Today

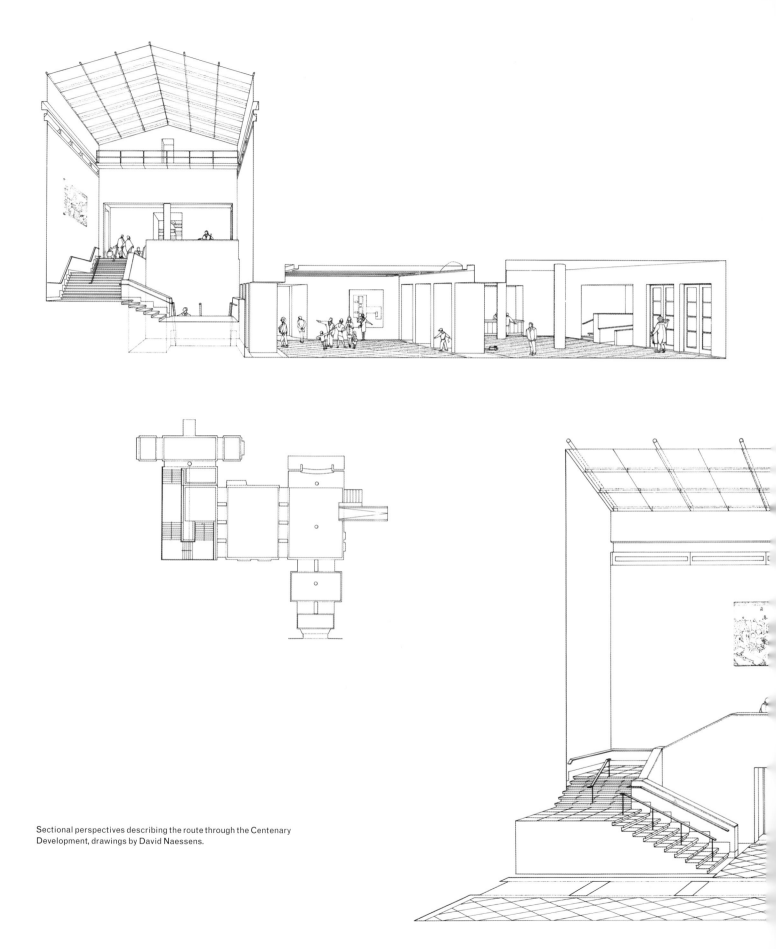

Sectional perspectives describing the route through the Centenary Development, drawings by David Naessens.

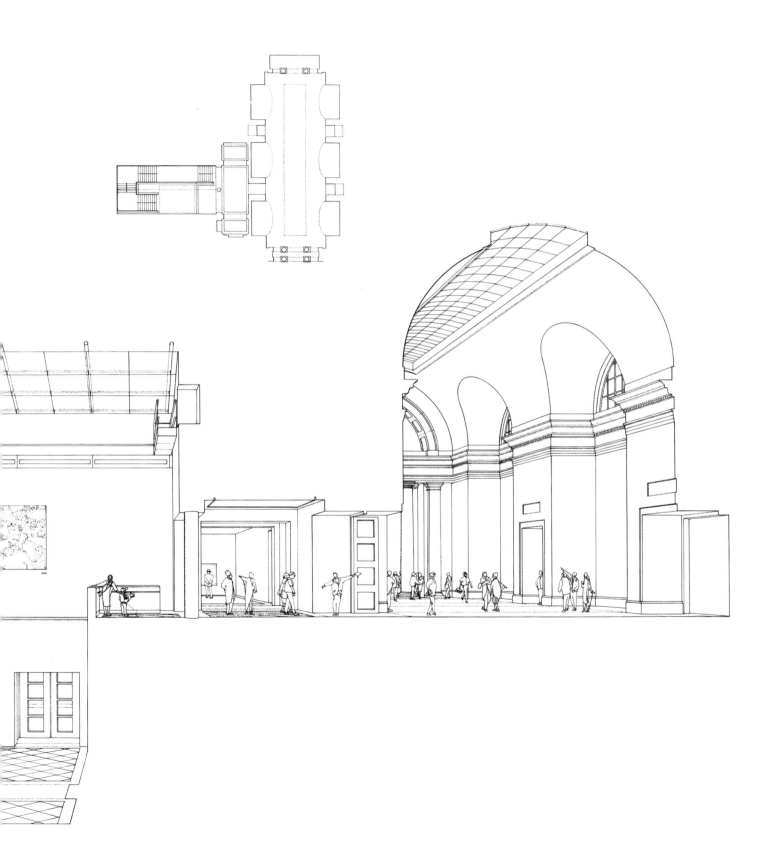

Opposite View of the Friends' Room, renovated, © Martin Charles.

Above View of the re-modelled cafe, © Martin Charles.

Any misgivings about the suitability of the spaces for temporary exhibitions at Tate Modern were dispelled by John Miller's designs for a sequence of variable spaces, alternating openness with enclosure, natural with artificial light (and a combination of the two) and grand sweeps and perspectives, with pauses for intimacy and reflection.
Henry Meyric Hughes, *Times Higher Education Supplement*

2002

MATISSE PICASSO EXHIBITION
Tate Modern
John Miller + Partners

The artificial lighting in Tate Modern's galleries earmarked for the exhibition gave a curious mist-like effect. This was a challenge, as were the distracting rectangular metal floor grilles. The curatorial team were determined that they should be changed. Suspended light fittings were introduced and timber substituted for metal grilles. The innovation was to make the temporary room partitions thicker than normal and to leave vertical 'slots' where partitions met surfaces at right angles. The ends of the partitions were then chamfered and this introduced enticing perspectives into adjoining spaces.

Views of the Matisse Picasso exhibition, ©Tate, London 2009, © Succession Picasso/Dacs 2009, © Succession Henri Matisse/Dacs 2009.

2002

WOKING ART GALLERY
John Miller + Partners

The competition was for the selection of an architect. But all competitors produced scheme designs. Much was made of the need for an 'iconic' building at the briefing meeting. Victoria Way on the southern side is lined with office buildings which aspire to iconic status. John Miller + Partners' proposal is in contrast to them. The site is long and narrow fronting Victoria Way on the south side and the Basingstoke Canal to the north.

The scheme is no more than three storeys at its west end descending to a single storey to the east. The entrance divides the gallery spaces from the administration and education suite in a three-storey pavilion. A glazed foyer runs parallel to the canal and contains the cafe/restaurant. The stepped section provides gallery spaces with a spatial connection to the foyer. The canal side, the 'quiet side', is open to the canal walk whilst the noisy Victoria Way is screened by a solid exterior wall with window openings. The objective is to make a sense of place and to earn 'landmark status' through use.

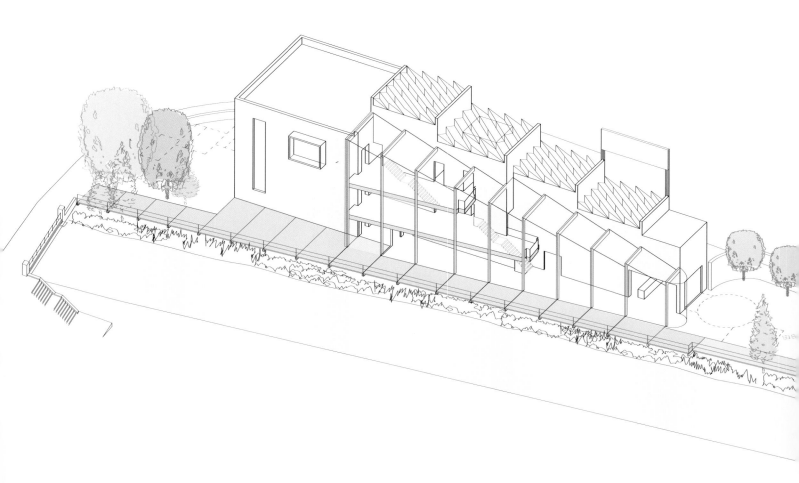

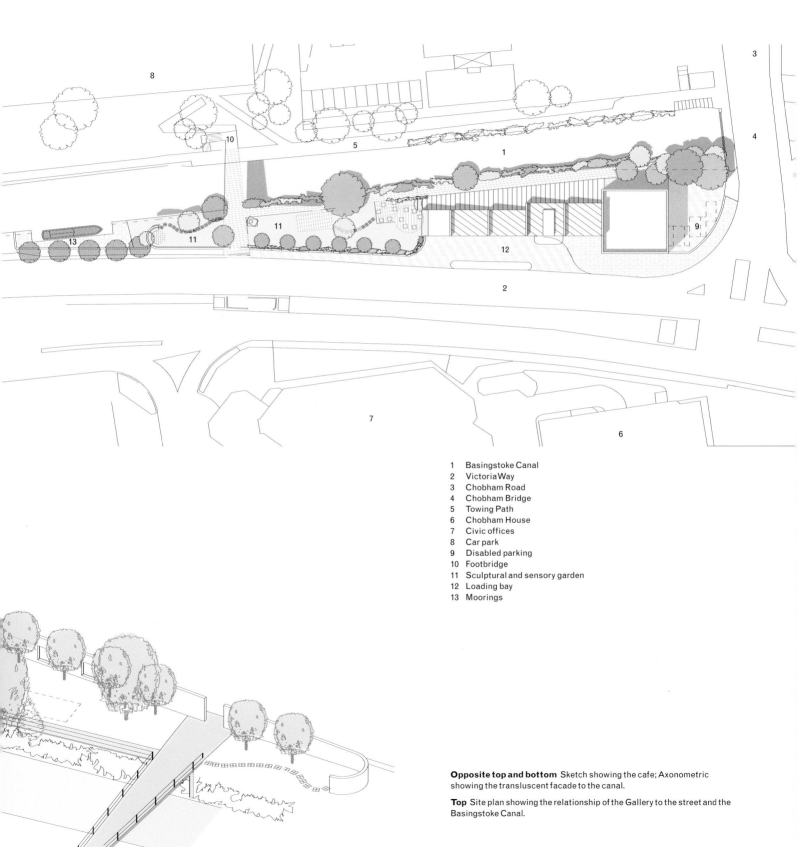

1   Basingstoke Canal
2   Victoria Way
3   Chobham Road
4   Chobham Bridge
5   Towing Path
6   Chobham House
7   Civic offices
8   Car park
9   Disabled parking
10 Footbridge
11 Sculptural and sensory garden
12 Loading bay
13 Moorings

Opposite top and bottom Sketch showing the cafe; Axonometric showing the transluscent facade to the canal.

Top Site plan showing the relationship of the Gallery to the street and the Basingstoke Canal.

Top to bottom Elevation; Sections.

Opposite top to bottom Second floor; First floor; Ground floor; Basement.

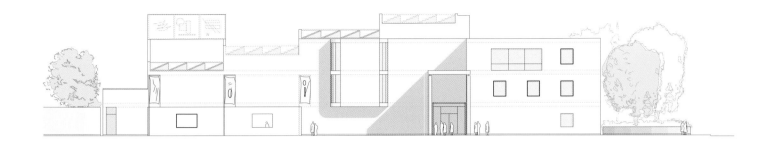

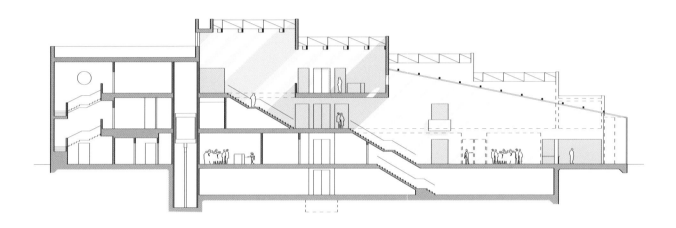

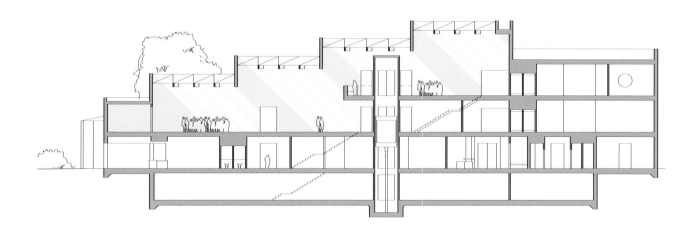

1 General store
2 Exhibition store
3 Museum store
4 Workshop
5 Plant
6 Cafe
7 Kitchen
8 Refuse
9 Children's activity
10 Bookshop
11 Loading
12 Receiving room
13 Office
14 Store
15 Enquiries
16 Entrance
17 Lockers
18 Family room
19 Education
20 Male WC
21 Female WC
22 Cloakroom
23 Exhibition
24 Multimedia galleries
25 Offices
26 History galleries
27 Corporate hire

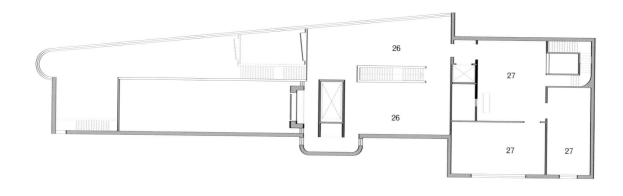

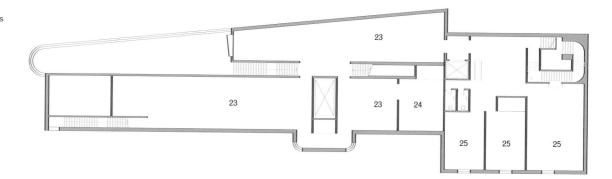

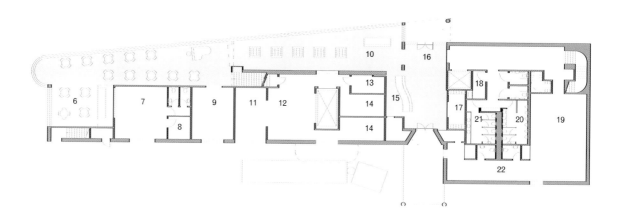

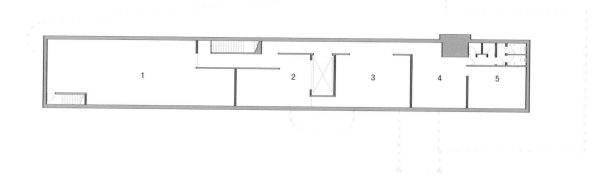

PLAYFAIR PROJECT
National Galleries of Scotland
John Miller + Partners

In 1999 John Miller + Partners won a limited international competition for a project to unite the architect William Playfair's National Gallery of Scotland (NGS) of 1845–1858 with his Royal Scottish Academy (RSA) of 1822–1826 and 1831–1836. The two buildings sit on an artificial mound connecting the Edinburgh Old town to the New.

Playfair shifted the National Gallery's alignment with the Academy, providing a glimpse of it from Prince's Street and similarly one of the RSA from the approach from the Old Town. This shift suggested the position of John Miller + Partners' stepped pyramid between the two buildings, rotated sufficiently to present a second side to the pedestrian approaches and thus emphasising its three-dimensional form. It serves to 'turn' the visitor towards the entrances of the two buildings.

It has a rooflight directly over the enquiry desk in the concourse below. The plateau is punctured with 11 circular rooflights to enliven the concourse.

Phase one, completed in 2003, consists of stabilising the foundations of the RSA. It includes the restoration of the existing first floor RSA galleries , the renewal of the gallery's artificial lighting, the provision of a new passenger lift and stairs in preparation for the connection to the phase two concourse, the creation of a stone door in the RSA facade giving access to an art handling lift for large artworks, and the conversion of store rooms into a new gallery on the lower floor.

Phase two is entirely new-build. Excavated space below the plateau of the mound provides a generous concourse approached from the gardens, a three tiered restaurant with views onto the gardens, a gallery shop, a new IT gallery, an education suite, a lecture theatre and a means of connecting the NGS to the RSA via lifts and stairs.

1   National Gallery
2   Royal Scottish Academy
3   Prince's Street
4   Railway cutting
5   Pyramid

Above View of the Royal Scottish Academy from George Street, © Keith Hunter.

Opposite Site plan showing the railway cutting and Prince's Gardens east and west with the two Neo-Classical buildings on the Mound.

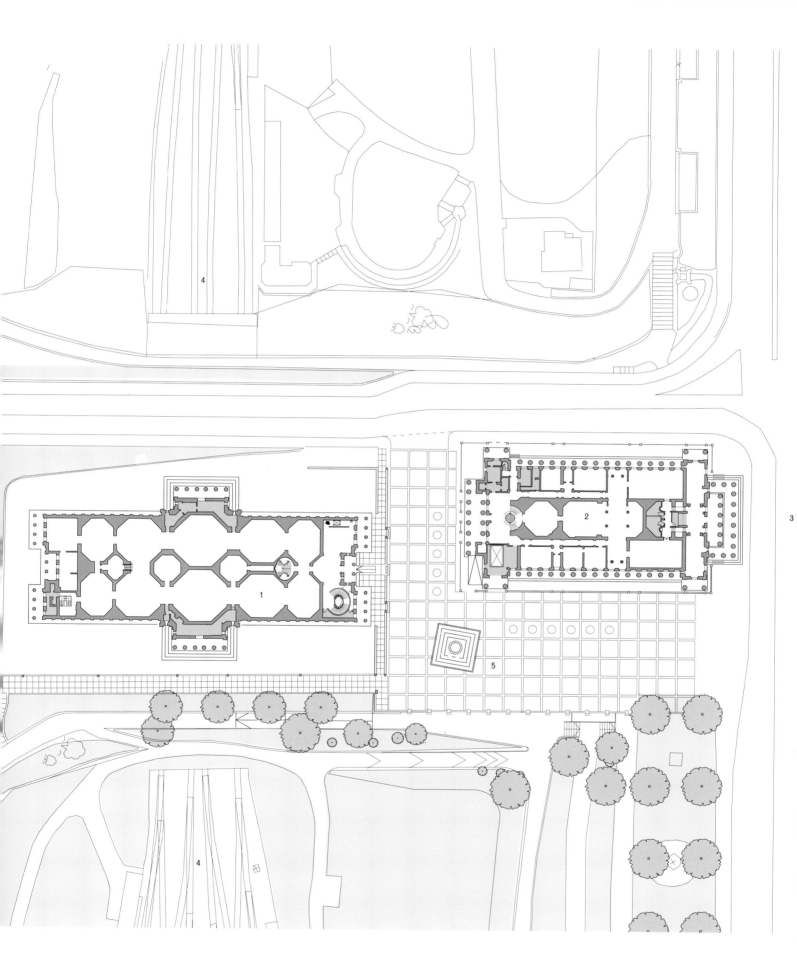

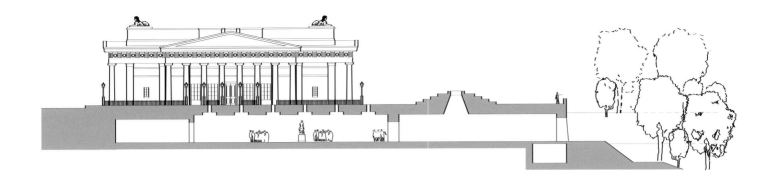

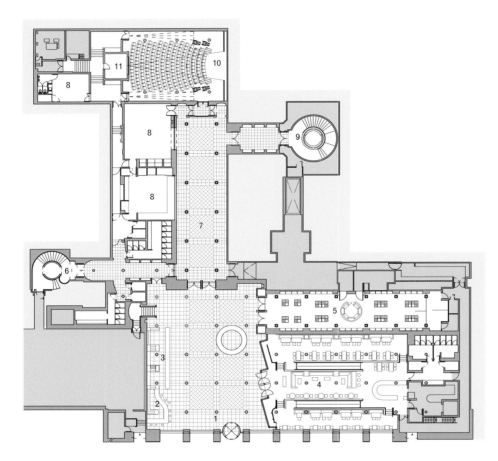

1   Entrance from Prince's
     Gardens east
2   Bar
3   Cloaks
4   Restaurant
5   Shop
6   Stairs and lift from the NGS
7   Gallery
8   Education
9   Stairs and lift from the RSA
10 Lecture theatre
11 Projection

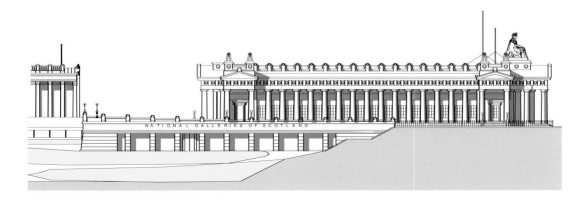

Opposite top to bottom Section through the link building with the RSA behind; Concourse level; Elevation from Prince's Gardens east.

Top and bottom First floor; View of the link building from Prince's Gardens east, © Keith Hunter.

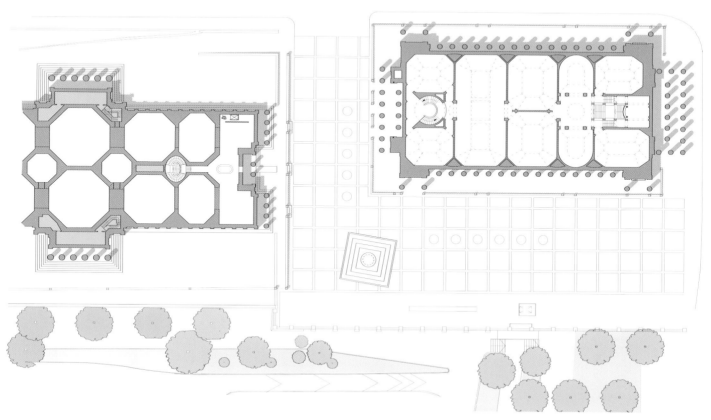

PLAYFAIR PROJECT 249

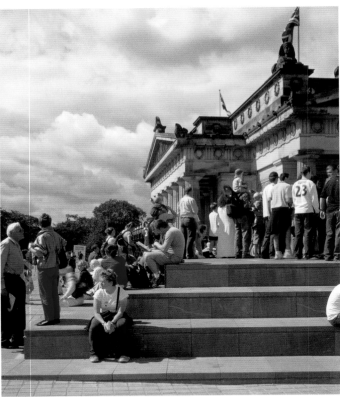

Clockwise from top left View of the reception area; The stepped pyramid during the Edinburgh Festival, © Keith Hunter; Detail plan of the stepped pyramid.

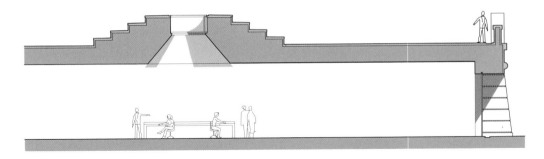

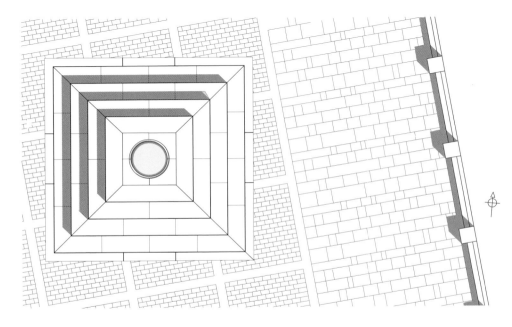

Left, top to bottom Detail showing access to the art handling lift through a pivoting section of the external stone wall with the existing door integrated within the wall to form a pass door.

Right Elevation and plan.

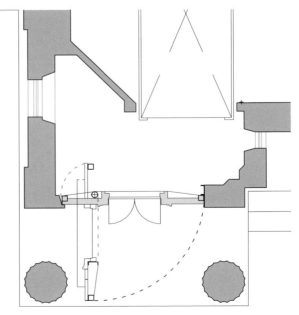

Clockwise from top left Lobby to the lift to Royal Scottish Academy above; The Clifford Room on the ground floor of the Royal Scottish Academy; The IT Gallery looking towards the gardens, © Keith Hunter.

The National Gallery of Scotland has unveiled the Weston Link, which unites the Gallery with the newly refurbished Royal Scottish Academy in a development that includes spacious new public facilities. This challenging task has been accomplished with great sensitivity as well as flair by John Miller + Partners.

Michael Hall, *Apollo*, September 2004

Top and bottom Weston Link lecture theatre; Weston Link shop, © Keith Hunter.

Overleaf Reception desk in the Farmer Concourse, © Keith Hunter.

Left and opposite Details of the circular lift connecting the Royal Scottish Academy to the Weston Link building, © Keith Hunter.

Below Renovated gallery at the Royal Scottish Academy with Cenatorial installation for the first exhibition, © Keith Hunter.

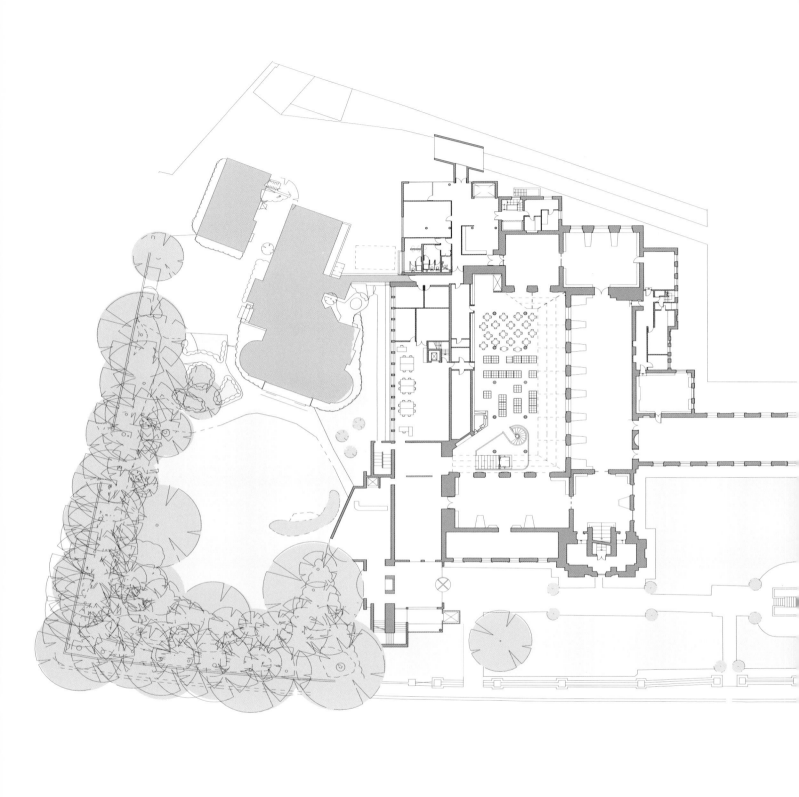

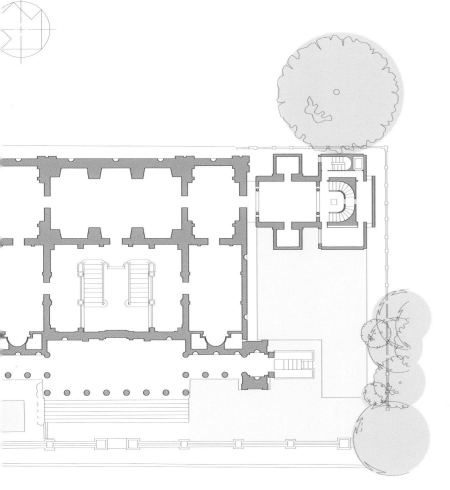

2004

COURTYARD DEVELOPMENT, FITZWILLIAM MUSEUM
Cambridge
John Miller + Partners

George Basevi was the Museum's original architect. The Museum was unfinished at the time of his death in 1845 and CR Cockerell took over, to be in turn superseded by EM Barry, who redesigned the entrance hall. The Founders Building was finished in 1875 fundamentally to Basevi's design. The galleries were later extended by Smith and Brewer between 1924 and 1936.

This was the context in which a feasibility study was commissioned in 1995 to identify sites for development.

In 1997, a design for a Northern Extension was proposed. Its proximity to Peterhouse and the absence of support from English Heritage caused this scheme to be abandoned. A proposal for an infill scheme for the Courtyard followed in 1998. This included an extension facing Trumpington Street and the excavation of the front gardens for storage. It proved to be too costly. The Heritage Lottery Fund advised that a submission should be for the courtyard only. A successful submission on this basis was made in 1999/2000.

The Courtyard Scheme: the site is bounded on three sides by the Smith and Brewer extension. The fourth side is bounded by a 1975 extension by David Roberts. This has been partly demolished to accommodate the new work. It consists of the courtyard infill, the improvement of adjacent accommodation, and an expanded southern entrance, convenient for group visits and for visitors with disabilities.

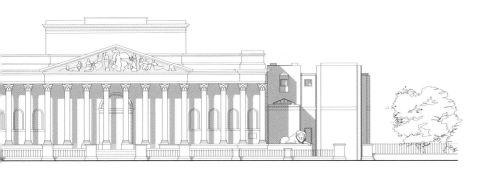

Clockwise from top left Ground floor; First floor; Section.

Opposite clockwise from top left View of the entrance foyer,
© Dennis Gilbert/View; View of the winter garden with shop and cafe
to the left, © Dennis Gilbert/View; Long section.

1   Entrance
2   Library
3   Shop
4   Cafe
5   Winter garden
6   Existing gallery
7   New gallery
8   Workshops/offices
9   Marlay gallery
10 Lower ground floor
11 Ground floor
12 Mezzanine
13 First floor

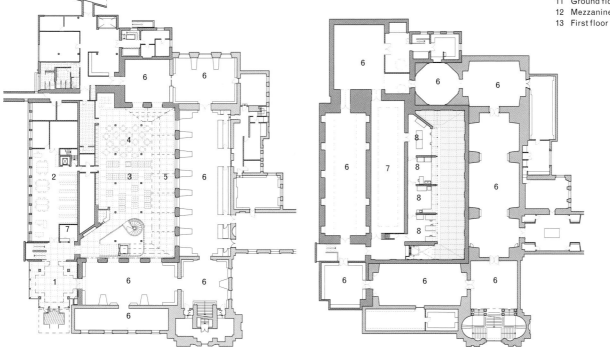

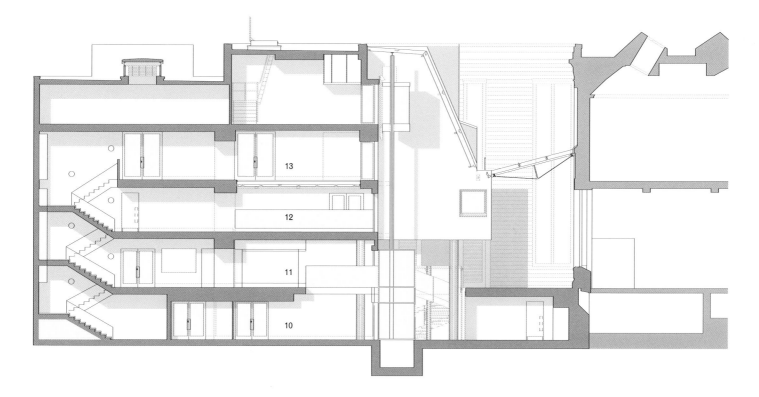

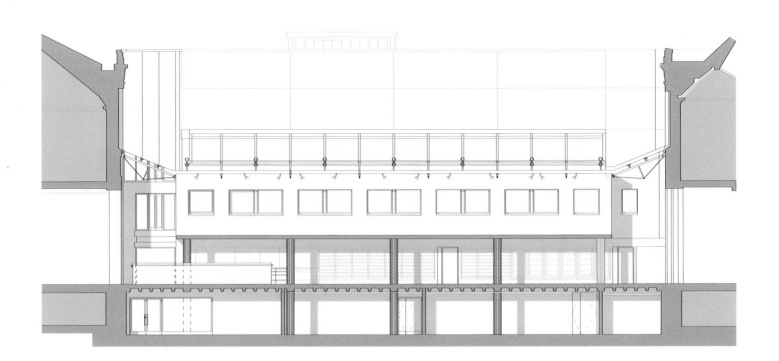

Miller and his team, who earlier enhanced the Whitechapel Art Gallery, the Serpentine Gallery, and Tate Britain's extension, know precisely how to invigorate without betraying the intrinsic character of an older building. While refusing to call undue attention to itself, Miller's architecture provides an uplifting experience for anyone who enters the new ground floor arena.

Richard Cork, *Cambridge Future*

Opposite Detail of the glazed lift, © Dennis Gilbert/View.

Top and bottom Glazing to the winter garden; View from the Marlay Gallery to the winter garden, © Dennis Gilbert/View.

Overleaf Detail of glazing to the winter garden, © Dennis Gilbert/View.

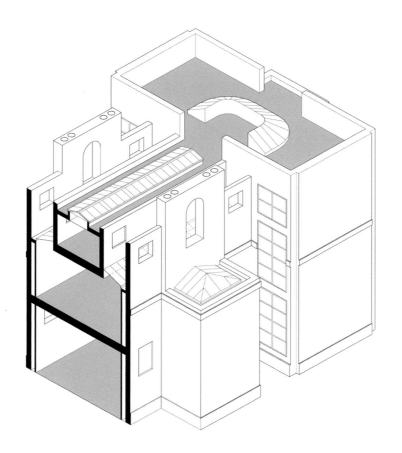

John Miller + Partners have a achieved a quiet triumph. The extension which has added about 3,000 square metres of floor space is designed in Miller + Partners habitual cool modernist idiom, its sleek lines forming a well considered contrast with the brick and ashlar of Smith and Brewer's internal facades.

Michael Hall, *Apollo*

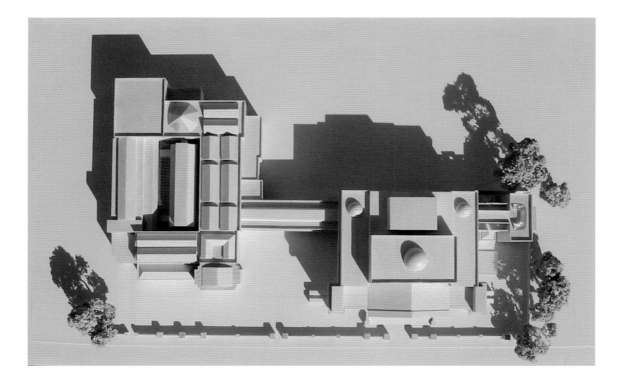

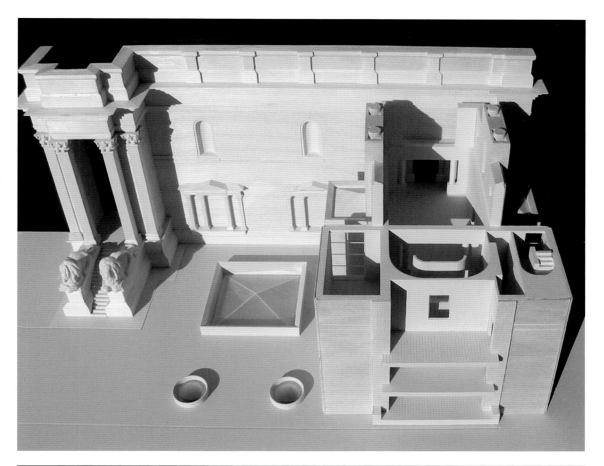

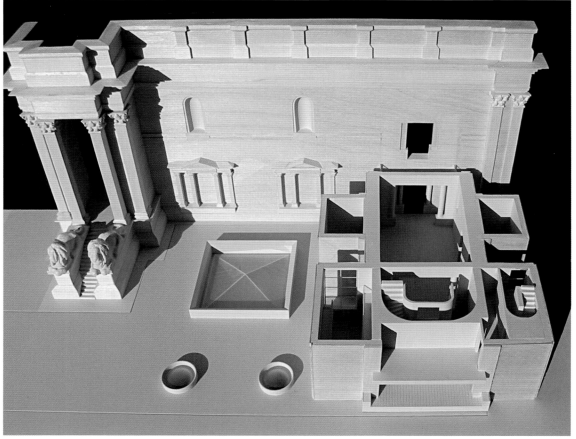

BRINDLEY ARTS CENTRE
Runcorn, Cheshire
John Miller + Partners

John Miller + Partners' first scheme of 1997 proved to be too ambitious. The foyer was lavish and the ancillaries extensive. Accordingly the scheme was redesigned with reduced accomodation.

The final design for the new Arts Centre reduces the circulation area substantially. It obtained funding from the Arts Council Lottery Fund in 2000, and from North West Arts.

The site is immediately north of the Bridgewater Canal. It slopes up from the town centre towards the canal with views towards the Mersey Bridge.

The circular auditorium, seating 420, with a deep stage and fly-tower, is designed for drama, speech, music and dance. It has high level technical galleries, acoustic baffles and wall linings to accommodate a variety of acoustic needs.

The auditorium is part enclosed by a top-lit double-height foyer. The bar, social spaces and education workshops are attached to it. The cafe at the upper level looks over the foyer and has access to a south-facing terrace fronting the canal. A lift and stairs connect the upper tiers of the auditorium to the foyer at first floor level via a bridge. There is also an exhibition space, for the display of art at first floor and a double-height studio, designed for flexible use, including cinema, dance and workshop performances, in a variety of seating configurations for up to 120 occupants.

Ancillary spaces include workshops, loading, storage, dressing rooms and administration.

The external materials are striped red and blue brick evoking the industrial context, with the main auditorium copper clad. Internal finishes include timber and resin stone floors, a maple-lined auditorium and plastered walls.

The project incorporates passive energy cooling systems utilising the thermal capacity of the building mass and fresh air ventilation for occupants' comfort.

The site is planted with retained mature trees and augmented with additional structured landscaping. Public access is either by foot, from the High Street or towpath, or by car and coach with drop off points planned near to the public entrance with service access and parking to the rear.

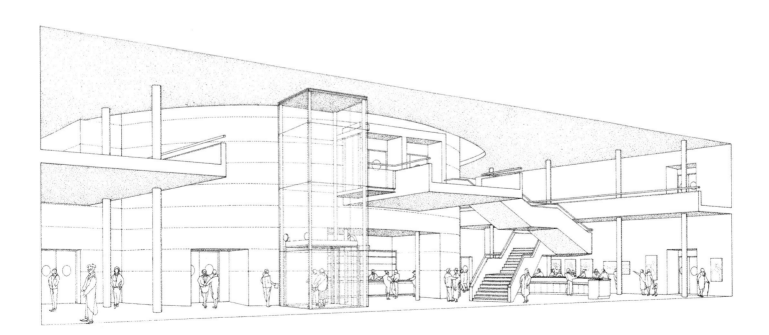

Above View of the entrance hall, preliminary perspective by David Naessens.

Opposite Plans of the preliminary scheme, for the first Lottery application.

1 Entrance
2 Foyer
3 Box office
4 Bar
5 Cafe
6 Stage
7 Auditorium
8 Studio one
9 Multi-purpose room
10 Control room

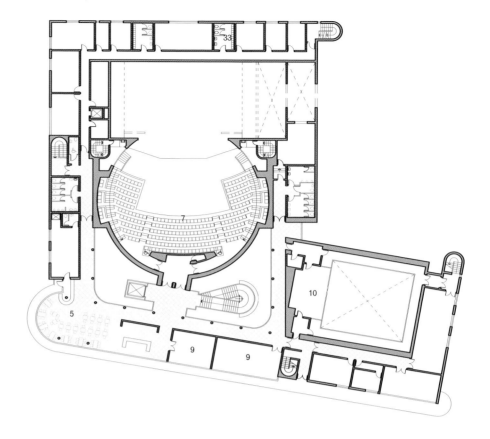

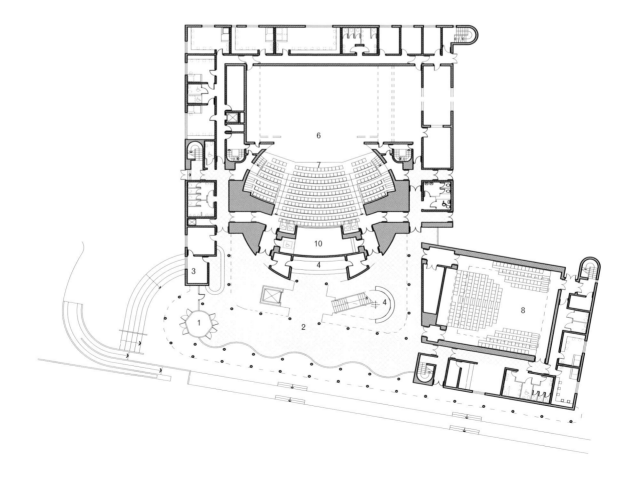

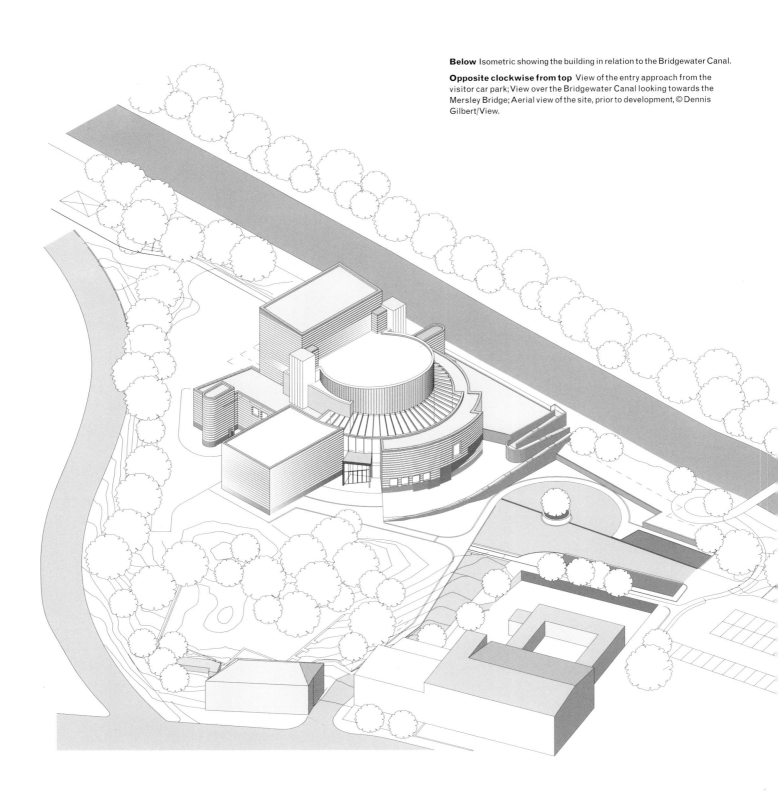

Below Isometric showing the building in relation to the Bridgewater Canal.

Opposite clockwise from top View of the entry approach from the visitor car park; View over the Bridgewater Canal looking towards the Mersley Bridge; Aerial view of the site, prior to development, © Dennis Gilbert/View.

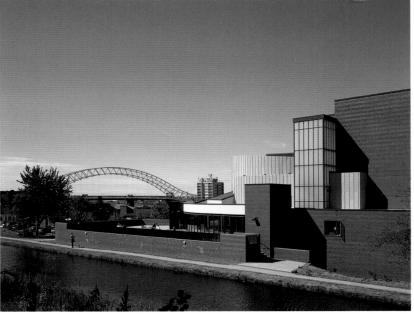

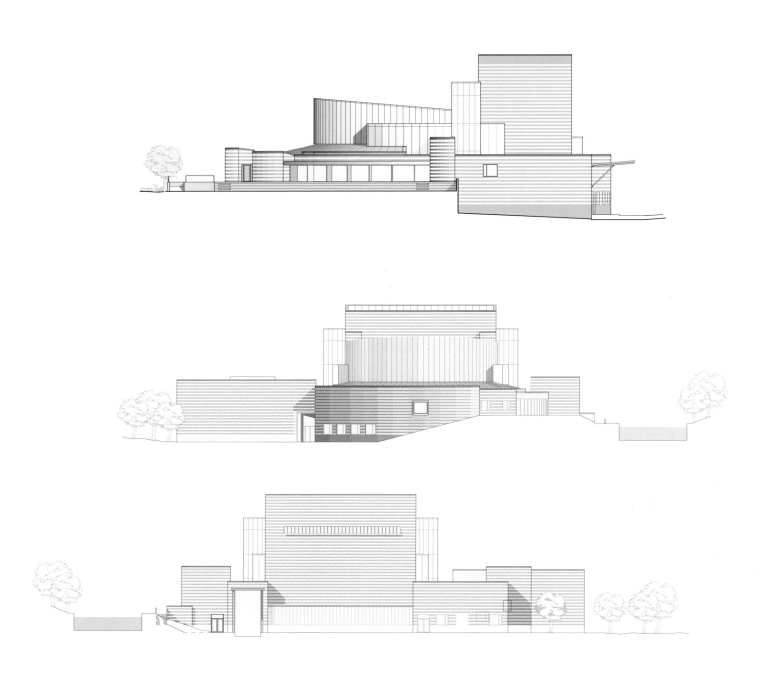

Top to bottom South elevation; West elevation; East elevation.

Opposite top and bottom First floor; Ground floor.

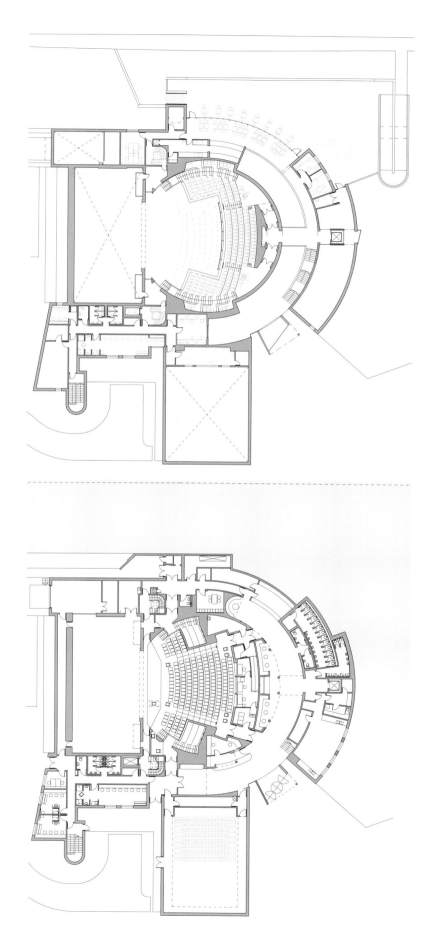

Opposite View of the stairs and bridge to the auditorium,
© Dennis Gilbert/View.

Top to bottom Bridge; View of the cafe with the terrace beyond,
© Dennis Gilbert/View.

TRADITION AND INNOVATION
Kenneth Frampton

> The ambiguity which truly matters, the sense giving ambivalence, the genuine foundation on which the cognitive usefulness of conceiving human habitat as the 'world of culture' rests, is the ambivalence between 'creativity' and 'normative regulation'. The two ideas could not be further apart, yet both are—and must remain—present in the composite idea of culture. 'Culture' is as much about inventing as it is about preserving, about discontinuity as much as about continuation, about novelty a much as about tradition: about routine as much as about pattern breaking, about norm following as much as about the transcendence of the norm; about the unique as much as about the regular; about change as much as about monotony of reproduction; about the unexpected as much as about the predictable.
> Zygmunt Bauman, *Culture as Praxis*, 1999

Both Alan Colquhoun and John Miller, the founders of the original partnership of Colquhoun + Miller, came to their initial maturity in the heyday of the British New Brutalist movement. Colquhoun was one of three architects working for London County Council who were engaged in the design of a prototypical, narrow-fronted, duplex apartment block completed in Bentham Road, London in 1955, while Miller, nine years younger, came to his initial maturity working as an assistant to Tom Ellis of Lyons Israel and Ellis on the realisation of the Old Vic Theatre Workshop, London, in 1958. Both the Bentham Road block and the Old Vic Workshop were manifestations of a reinterpreted modernity, which was more demanding than the socio-democratic, stylistic populism of the 1951 Festival of Britain. Both of these otherwise unrelated works tended to emphasise the ethical rather than the aesthetic dimension, to coin the distinction elaborated by Reyner Banham in his book, *The New Brutalism*, of 1956. Through such affinities, the partnership, established at the end of 1962, favoured a mediated modernity, one which would have recourse to traditional materials and geometrical forms of composition; that is to say, features that were not prevalent in the work of the pre-war avant-garde.

The Forest Gate High School, completed in the Borough of West Ham, London in 1965, established the reputation of the firm overnight with a work of exceptional maturity, summating the best of the modern fair-faced brick tradition both in Britain and elsewhere. Evocative of such distinguished pre-war works in brick as that of Dudok in Hilversum or Mies Van der Rohe in Krefeld, the Forest Gate School was also part of an evolving Brutalist sensibility, as could be found at the time in such works as Louis Kahn's Yale Art Gallery of 1952 or James Stirling's competition entry for Churchill College, Cambridge of 1958. What distinguished the design of Forest Gate from these precedents was not only the rational rhythmic distribution of the classrooms about a central square assembly hall and the accompanying diagonal composition bounded by the larger square of the school's playground, but also the consummate skill with which the school was fenestrated. Thus apart from the curtain wall glazing of the individual classrooms, the load-bearing, brick walls which constituted the main body of the building were deftly punctuated by precisely proportioned windows. What was truly remarkable about this work, apart from the indebtedness of the hall to Frank Lloyd Wright's Unity Temple of 1906, was the way in which it rendered the programme of a school as a city-in-miniature, complete with covered play areas, a monumental entry stair, workshops, a stage and a gymnasium connected to the first floor of the building by a bridge. One may note in passing the affinity between this work and the solid brick syntax of Caius College, Cambridge, designed in 1962 by Patrick Hodgkinson, within the Cambridge office of Leslie Martin, where Miller worked for two years following his initial apprenticeship with Lyons, Israel and Ellis.

The Chemistry Building of the Royal Holloway College, realised to the designs of Colquhoun + Miller at Egham in Surrey in 1971, adopted a distinctively different *parti pris*, in large measure because it was structured according to newly evolved standards for the planning and servicing of university laboratories as had been developed by the Martin office in collaboration with the engineers Ove Arup and Partners. Axially organised and sectionally displaced as it stepped down a steeply sloping site in three large increments, this chemistry building was articulated in the transverse direction by a tartan grid of split beams and columns within which it accommodated the necessary ducts for servicing the laboratories.

Apart from the clarity and heroic scale of its structure, reminiscent of work of the engineer E Owen Williams at his best, what guarantees this building its nobility is the way in which it is accessed via a pedestrian walkway which bypasses the open loggias on either side of the central three-bay portico. The latter performs the doubly symbolic function of establishing the entry and supporting the library above. The panelled opaque face of this top-lit library, raised above the walkway, bestows a palatial monumentality on the work which serves to connect it, however incidentally, to the pre-war Italian Rationalist tradition; to Pietro Lingeri's Trades Union Building, Como, 1938–1943, and Giuseppe Terragni's unrealised proposal for a reception building for the EUR '42 site situated on the outskirts of Rome.

One of the most ingenious aspects of this design is the split-level accommodation of pedestrian movement at the point of entry, which incorporates a bi-axial, top-lit, transverse ramp system affording access to top-lit lecture halls situated partially below grade on the other side of the pedestrian walkway. This same system continues upward to access a range of seminar rooms, situated below the library, half-a-floor above the entrance. With regard to the section, one notes the way in which the entire building is integrated into the topography, along with the continuous arcades which flank the sides of the building, while stepping at intervals in accordance with the fall of the ground. By virtue of these arcades one may gain access to the entry portico under cover from the lowest part of the site.

These arcades, combined with the reiterated ABA Palladian rhythm of the tartan grid, help to bestow upon the whole an ambivalent identity, one that is divided between, on the one hand, an austere, aesthetic factory and, on the other, the aura of a baroque palace discretely inserted into a bucolic landscape. In the last analysis, the overall character of this work derives in some measure from the way in which it serves as a foil to the nearby Neo-Gothic, red brick pile of the original Holloway College dating from the last quarter of the nineteenth century. Entirely constructed of fair-faced concrete and clad with standard aluminum glazing, the rigorous, canonical nature of this achievement has, in my view, never been sufficiently recognised.

A work of comparable authority will shortly follow, taking the form of a rather atypical, high-tech vacation house designed by John Miller and Su Rogers for their own occupation in 1972. Known as Pillwood 1, this mono-pitched, glass house is situated on a narrow stepped site on the edge of Pill Creek, a tributary of the Fal estuary. Constructed out of a tubular steel frame with concrete floors and GRP modular panels, the bulk of the house is faced with greenhouse glazing, thereby rendering what is essentially a house in the form of a conservatory. The plan is ordered about six virtual squares in which the living area takes up four of the squares and the dining/kitchen two. Dining takes place on a multi-purpose mezzanine overlooking the double-height living volume, the two levels being linked by an open spiral stair. Sliding modular wall panels enable one to increase or decrease the sub-division of the interior according to the density of the occupation. Through this open-ended play with sliding partitions, that which is living space during the day may well become a sleeping area at night.

These nocturnal transformations are facilitated by a central cylindrical spiral stair situated to the rear of the house. As with the laboratory building, the house comprises an axial, tripartite composition which is stepped in section. What is topographically felicitous in this work is the way in which its conception depends on a pre-existing retaining wall that divides the site for much of its length. The house is grounded on a shallow earthwork which, studded with square pavers, forms a terrace around its three sides at grade. A paved walkway running along the higher part of the site affords access to the back entrance of the house and to an auxiliary stair leading down to the lower level. Two factors come to mind when one looks back at this work; the one prospective, the other retrospective. On the one hand, it has a prototypical character in as much as it could have been seen as a pilot-study for a future building system. On the other, it directly evokes tradition, in as much as both the structure and the glazing recall the Crystal Palace of 1851.

The single-storey Pillwood 2, initially designed on an adjacent site, remains unrealised after more than three decades, postponing, as it were, the fulfilment of a composition that would have linked the two houses, both being designed in an equally minimalist manner. Less experimental than the initial house, Pillwood 2 combines a light, tubular steel frame with a conventional built-up flat roof along with a load-bearing storage wall to the rear of the site. At the same time, the project suggests that the house would have been as elegantly detailed as Pillwood 1, with six, full-height sliding plate-glass doors separating the house from a podium-terrace overlooking the creek. Accessed by a similar walkway, at the upper level to the rear of the site, this simple residence was designed as a layered composition, beginning with a storage wall and a parallel top-lit corridor and ending with a continuous terrace, four bays in length, shielded from the sun by a light tubular steel pergola. The living room was chamfered in plan so as to take advantage of the orientation and an oblique view over the creek. The spatial layering of the house is stabilised, as it were, through three moves; by a wrap-around terrace at the western end of the site, by the centralised tri-partite service core, and by two bedrooms, which are rotated through 90 degrees.

These two houses, designed for a unique site, were necessarily quite different from the general domestic line adopted by the office in the 1970s as we find, say, in a mono-pitched, two-storey farmhouse, projected by Colquhoun + Miller for Wales in 1972, or in the equally, mono-pitched, cluster-housing structured about a central spine and realised, in load-bearing brickwork, in Fenny Stratford in 1978. Arguably influenced by Thomas Sharp's study of the British linear village tradition, as set forth in his book *The English Village,* of 1953, the housing in Fenny Stratford could hardly have been more removed from the other domestic line of the office, namely a more urbane, although equally contextual manner, which we first encounter in Colquhoun + Miller's Caversham Road and Gaisford Street, infill development built in Camden Town in 1979. In this instance the architects were to achieve a subtle synthesis between a received Italianate manner and the abstraction of modern form that merits analysing in some detail, since it picks up on a local, shallow-pitched, hipped-roofed domestic manner that may be found throughout extensive areas of Camden Town. Thus in order to complete the missing half of a semi-detached villa on the Caversham Road frontage, the architects adopted several ingenious devices. In the first place, they extended the original shallow pitched slate roof over the newly restored missing half of the semi-detached unit; in the second, they echoed as far as possible the string courses and proportions of the existing villa. In this instance they proceeded to light the bedrooms of the upper duplex units through side-lit bulkheads, thereby manipulating the form of the new fenestration so as to play off the window pattern of the adjacent house. However, as one passes through the lot to the Gaisford Street frontage this hybrid syntax becomes more modern abstract; that is to say, it is transformed into a strictly abstract, orthogonal mass-form with rectilinear window openings, which are to be seen as being little more than the well-proportioned outcome of its internal organisation. Within this context, the eventual omission of a mid-block community centre is to be regretted in that it would have not only mediated between the different expressive modes of these frontages, but it would have also made sense of the large opening let into Gaisford Street facade. Colquhoun + Miller would go on to apply this hybrid syntax to two, new, semi-detached 'villas,' set side-by-side to form a fan-shaped composition, that they saw realised in Church Crescent, London, in 1984.

From Caversham Road onwards, the low- to medium-rise domestic work of the office moves towards a more popularly accessible syntax based in part on a return to the abstract yet partially traditional language that we can find in the work of such proto-modern architects as Josef Hoffman and CR Mackintosh. We should also again acknowledge the influence of Wright evident in both Caversham Road and Church Crescent and above all in the two housing estates that the office designed for the new town of Milton Keynes in the late 1970s. In all four instances the Wrightian trope is evident in the subtle monumentalisation of the form through emphasising the string course of the first floor cill height that is kept as high as possible under deep over-hanging eaves. Thus, the one-off infill housing built in London will be a prototype for the low-rise housing manner of the office, particularly as this is manifest in the residential estates that they would build in Milton Keynes; that is to say, Two Mile Ash, 1973–1984, and Oldbrook II, 1976–1982. While both of these estates are in brick and have hipped, shallow-pitched roofs, they differ in that the first of the two schemes consisted of 54 units built for sale. In effect, this was a speculative project which indirectly reflected the decline of the welfare state and the increasing privatisation of society under the Thatcher government. Aside from deeply overhanging eaves, hip roofs and a pavilionated composition of semi-detached houses an attempt is made in both schemes to unify the free-standing semi-detached houses with pergolas. Of the two schemes, Oldbrook II will possibly come closer to the garden city ethos of the pre-war era. In this instance, one should also note the passing influence of MH Baillie-Scott via his contribution to Hampstead Garden Suburb in 1909. However, the most important difference between these two estates resides in the fact that unlike Two Mile Ash, Oldbrook II is not only larger but also designed as a coherent three-storey street layout, terminating in two-storey, pavilionated gateway blocks at the end of each street. The other distinguishing feature in the three-storey street units is their wood-panelled, up-and-over, built-in garages doors along the street. However, despite this civic tone, the architects were only too explicit about the difficulty they experienced in their attempting to introduce a feeling of urbanity into these developments. As they wrote of Oldbrook II:

> The programme called for 152 dwellings for families of two to seven people, the majority of which should consist of houses with integral garages. The layout attempted to create an urban scale by stressing the street as the locus of the *res publica* and contrasting this to the *res privata* of gardens and children's play spaces. The scheme illustrates the difficulty of establishing an urban environment in a context that is fundamentally suburban in concept. Our preference was for three-storey terraces, but our client preferred two storeys, and the resultant layout is a compromise between the two.

Such an ideological split did not arise with the nine-storey bachelor apartment block that the office saw completed to its designs in Hornsey Lane in 1980. This may have been largely due to the fact that it was a one off, rather specialised block built on the site of a pre-existing house in the midst of luxurious upper class suburban neighbourhood from the turn of the century. Irrespective of the site, this was the invention of a totally new type, comprising one room units, grouped in pairs, about shared bathrooms and kitchenettes. Since the service elements occupied a narrower bay, the main face of the building could be organised according to the familiar ABAABA Palladian rhythm. This syncopation was emphasised by the alternating width of the glass block spandrels, the luminosity of which gave a particularly modern inflection to the overall structure, otherwise rendered in brick throughout.

With the refurbishment and extension of the Whitechapel Art Gallery, completed in the East End of London in 1985, the recasting of art galleries and museums began to emerge as a major genre of the practice. In this amplification and renovation of a late nineteenth century gallery, the affinity of the office for the English Free Style came to engage with the style itself, in as much as the original building designed by CH Townsend in 1898 exemplified this manner. Close to the Art Nouveau of the Glasgow School, the original building was equally affected by the transatlantic Neo-Romanesque rhetoric of HH Richardson and by the sobriety of Lethaby's Arts and Crafts ideology. This much is evident from the original elevation, featuring a mural by Walter Crane which would unfortunately never be executed. Subject to an ingenious yet delicate intervention, the Whitechapel Gallery was refurbished in such a sensitive manner as to make it seem as if the various new components had always been there. At its completion, it was difficult to imagine how the building had been prior to the re-arrangement. This was particularly true of the white, Mackintosh-like gridded apertures to the entrance doors plus the Wagnerian detailing of the main stair which imparted to the institution a sense of freshness without disturbing the form of the original galleries. A similar restraint was evident in the transverse straight flight introduced at the end of the ground floor gallery space, which served to link the principal exhibition space to a new cafe on the mezzanine and a new exhibition space and education room on the floor above. These new facilities, including a service entrance and a lecture theatre at grade, were built on a sliver of land accessed from an existing alleyway. Faced in precision brickwork, these additions were extremely discrete, save for the bay-window of the cafe with its gridded fanlights, and a semi-circular projection at the top of the new stair that provided a window from which to overlook the addition.

The second half of the 1980s would be the occasion of a fundamental change in the structure of the partnership as Colquhoun becomes increasingly engaged with teaching in the United States. The expansion of the partnership to include Richard Brearley in 1976, Su Rogers in 1986 and John Carpenter, who became a salaried partner at around the same time, led eventually to a re-constitution of the office as John Miller + Partners in 1990. These years also saw the practice increasingly involved with one-off, small scale university buildings, beginning with the Stevens Building, for the Royal College of Art, London, completed 1991. This three- to five-storey, in-fill block inserted into a typical London mews, was set to the rear of the main RCA building. This faculty/studio annex was partially related to the syntax employed in the Whitechapel Art Gallery. The common reference was once again the English Free Style. The gridded clerestory fenestration employed in this annex testifies to this connection, as do the tall studio windows at the top of the block facing the mews. Dualistically organised, this structure is focused about a top-lit central exhibition space, three storeys in height, distantly reminiscent in its spatially unifying role of the full-height stair hall in Mackintosh's Glasgow School of Art. The contextual inflection embodied in this building, takes place at more than one level, not only because of its modulation with regard to the scale and grain of the surrounding mews and its frontage onto Queen's Gate but also possibly because of the quiet allusion to Mackintosh's masterwork, since this had been the point of departure in Cadbury-Brown's design for the main building of the College, completed in 1963.

The 1990s would see the office increasingly involved with the provincial university as a client, beginning with the canonical Queen's Building, realised for the University of East Anglia in Norwich in 1994, which is the first occasion on which John Miller + Partners would formulate a new medium-scaled, academic type combining a low-rise, bar-building housing faculty offices and seminar rooms with a cylindrical structure accommodating the more honourific public elements of the programme, such as the entry, the main lecture theatre, common rooms, etc.. This type-form will be given an even more didactic formulation in the Ramphal Building for the University of Warwick of 1995, where a two-storey cylindrical element is symmetrically bracketed by the bi-lateral arms of a four-storey faculty structure L-shaped in plan. In this instance, the cylinder is occupied by a large, fan-shaped lecture hall, the left-over space is taken up by so-called "break-out" space. The University of Warwick will also be the client for a much more comprehensive faculty building, built in three phases, starting with a quadrant lecture hall snugly positioned between the arms of a symmetrical faculty building. In subsequent phases, this conjunction will expand along the axis of one of the arms which will be treated as a multi-storey galleria with individual faculty offices running along one side of the top-lit, axial space, and seminar rooms being ranged along the other. Study wings, canted at 30 degrees, branch out from this central galleria at three points so as to create three interconnected teaching wings, enclosing two open-air courtyards between them. Here we are momentarily within the province of innovation rather than tradition since, in many respects, this is the invention of an unprecedented academic type, designed to afford different views from the classrooms both within and without the complex. In many respects, one may regard this work as the culmination of the practice's involvement with the evolution of new forms of accommodation.

From the late 1990s onwards, the play of the practice between tradition and innovation will assume a particularly sensitive character in that the office will become successively engaged in the rearrangement, amplification and refurbishment of a series of galleries. In sequence, these will range from an extension to George Basevi's Fitzwilliam Museum, Cambridge, with a design won in a limited competition in 1993, to the Serpentine Gallery in Hyde Park, London, completed in 1998, and the conversion of the existing Tate Gallery into the Tate Britain realised in 2001, ending with the transformation of the two Neo-Greek temples that made up the so-called Playfair Project, completed in Edinburgh in 2004. It is significant from the standpoint of tradition that all of these institutions were designed by distinguished architects: CR Cockerell and EM Barry who completed Basevi's Fitzwilliam Museum in 1875; Sidney RJ Smith, Romaine Walker and the American architect John Russell Pope who together assembled the Neo-Classical body of the Tate Gallery between 1895 and 1937; and finally, William Playfair who was the original architect of the Royal Scottish Academy, 1822–1826, and the National Gallery of Scotland, 1850–1859.

The Serpentine, being the smallest of these institutions, was also the most modest, with the architects limiting their intervention to a few salient moves. As in the Whitechapel Gallery, the crucial move was to recast the entry along with a new bookshop, adjacent toilets and a discrete lift and stair linking to the offices above. A new education room was provided in the space which had been previously occupied by the entry, while the galleries themselves, including the central rotunda, were left unmodified. The other substantial alteration was to provide a roof terrace which could be readily accessed from the staff offices.

John Miller + Partners became the architects for the extension of the Fitzwilliam Museum in Cambridge by winning two successive competitions, one in 1993 and the other in 1995, neither of which came to fruition due to local opposition from Peterhouse College. Despite these frustrating delays the extension was finally realised in the embodiment of a courtyard at the southeastern end, as had been originally designed by Smith and Brewer in the inter-war years and partially enclosed by David Roberts in 1975.

John Miller + Partners converted this architectonic legacy into a three-storey structure comprising a top-lit entry, a cafe, a bookshop, and an orientation space on the ground floor with offices and additional galleries on the two floors above. The discrete zenithal lighting of the atrium around which this accommodation is assembled plays off against the Neo-Georgian, brick-faced enclosure designed by Smith and Brewer.

The so-called Centenary Development of the Tate Britain involved a similar wholesale addition to one side of an existing Neo-Classical composition. On this occasion the intervention entailed the creation of a total new side entrance, so as to accommodate the large numbers of people currently attending temporary exhibitions. The architects developed the initial brief about the nexus of a generously scaled entrance and stair hall with the stair feeding into the cross axis of the original Duveen Gallery. Approached by ramp and a short stair set against the western Atterbury Street frontage, this stair hall gave access in depth to cloakrooms, a bookshop and a cafeteria at the lower level, while the stair rises to serve the new barrel vaulted Linbury Galleries, inserted into a space that was previously occupied by a courtyard in the northwest corner of the complex. The discrete ingenuity of this entire exercise is such as to lead one to underestimate the exceptional quality of the result from the generous proportions and shallow going of the main stair to the clerestory lighting and the consistent use of shadowless curves between the walls and the ceiling throughout. The pale limestone paving of the entrance hall is offset by black columns while elsewhere in the top-lit galleries plain wooden floors are sharply articulated from the walls by a minimal recess. The modesty and precision of this work along with its harmonic relationship to the syntax and scale of the original building makes it hard to believe that the net effect of the intervention was to expand the total area of the building by a third.

The Playfair Project, situated just off Princess Street in the heart of Edinburgh, was a much more complex undertaking in that it entailed rearranging and linking two adjacent Neo-Classical structures as originally designed by William Playfair; the Royal Scottish Academy, 1830–1835, and the National Gallery of Scotland, 1850–1857. Where the former is entered from Princess Street via a peripetal portico, the National Gallery is not entered via the two separate porticoes on the cross axis of the building but from the long axis facing the RSA building. These respective entries are approached from a podium—the so-called mound, raised above the *datum* of the surrounding streets. The parti of the project, designed in two phases, was to build beneath the podium so as to provide a new concourse serving both buildings, one which could be entered from the East Princes Street Gardens, running parallel to the railway. The result has been the creation of a generous colonnaded foyer, measuring three by five bays, leading directly to a lecture hall at the end of the principal axis. A stair and a secondary foyer conducts the visitor to a circular stair and cylindrical glass lift leading up into the Royal Scottish Gallery above. The shaft of this light is lined in Pouilleney limestone, while from within the lift one can look up to a conical zenithal light overhead. The details throughout this sequence are of the highest quality, highlighted by the fact that stair nosings and handrails are all in bronze. Aside from providing quasi-subterranean access to both buildings the main foyer houses a museum shop to the rear of the undercroft and a restaurant facing out over the gardens. The paved surface of the refurbished and slightly widened podium includes a shallow pyramid, four steps high, with a central zenithal light, that affords a canted, geometric counterform mediating between the misaligned axes of Playfair's original Greek temples. It is typical of the latent playfulness of the practice that it would conclude this discrete museological intervention with such a catalytic gesture that does nothing to disturb the eccentric order of Playfair's original composition. In addition to this, the new Caithness paving of the mound is punctuated by eleven circular rooflights illuminating the space below.

All of this brings us to the most significant free-standing building that the practice has realised of recent date, namely, the Brindley Arts Centre, situated on a wooded slope to the north of the Bridgewater Canal overlooking Runcorn town centre, with a distant view of the Mersey. Completed in 2004 for the Halton Borough Council, this structure houses two separate auditoria; the first with a proscenium and a fly-tower seating 420 and the second, a poly-functional space designed for theatre, dance and cinema, with flexible seating for a maximum of 120. The third public programmatic element in the scheme is an exhibition space and educational workroom. In the design as built, the main auditorium gives rise to an equally drum-like structure with a top-lit galleria separating the auditorium proper from a bar, a cafeteria, and terrace facing south. The interior of the theatre has a somewhat provisional feel to it, due in part to the undulating concrete surfaces lining the sides of the auditorium. This acoustical surface is set against flat modular panels painted blue to match the upholstery of the seating. Flanking side walls close off the parterre from the upper circle as it descends towards the stage. The soffit of this volume is rendered a recessive surface, punctuated by spot lighting. Passive energy is used for cooling and ventilating the auditorium by exploiting the structure for thermal storage. Floor-to-ceiling glazing divides the cafeteria from its terrace, while the exterior of the theatre is clad in copper sheeting with standing seams. The orthogonal ancillary spaces including the black box theatre, the fly tower and a perimeter wall bounding the site are all faced in alternating courses of blue and red brickwork, somewhat evocative of industrial vernacular.

Two relatively modest works situated virtually at either end of the firm's four decades of practice seem in retrospect to embody reciprocal poles that in an uncanny manner have a very similar scale and mood. The first of these is the long since demolished Weinreb + Douma print and map shop, realised by Colquhoun + Miller in Bloomsbury Way, London, at the end of the 1960s. Warmly furnished and subtly lit, this restrained, generously planned and well-appointed shop may be seen, across almost half a century, as having much in common with the two bedroom, two-storey penthouse that John Miller and Su Rogers recently completed for their own occupation in the nearby Chancery Lane area of London. What these two works share, apart from their mutual articulation of free-standing, cylindrical columns, painted white, is a lyrical spirit and feeling for intimacy that is rarely seen in architecture today. Both works speak of the emancipatory modern tradition, of the unfashionable, unfurnished modern project; the one from a lost cultural past, when, to coin the phrase, "the flag was in the breeze," and the other, from the challenging present, with a work that insists on asserting the same values of lightness, efficiency and warmth that this practice has always cultivated and which it has invariably tried to demonstrate in the evolution of its work.

Above The Beauchamp Building, view looking east. Opposite Weinreb + Douma print and map shop, London.

CHRONOLOGY

1961–1989
COLQUHOUN + MILLER

1961–1965 Forest Gate High School, London
Client: London Borough of West Ham
Team: Paul Yarker

1964 Gallery for Precolumbian Art, London (unrealised)
Client: Miss Kemper

1964 House, Surrey (unrealised)
Client: Mr B Lodge

1964 Office Conversion, London (unrealised)
Client: Reuters
Team: Geoffrey Wigfall

1965–1971 Chemistry Building Royal Holloway College
Client: Royal Holloway College
Team: David Bryan, Chris Cross, Edward Jones, Tony Musgrove

1966 Library, London (unrealised)
Client: Mr B Drummond

1966 Shop Conversion, Covent Garden, London
Client: Miss Christina Smith

1967 House, Surrey (unrealised)
Client: Mr Leslie McCombie

1968–1969 Print and Map Shop, London
Client: Weinreb + Douma
Team: Madhu Sarin

1970–1973 Clifton Cannon Lee School, Yorkshire
Client: West Riding of Yorkshire
Team: Dougal Campbell, David Bryan, Roger Barcroft

1971 House Conversion, Marylebone, London
Client: Durrants Hotel
Team: Alan Basing

1970–1973 Lower House Farm, Wales
Client: Mr Lyman Dixon

1972–1974 Pillwood 1, Cornwall
Client: Mr and Mrs Marcus Brumwell
Awards: RIBA Regional Award 1975
Team: Roger Barcroft

1972–1974 Melrose Avenue Activity Centre, Milton Keynes
Client: Milton Keynes Development Corporation
Awards: Structural Steel Award Highly Commended 1974
Team: Russel Bevington, John Parker, Simon Winstanley

1973 Holiday Chalets, Aviemore, Scotland (unrealised)
Client: Time Off Properties
Team: Roger Barcroft, Simon Winstanley

1973 Coca Cola Factory
Client: Invited Competition
Team: Simon Winstanley

1973–1976 Old Persons' Home, London
Client: London Borough of Haringey
Team: Richard Brearley, Shinici Tomoe

1974–1976 Welbourne Road and Tenterden Road Activity Centre
Client: London Borough of Haringey
Team: Roger Barcroft, Simon Winstanley

1974 Housing, Fenny Stratford, first project (unrealised)
Client: Milton Keynes Development Corporation

1974 Pillwood 2, Cornwall (unrealised)
Client: Mr John Raynes
Team: Simon Winstanley

Richard Brearley (1975–present) and Simon Winstanley (1975–1978) become Partners

1975 Colnaghi's, London (unrealised)
Client: Colnaghi's
Team: Simon Winstanley

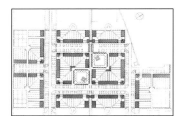

1975 Two Mile Ash Housing, Milton Keynes, first project (unrealised)
Client: Milton Keynes Development Corporation
Team: Peter Roy, Simon Winstanley

1975 Prince Road, Croydon (unrealised)
Client: GLC
Team: David Nixon

1975–1979 Housing, Caversham Road and Gaisford Street
Client: London Borough of Camden
Team: Innes Lamunière, David Nixon, Shinichi Tomoe

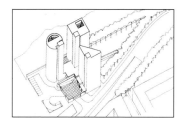

1977 Housing Millbank, London
Client: Open Competition
Team: Peter Roy, Simon Winstanley

1976–1978 Vernacular Housing, Fenny Stratford
Client: Milton Keynes Development Corporation
Team: Innes Lamunière, Shinichi Tomoe, Simon Winstanley, Richard Brearley

1976–1982 Housing, Oldbrook II, Milton Keynes
Client: Milton Keynes Development Corporation
Awards: Public Sector New Housing Highly Commended 1984, Civic Trust Awards Highly Commended 1984, Architectural Design Project Award 1982, Housing Design Awards 1983
Team: John Hunter, Shinichi Tomoe

1978 Dada and Surrealism Reviewed, Hayward Gallery
Client: Arts Council of Great Britain
Team: Innes Lamunière, Shinichi Tomoe

1978–1980 Housing, Hornsey Lane, London
Client: London Borough of Haringey
Team: John Hunter, Shinichi Tomoe

1978–1985 Whitechapel Art Gallery, London
Client: Trustees of the Whitechapel Gallery
Awards: European Prize for Architecture 1988, RIBA Regional Award 1988, Shortlisted for the Mies van der Rohe Pavilion Award for European, Architecture Barcelona 1988–1992, Civic Trust Award 1987, North Thames Architectural Society Award 1986, Summer Exhibition, Royal Academy 1984
Team: Peter Bernamont, John Carpenter, Norman Chang, Graham Smith

1979 Taoiseach Residence and Guest House
Client: Open Competition
Team: Chris Hay, Peter Jones, Shiela O'Donnell

1979 Theatre Workshop, Egham (unrealised)
Client: Royal Holloway College
Team: Shinichi Tomoe

1979 The Arts of Bengal Exhibition
Client: The Whitechapel Gallery in Association with the Victoria and Albert Museum

1980 10 Twentieth Century Houses, Travelling Exhibition
Client: Arts Council of Great Britain
Team: Shiela O'Donnell

1981 Housing Central, Milton Keynes (unrealised)
Client: Milton Keynes Development Corporation

1981 Picasso's Picassos Exhibition, Hayward Gallery
Client: Arts Council of Great Britain and the Hayward Gallery

1981–1984 Housing Shrubland Road and Albion Drive, London
Client: London Borough of Hackney
Awards: Architectural Design Award 1986, Civic Trust Award 1985
Team: Norman Chang, John Hunter, Graham Smith

1981–1984 Housing Church Crescent, London
Client: London Borough of Hackney
Team: Norman Chang, John Hunter, Graham Smith

1982 Sir Christopher Wren Exhibition
Client: Whitechapel Art Gallery

1982–1984 Housing, Two Mile Ash, Milton Keynes
Client: Milton Keynes Development Corporation
Team: John Carpenter, John Hunter

1983–1985 Housing, Willen Park 2, Milton Keynes
Client: Milton Keynes Development Corporation
Team: Graham Smith

1984 Adolf Loos Travelling Exhibition
Client: Arts Council of Great Britain

1984–1985 Housing, Shenley Lodge, Milton Keynes
Client: Milton Keynes Development Corporation
Team: John Carpenter

Su Rogers (1986–present) becomes Partner

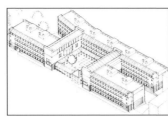

1986 Medical Research Laboratories, winners of Invited Competition (unrealised)
Client: University of Cambridge
Team: Norman Chang, Esmonde O'Briain

1986 Gibralter East Coast Development
Client: Wimpey Trocom
Team: Graham Smith, Norman Chang

1986 National Gallery Extension London, Invited Competition
Client: Trustees of the National Gallery
Team: John Carpenter, Norman Chang, Avtar Lotay, Graham Smith, Patrick Theis, Hester Gray

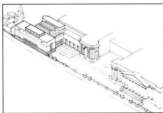

1986 Fitzwilliam Museum Sculpture Court (unrealised)
Client: The Trustees of the Fitzwilliam Museum
Team: Norman Chang, Esmonde O'Briain, Dean Smith, Patrick Theis

1986 Generic House
Client: Ashby and Horner Team Contracts Ltd.
Team: Norman Chang

1986 Masterplan, Tate Gallery, London
Client: Trustees of the Tate Gallery
Team: Tim Boyd, Norman Chang, Esmonde O'Briain, Graham Smith

1986 Regent Street Polytechnic, London (unrealised)
Client: Polytechnic of Central London
Team: Norman Chang, Tim Boyd

1986 Housing, Walnut Tree, Milton Keynes
Client: Milton Keynes Development Corporation
Team: Graham Smith

1986 Thamesmead Housing, London
Client: Thamesmead Development Corporation
Team: Norman Chang

1987 Messepalast, Vienna
Client: Invited Competition
Team: Norman Chang, Nick Pham, Graham Smith, Tim Boyd

1986–1991 Stevens Building Royal College of Art, London
Client: the Rector and Council of the RCA
Team: Tina Bird, Tim Boyd, John Carpenter, Norman Chang, Louise Cotter, Hester Gray, Neil Harkness, Simon Lanyon-Hogg, Alex Michaelis, Pankaj Pandara, Dean Smith, Chris Roache, Graham Smith, Patrick Theis, Mark Titman

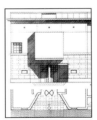

1987 Staedel Institute of Art, Frankfurt, Invited Competition, second prize
Client: Trustees of the Staedelsches Kunstunstitut
Team: Norman Chang, Patrick Theis

1987 IBA Housing, Berlin, Invited Competition
Client: IBA
Team: Tim Boyd, Norman Chang, Nick Pham, Graham Smith, Patrick Theis

1987 Housing, Woodall House, London (unrealised)
Client: London Borough of Haringey
Team: Tim Boyd, Patrick Theis

1987 Norwegian YMCA London, Invited Competition
Client: Norwegian YMCA
Team: Patrick Theis

1987 The Lodge, Tate Gallery, London
Client: Lord Peter Palumbo
Team: Patrick Theis

1987 Duveen Axis, Tate Gallery
Client: The Trustees of the Tate Gallery
Team: Norman Chang, Graham Smith

1987 Hawley Lock Development, London (unrealised)
Client: Trevor Clarke
Team: Patrick Theis

1988 Samsung Gallery, Tate Gallery, London (unrealised)
Client: The Trustees of the Tate Gallery
Team: Graham Smith

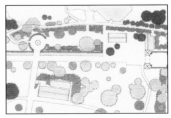

1988 Entrance sequences to Kew Gardens, Invited Competition
Client: Kew Garden
Team: Bryn Riches

1988 New Offices for Logica (unrealised)
Client: Logica
Team: Bryn Riches

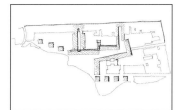

1989–1991 Housing, Alcoy, Spain (unrealised)
Client: Generalalitat Valencia
Team: John Carpenter, Bryn Riches, Patrick Theis, Neil Harkness

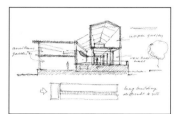

1989 Rowing Museum, Henley on Thames, Invited Competition
Client: The Rowing Museum

1987–1988 Students' Housing, Churchill College, Cambridge
Team: Tim Boyd

1989 Tate Gallery St Ives, Invited Competition
Client: The Trustees of the Tate Gallery
Team: Tim Boyd, Graham Smith

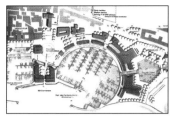

1990 Masterplan for La Ciotat Docks, France (unrealised)
Client: Aménagement du Littoral du la Ciotat
Team: Bryn Riches in collaboration with Bernard Terrazi, Marseille

1990–1991 The Gulbenkian Hall RCA, London
Client: The Rector and Council of the RCA
Team: John Carpenter, Tim Boyd

1992 Five Buildings by Colquhoun + Miller, exhibition at the Royal College of Art
Client: The Rector and Council of the RCA
Team: John Carpenter

1990–1992 Nomura Gallery 1 and 2, Tate Gallery
Client: The Trustees of the Tate Gallery
Team: Tim Boyd, Norman Chang, Hester Gray, Graham Smith,

1992 Tate Gallery Shop
Client: The Trustees of the Tate Gallery
Team: John Carpenter, Hester Gray, Graham Smith

1992 Science Building, University of Portsmouth, Invited Competition
Client: University of Portsmouth
Team: Jo Eade, Tim Boyd

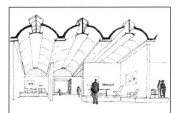

1992 Geffrye Museum, Invited Competition
Client: Trustees of the Geffrye Museum
Team: Tim Boyd, Graham Smith

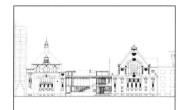

1992 Kestner Art Gallery Hanover, Invited Competition
Client: The Trustees of Hanover Art Gallery
Team: Bryn Riches

1991–1994 The Twentieth Century Galleries, National Portrait Gallery, London
Client: The Director and Trustees of the National Portrait Gallery
Awards: Civic Trust Commendation 1996, Museum of the Year Award—Best Museum of Social History 1994, British Gas Adapt Award—Highly Commended—For Access for the Disabled 1994, Holiday Care Award—For Access for the Disabled 1994
Team: Tim Boyd, Hester Gray

1991–1994 Queen's Building, University of East Anglia
Client: The University of East Anglia
Awards: Civic Trust Commendation 1997, Lighting Design Award 1995, RIBA National Award for Architecture 1994, RIBA Regional Award for Architecture 1994
Team: John Carpenter, Umberto Emoli, Hester Gray, Neil Harkness, Soraya Khan, Bryn Riches, Patrick Theis

1991–1994 Elizabeth Fry Building, University of East Anglia
Client: The University of East Anglia
Awards: Building Services Energy Efficiency Award 1999, Civic Trust Commendation 1997, Building Construction Industry Award 1996, RIBA Regional Award 1995
Team: Umberto Emoli, Neil Harkness, Soraya Khan, Patrick Theis

1993–1995 Ramphal Building, University of Warwick
Client: The University of Warwick
Team: Jo Eade, Graham Smith

1993 Manchester City Art Gallery (unrealised)
Client: Manchester City Council
Team: John Carpenter, Graham Smith

1994 Tate Gallery North West Quadrant, first study (unrealised)
Client: The Trustees of the Tate
Team: Tim Boyd, John Carpenter, Graham Smith

1993 Friends' Room, Tate Gallery
Client: The Trustees of the Tate Gallery
Team: Hester Gray

1993 Royal Northern College of Music, Invited Competition
Client: Manchester University

1995 Grosvenor Museum, Chester (unrealised)
Client: Chester City Council
Team: Graham Smith

1995 Hermitage Riverside Development, Invited Competition
Team: in collaboration with Rick Mather, Michael Wilford, Dixon Jones. Pollard Thomas Edwards

1995 Art Now Space, Tate Gallery
Client: The Trustees of the Tate Gallery
Team: Patrick Theis

1995 Manchester City Art
Gallery, Invited Competition
Client: Manchester City Council
Team: John Carpenter,
Graham Smith

1996 Latymer Centre for
Performing Arts, Invited Competition
Client: Latymer School

1996 Corpus Christie College,
University of Cambridge, Invited
Competition
Client: Corpus Christie College
Team: Kristine Ngan

1996 City Museum and Art
Gallery, Stoke on Trent (unrealised)
Client: Stoke on Trent City Council
Team: Kristine Ngan

1996 Dundee City Art Centre,
Invited Competition
Client: Dundee City Council
Team: John Carpenter

1996–1998 Serpentine Gallery,
Hyde Park
Client: The Trustees of the
Serpentine Gallery
Team: John Carpenter, Umberto
Emoli, Hester Gray

1996–1998 Shackleton Memorial
Library, University of Cambridge
Client: Cambridge University Estates,
Management and Building services
Awards: RIBA Regional Award
for Architecture 1999
Team: Jo Eade, Umberto Emoli,
Kristine Ngan

1996–2001 Tate Britain
Centenary Development
Client: The Trustees of the Tate
Awards: RIBA Regional Award
for Architecture 2002, Short-
listed for RIBA Special Award
Team: Patrick Bankhead, Tim
Boyd, John Cannon, John
Carpenter, Kate Hare, Stuart Hill,
Kristine Ngan, James Nelmes,
Graham Smith, Seamus Thornton

1997 Buckingham Palace,
Queen's Picture Gallery,
Invited Competition
Client: Royal Household
Team: Jo Eade

1997 Fitzwilliam Museum,
Northern Extension (unrealised)
Client: Cambridge University
Estates, Management and
Building services
Team: Jo Eade

1997 National Youth Centre for
Performing, Invited Competition
Arts Gloucester Docks
Client: University of Gloucester

1997 Norfolk Record Office,
University of East Anglia,
Invited Competition
Client: Norfolk County Council
Team: John Carpenter

1997–1998 New Cafe,
Tate Britain
Client: The Trustees of the Tate
Team: John Carpenter, Umberto
Emoli, Graham Smith

1998 The Whitechapel Art
Gallery, Arts Council
Refurbishment
Client: The Trustees of the
Whitechapel Gallery
Team: Umberto Emoli, Bryn
Riches, Kristine Ngan

1998 The Museum of World
Culture, Gotenburg, Sweden,
Open Competition
Client: The Trustees
Team: Kristine Ngan

1999 The Ashmolean Museum,
Oxford, Invited Competition
Client: Trustees of the
Ashmolean Museum
Team: Kristine Ngan

1999 Mid-Wales Art Centre
Client: Invited Competition

1999 Four Camden Architects
Exhibition
Client: Prince of Wales Foundation
Team: John Carpenter

1999–2000 Guildhall Visitors'
Centre Leicester
Client: Leicester City Council and
Leicester Cathedral Authority
Team: Umberto Emoli

John Carpenter (2000–2007)
becomes partner

2000 Inside Outside Project,
Royal College of Art (unrealised)
Client: The Rector and Council
of the RCA
Team: Soraya Khan, Patrick Theis

2001 London Transport
Museum, Invited Competition
Client: London Transport Museum

2001 Wilton's Music Hall
London, Invited Competition
Client: Broomhill Trust

2001 Painter's Studio, London
Client: Harriet Miller
Team: Stuart Hill

2001 Victorian Nudes
Exhibition, Tate Britain
Client: The Trustees of the Tate
Team: Deborah Denner

2001 The Hyman Kreitman
Research Centre, Tate Britain
Client: The Trustees of the Tate
Team: Patrick Bankhead,
Kristine Ngan

2002 Herbert Art Gallery
Coventry, Invited Competition
Client: Coventry City Council

2002 Woking Galleries,
Invited Competition
Client: Woking Art Gallery
Team: John Carpenter

2002 Holbourne Museum, Bath,
Invited Competition
Client: Holbourne Museum
Team: Daisuke Harada

2002 Picasso Matisse
Exhibition, Tate Modern
Client: Trustees of the Tate
Team: Deborah Denner

2002 Clare Hall Student
Accommodation, University
of Cambridge (unrealised)
Client: Clare Hall
Team: Kate Hare

2002 Exhibition La Biennale
di Venezzia
Client: Mostra Internazionale
du Architectura
Team: Patrick Bankhead,
John Cannon, John Carpenter,
Deborah Denner, Stuart Hill,
James Nelmes, Seamus Thornton

2000–2003 Newnham College
Library, University of Cambridge
Client: The Principal and Fellows
of Newnham College
Awards: Summer Exhibition,
Royal Academy 2001, David
Urwin Design Award Civic Trust
Commendation 2004
Team: Deborah Denner,
Dai Hassuda, James Nelmes,
Kristine Ngan

2003 Newlyn Art Gallery
Cornwall, Invited Competition
Client: The Trustees
of Newlyn Art Gallery
Team: Kristine Ngan

2003 Whipple Museum, University
of Cambridge (unrealised)
Client: Estate Management
and Building Services
Team: Daisuke Harada

2003 School of Midwifery
and Nursing, University of
Southampton, Invited Competition
Client: Southampton University
Team: Jo Eade

2003 The Royal Museum
Edinburgh, Invited Competition
Client: The Trustees
of the Royal Museum
Team: John Carpenter

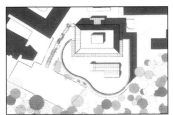

2003 Bedford Library Extension Royal Holloway College, Invited Competition
Client: Royal Holloway College
Team: Deborah Denner

2003 Middlesbrough Town Hall Masterplan, Invited Competition
Client: Middlesbrough City Council
Team: John Carpenter

2003 Lyceum Theatre, Central Library + Graves Art Gallery, Sheffield, Invited Competition
Client: Sheffield City Council
Team: John Carpenter

2004 Greenock Arts Guild Theatre, Invited Competition
Client: Greenock Arts Guild Theatre
Team: Patrick Bankhead

2004 Old College Quad, Edinburgh University, Invited Competition
Client: Edinburgh University
Team: Deborah Denner

1999–2004 The Playfair Project, National Galleries of Scotland
Client: The Trustees of the NGS
Awards: Exhibited at La Biennale di Venezzia 2002, Non-member's Award at the Royal Academy Summer, Exhibition 2000 sponsored by *The Architects' Journal*/Bovis Lend Lease, The Worshipful Company Of Chartered Architects Measured, Drawing Prize 2000 at the Royal Academy Summer Exhibition 2000
Team: John Canon, John Carpenter, Mary Comerford, Stuart Hill, Rita Makanjee, James Nelmes, Seamus Thornton

2000–2004 Courtyard Development Fitzwilliam Museum, University of Cambridge
Client: Estate Management and Building Services
Awards: RIBA Regional Award, Civic Trust Commendation, Short-listed for the Gulbenkian "Museum of the Year Award"
Team: Natalie Bagnould, Mary Comerford, Kate Hare, Rita Makanjee

2004 Glyn Vivian Art Gallery Swansea, Invited Competition
Client: Swansea City Council
Team: John Carpenter

2004 St Mary's York, Invited Competition
Client: The Diocese of York
Team: Kristine Ngan

2005 The Wellcome Trust London, Invited Competition
Client: The Welcome Trust
Team: John Carpenter, Kate Hare

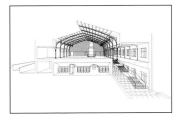

2005 The British Empire and Commonwealth Museum, Bristol (unrealised)
Client: The Trustees of the British Empire and Commonwealth Museum
Team: Paul Barke-Asuni, Kristine Ngan

2005 Albert Memorial Museum, Exeter, Invited Competition
Client: Exeter City Council
Team: John Carpenter, Daisuke Harada, Kate Hare

2005 Art Gallery and Library, Tonbridge Wells, Invited Competition
Client: Kent County Council
Team: Deborah Denner

2005 National Portrait Gallery, Ottawa, Canada, Invited Competition
Client: Ottawa City Council
Team: John Carpenter, Kristine Ngan

2005 Private House, London
Client: Sir Nicholas Serota
Team: Deborah Denner

2006 Library Extension Emanuel College, University of Cambridge, Invited Competition
Client: Emanuel College
Team: Uli Kraeling

2006 IOTA Gallery Ramsgate (unrealised)
Client: Isle of Thanet Arts
Team: John Carpenter

2006 Heritage Arts Centre Shrewsbury, Invited Competition
Client: Shrewsbury City Council
Team: Uli Kraeling

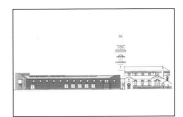

1999–2007 The Embroiders' Guild Manchester (unrealised)
Client: the Embroider' Guild
Team: Mary Comerford, Daisuke Harada, Uli Kraeling

1999–2007 Warwick University Business School, Faculty of Social Science (three phases)
Client: University of Warwick
Team: John Carpenter, Paul Barke Assuni, Deborah Denner, Jo Eade, James Nelmes, Kristine Ngan

2001–2005 The Brindley Arts Centre, Runcorn, Cheshire
Client: Halton Borough Council
Awards: Exhibited at the Venice Biennale 2002, Non Member's Award at the Royal Academy, Summer Exhibition 2000 sponsored by The Architect's Journal / Bovis Lend Lease, RIBA Award 2005
Team: Patrick Bankhead, Paul Barke Assuni, Deborah Denner, Jo Eade, Mark Jeffs, Rita Makanjee, Kristine Ngan

2004–2006 Media Centre, University of Essex
Client: University of Essex
Team: Patrick Bankhead, Mark Jeffs, Stuart Hill

2005 Antony Caro Exhibition, Tate Britain
Client: The Trustees of the Tate
Team: Deborah Denner

2005–2008 Westwood Teaching Centre, University of Warwick
Client: University of Warwick
Team: John Carpenter, Deborah Denner

2006 John Miller receives CBE

ACKNOWLEDGEMENTS

We would like to thank the following who have made possible the publication of this book; the architects, colleagues and the many consultants who have worked with both Colquhoun + Miller and John Miller + Partners over the last 48 years, for their enthusiasm and contribution to the work of the two practices; with a special thanks to the Partners Simon Winstanley and John Carpenter and to the Associates Graham Smith, Bryn Riches, Patrick Theis, John Cannon and Kristine Ngan; to our clients for their patience support and trust; to Kenneth Frampton, Robert Maxwell, Nicholas Serota and Deyan Sudjic for their essays; to Tim Williment and Norman Chang for their help in sourcing the images illustrated; to Margaret Pope, our technical librarian for her superb photographic filing system and to Ziemowit Maj for his technical assistance and know-how; to Sarah Miller for her help with the editing; to Rachel Pfleger and Duncan McCorquodale at Black Dog Publishing. With a special thanks to John Hewitt, who provided the delicate axonometric drawings and to Sandra Lousada, who provided the personal photographs. We would also like to thank Sidell Gibson Architects for providing us with the space in which to prepare the book.

In conclusion we acknowledge that the selection of work by Colquhoun + Miller, included in the book, recognises the importance of Alan Colquhoun, not only to the work completed by the earlier practice, but also to the development of the later work of John Miller + Partners.

John Miller + Richard Brearley + Su Rogers, September 2009

© 2009 Black Dog Publishing Limited, the authors and architects
All rights reserved

Designed by Rachel Pfleger @ bdp

Black Dog Publishing Limited
10A Acton Street
London
WC1X 9NG

t. +44 (0)207 713 5097
f. +44 (0)207 713 8682
e. info@blackdogonline.com

All opinions expressed within this publication are those of the authors and not
necessarily of the publisher.

British Library Cataloguing-in-Publication Data.
A CIP record for this book is available from the British Library.

ISBN 978 1 906155 70 4

Black Dog Publishing is an environmentally responsible company.

architecture art design
fashion history photography
theory and things

black dog
publishing

www.blackdogonline.com   london uk